45 —
46.80

D1270591

MYTH AND METAPHYSICS

WILLIAM A. LUIJPEN

MYTH AND METAPHYSICS

Translated

by

HENRY J. KOREN

MARTINUS NIJHOFF / THE HAGUE / 1976

Translated from the original Dutch edition *Theologie is Antropologie* (Boom, Meppel, 1974).

© 1976 by Martinus Nijhoff, The Hague, Netherlands
All rights reserved, including the right to translate or to reproduce this book or parts thereof in any form

ISBN 90 247 1750 7

LUTHER COLLEGE LIBRARY
University of Regina

TABLE OF CONTENTS

PREFACE

This book is an attempt to interpret man's religious existence, an interpretation for which some of the groundwork was laid by the author's book PHENOMENOLOGY AND ATHEISM (Duquesne University Press, 2nd impression, 1965). That work explored the "denial" of God by the leading atheists and came to terms with the most typical forms assumed by their "denials". Nevertheless, I am not an adherent of atheism. The reason why it is possible to agree with many "atheists" without becoming one of them is that man can misunderstand his own religiousness or lapse into an inauthentic form of being a believer. What many "atheists" unmask is one or the other form of pseudo-religiousness which should be unmasked. On the other hand, I have also constantly refused to identify religiousness with such inauthentic forms and to define it in terms of those forms — just as I refuse to identify the appendix with appendicitis, the heart with an infarct, the psyche as a disturbance, and marriage as a fight.

The book offered here has been written since the rise of the radical "God is dead" theology. This "theology" without God has often been presented as the only form of theological thought still suitable for "modern man". As the reader will notice, I reject the brash facility with which some "modern men" measure the relevance of "anything" by its "modernity". There exists a kind of ingenuous tendency to use the qualifier "modern" as an infallible "pass" (Heidegger) or criterion to distinguish meaningful questions and answers from others that are meaningless. With such a criterion one can then achieve quick results in the realm of religion, as well as with respect to the "standpoints" occupied by the various "religions" toward the crucial questions of life : those "standpoints" simply are nothing but "taboos".

Such an attitude gives rise to two questions. First of all, who is really "modern"? Those who have turned their backs to all religiousness or the Jesus people? Whatever one thinks about the Jesus people, they show at least that so-called "modernity" is not so reliable that it can function as an infallible criterion. Besides, there are many philosophers for whom the so-called « modern man" simply is a symptom of degeneration, a man who lives in "forgetfulness of Being". And in the eyes of these philosophers, this means that the "modern man's" essential ability to "see" has also degenerated. A few do not hesitate to say that "modern man" is blind in many respects.

The second question is connected with this. Isn't it possible that religiousness implies a specific way of "seeing"? No one is entitled to answer this question, either affirmatively or negatively, from an *a priori* standpoint. If, however, religiousness does indeed imply a specific form of "seeing", it would be folly to ask one afflicted with various forms of "blindness" whether there is anything to "see".

At the same time, let us also mention something else here—viz., the ineptness with which some people defend man's religiousness. The claim is made that "modern man's" rationality has no right whatsoever to speak. Such a claim would appear to imply that religiousness is a form of infantilism.

In all this I have not said anything as yet about my own standpoint. Anticipating ideas that will be explained in this book, I may say that I have tried to interpret religiousness as implying a specific form of rationality, of "seeing". The philosopher dwells in "the wonder of all wonders" that there is something to "see". This wonder is his own existence as rationality. The philosopher has no right to impose any *a priori* limitations on the possibilities of man's rationality. What the religious man means when he calls "God" becomes "visible" to the philosopher who abstains from making such limitations. It is at this point that philosophy becomes theology.

This book's description and explanation of my view—offered only as a kind of proposal—is preceded by an inventory of the standpoints taken today with respect to the "affirmation" of God made in myth and metaphysics. The purpose of this inventory is not merely to bring some order into the bewildering variety of expression used by many writers, but also to prepare my own personal standpoint by a critical reflection on myth and metaphysics. Even reflection, however, is not more than a "proposal".[1]

---

[1] Chapter Two of this book and a few shorter passages have been taken in a slightly modified form from the author's previous work, *Theology as Anthropology*, Duquesne University Press, 1974.

CHAPTER ONE

MYTHICAL SPEAKING "ABOUT" GOD

One who wishes to make an inventory of the various standpoints with respect to the "affirmation" of God must also consider the different ways of looking at the meaning of symbolic and mythical speaking "about" God. There are several ways of doing this. Symbols and myths are studied by many sciences, such as psychology, sociology, psychoanalysis, literary science, cultural anthropology and linguistics. From their own specific standpoints these sciences address *different* questions to symbols and myths. The questioning attitude of a particular science determines at once the *kind* of answer that will be received. This rule applies also to the phenomenology of comparative religion when it discusses *religious* symbols and myths : it, too, speaks in a *specific* way and endeavors to arrive at a *specific* way of understanding.

Philosophy, however, doesn't approach symbols and myths in the same way as the phenomenology of comparative religion. The latter remains within the order of the symbolic when it tries to understand symbols and myths. It looks for connections, analogies and systematizations in the world of symbols. Its "understanding" is, as Paul Ricoeur expresses it, extensive and panoramic, it is interested but not involved.[1] The understanding of the internal connections and the systematization of the world of symbols, the understanding of symbols through symbols could be called the "truth" of the phenomenology of comparative religion.[2]

---

[1] "Ce niveau ne peut être qu'une étape, celle d'une intelligence en extension, d'une intelligence en extension panoramique, curieuse, mais non concernée". P. Ricoeur, *Finitude et Culpabilité*, II, La symbolique du mal, Paris, 1960, p. 329.

[2] "En effet la question de la vérité y est sans cesse éludée; s'il arrive au phénoménologue d'appeler vérité la cohérence propre, la systématicité du monde des symboles, il s'agit d'une vérité sans croyance, d'une vérité à distance, réduite, d'où a été expulsée la question : est-ce que je crois cela, moi"? P. Ricoeur, *o.c.*, p. 329.

The phenomenologist of religion *himself*, however, is not involved. In the phenomenology of comparative religion there is no room for the question, Do I myself believe this? To use again Ricoeur's language, in the phenomenology of religion one passes from one symbol to another without being *oneself* "somewhere" there.[3]

This non-committal attitude of the phenomenologist of comparative religion is *not* that of the philosopher. He *does* ask the question, Do I myself believe this? Not of course in the sense that he asks the philosophical question about the truth with respect to each and every symbol and myth, but in the sense that he endeavors to understand the essence of man's symbolizing and mythical consciousness. He investigates in what sense symbolic and mythical consciousness stands in truth-as-unconcealedness.

Within the search for the philosophical truth of religious symbols and myths one can discern different standpoints. There are thinkers who reject mythical speaking in order to give a foundation to their "denial" of God. Others do the same to purify their "affirmation" of God, but they reject only an interpretation of myths which, in their view, is untenable. Finally, there are thinkers who view mythical speaking as the only possible way of speaking "about" God. What they mean by this depends of course on their interpretation of mythical consciousness.

1. The Rejection of Myths and the "Denial" of God

The people who reject myths in order to give a foundation to their "denial" of God usually claim that the mythical consciousness is inferior to the consciousness of the positive sciences. They are unable to accept that man's authentic consciousness also implies a mythical dimension, that it is *essentially* also mythical. In their view, authenticity is exclusively guaranteed by rationality, i.e., the power to let meaning appear as *objective* meaning, by placing oneself critically at a distance.[4] Mythical consciousness, they say, is unable to distance itelf critically and thus is doomed to obfuscate objectivity by all kinds of "fictions", "fables", "fabrications" and "illusions".

It stands to reason that the prestige of the positive sciences induced these people to define the rationality which they oppose to mythical con-

---

[3] P. Ricoeur, *o.c.*, p. 329.

[4] G. Gusdorf, *Mythe et métaphysique*, Introduction à la philosophie, Paris, 1953, pp. 151-160.

sciousness as scientific rationality.[5] In this way myth and science became competitors. At first, they said, consciousness is mythical, but this consciousness is still primitive. Non-primitive, authentic consciousness is scientific. In the course of its development, then, consciousness entirely abandons its mythical phase. Auguste Comte is a well-known representative of this theory. He held that the human mind arrives at maturity through three stages, a theological stage, a metaphysical stage, and then the stage of positive science.[6]

In the theological stage man sees the phenomena of nature as dependent on supernatural causes : God, gods, or spirits. Comte sometimes calls this the "fictitious stage" because, in his attempts to connect the phenomena of nature with a transcendent cause, man relies exclusively on his imagination. Comte doesn't wish to imply that this first phase in the history of the human mind has been unimportant. On the contrary, because of man's primitive condition, any other kind of explanation was practically impossible. But this first step was also the one that made further development and the ultimate maturity of the human mind possible.[7] The Catholic religion, Comte held, occupies the first place in this stage of man's development.[8]

To Comte it was obvious that the transition from the theological stage, which relied only on the imagination, to the stage of positive science could not occur without an intermediary phase. Theology and physical science are so far apart that a transitional phase was needed to arrive at the maturity of positive science. Metaphysics offered this transition.[9]

The typical feature of this metaphysical phase is that it replaces the supernatural influence of God, gods and spirits by mysterious entities called "substances". In this way the explanation of nature's phenomena

[5] A.H. Krappe, *La genèse des mythes*, Paris, 1952, pp. 27-33.

[6] "Or, chacun de nous, en contemplant sa propre histoire, se souvient-il pas qu'il a été successivement *théologien* dans son enfance, *métaphysicien* dans sa jeunesse, et *physicien* dans sa virilité". A. Comte, *Cours de philosophie positive*, Paris, Schleicher Frères, Editeurs, 1907, I, p. 4.

[7] *Cours I*. p. 7.

[8] *Cours V*, pp. 158-259.

[9] "La théologie et la physique sont si profondément incompatibles, leurs conceptions ont un caractère si radicalement opposé, qu'avant de renoncer aux unes pour employer exclusivement les autres, l'intelligence humaine a dû se servir de conceptions intermédiaires, d'un caractère bâtard, propres, par cela même, à opérer graduellement la transition. Telle est la destination naturelle des conceptions métaphysiques". *Cours I*, p. 7.

is no longer connected with causes transcending nature, but appeals to causes lying within nature itself. These causes, however, are so subtle and abstract that anyone with sound reason must realize that, in the final analysis, only one thing has been done : strange names have been given to the phenomena themselves. In other words, these phenomena remain unexplained, for the so-called explanations are nothing but fancies.[10] Nevertheless, this intermediary stage is very important : it does away with the ideas of the theological stage and prepares the way for the definitive stage of the nature mind.

In the scientific stage of the mind's development everything becomes different. Now the mind turns to the phenomena of nature by way of *experience*. It is no longer interested in transcendent or immanent causes but only in the empirically verifiable *laws* by which the phenomena are interconnected.[11] Anyone who is acquainted with positive science, says Comte, should realize that this is the only method to be followed by the mature mind. In a word, the only valid road to knowledge is that of physical science.

It follows, of course, that the positive philosophy in principle encompasses the total range of phenomena. For it would be a contradiction to assume that, on the one hand, the mind holds fast to a primitive way of philosophizing and, on the other, has adopted a way of thinking that is wholly the opposite of that primitive approach.[12] In actual fact, however, that universal range of positive philosophy has not yet been reached.[13] There is still a big gap in the system; what is most urgently needed is a "social physics" and this science does not exist as yet.[14]

---

[10] *Cours I*, pp. 7-8.

[11] "Nous voyons, par ce qui précède, que le caractère fondamental de la philosophie positive est de regarder tous les phénomènes comme assujettis à des *lois* naturelles invariables, dont la découverte précise et la réduction au moindre nombre possible sont le but de tous nos efforts, en considérant comme absolument inaccessible et vide de sens pour nous la recherche de ce qu'on appelle les *causes*, soit premières, soit finales". *Cours I*, p. 8.

[12] *Cours I*, p. 11.

[13] "Tout se réduit donc à une simple question de fait : la philosophie positive, qui, dans les deux derniers siècles, a pris graduellement une si grande extension, embrasse-t-elle aujourd'hui tous les ordres de phénomènes? Il est évident que cela n'est point, et que, par conséquent, il reste encore une grande opération scientifique à exécuter pour donner à la philosophie positive le caractère d'universalité, indispensable à sa reconstitution définitive". *Cours I*, p. 11.

[14] "... il lui reste à terminer le système des sciences d'observation en fondant la *physique sociale*". *Cours I*, p. 12.

As soon as all fundamental views become homogeneous, *the* philosophy will have been reached. Then philosophy will never again change its character, and all further development will simply be a matter of new additions.[15] By the power of its universality, positive philosophy will confirm its natural superiority and simply take over the place of theology and metaphysics. In the future, only the "historical existence" of these early phases will be of any interest to men of research.[16]

"Theology will necessarily give up the ghost when it comes face to face with physical science".[17] Comte could hardly have expressed himself more clearly. It isn't necessary to combat the "affirmation" of God. There will be so much "progress" that at some point in the future people interested in history will ask themselves what has happened to that "affirmation". Then it will become evident that the backwardness of the theological phase in the mind's development has been overcome by positive philosophy without any struggle against God. Theological fancies and metaphysical abstractions will then appear to have been replaced by the affirmations of the positive sciences. The kingdom of God will then be finished forever, and God will have departed without leaving any unanswered questions.[18]

According to Comte, then, the "affirmation" of God is tied to mythical consciousness but this consciousness is only "provisional". The tendency to create "fictions" and "fables" in which gods and spirits are introduced to explain matters that should be explained scientifically will disappear. Accordingly, Comte rejected the "affirmation" of God because he wished to expedite the birth of scientific consciousness.

2. THE REJECTION OF MYTHS AND THE "AFFIRMATION" OF GOD

Christianity also has very often rejected the myths, but not in order to base a "denial" of God on this rejection. Its rejection originated with the author of the second Letter of Peter, who points out that he is not

[15] *Cours I*, pp. 12-13.

[16] "Ayant acquis par là le caractère d'universalité qui lui manque encore, la philosophie positive deviendra capable de se substituer entièrement, avec toute sa supériorité naturelle, à la philosophie théologique et la philosophie métaphysique, dont l'universalité est aujourd'hui la seule propriété réelle, et qui, privées d'un tel motif de préférence, n'auront plus pour nos successeurs qu'une existence historique". *Cours I*, p. 13.

[17] *Cours IV*, p. 108.

[18] H. de Lubac, *Le drame de l'humanisme athée*. Paris, 1945³, pp. 141-184.

following "clever myths" but has been an eyewitness of historical events.[19] The "clever myths" of other religions must be rejected, this author holds, because, in contrast to the Christian "affirmation" of God, theirs has no historical foundation.

The remarkable point of this view is that the authenticity of the "affirmation" of God is made dependent here on the historicity of certain events. Perhaps it would be better to say that this is "remarkable" *for us now* because in the past few decades the appeal to historical events has begun to be viewed in an entirely new light. For the author of II Peter, myths are fables and fictions, and the "affirmation" of God contained in them has no foundation because it has no *historical* basis. What the "clever myths" tell us is historically not true, and therefore these myths are fictions. It soon became obvious, however, that the so-called mythical events of other religions occur also in Christianity. Many non-Christian religions are familiar with incarnations, virgin births, ascensions into heaven and descents into hell. Such occurrences were called mythical elsewhere, but insofar as they occurred in Christianity they were judged to have *really* happened and *not* to be mythical.[20] The ancient Church Fathers called the myths of non-Christian religions "diabolical imitations" of Old-Testamental stories.[21]

In the past few decades, however, well-known writers have defended the view that there is no reason to call myths fictions simply because they do not relate historical events. These authors came to the realization that there is one possible standpoint from which myths must be recognized as "true",[22] even though they do not relate historical events in the sense in which historians do this.[23]

---

[19] II Petr., I, 16-19.

[20] John A.T. Robinson and David L. Edwards, *The Honest to God Debate*, London, 1963², pp. 265-266.

[21] R. Pettazzoni, *Essays on the History of Religion*, Leiden, 1954, pp. 24-25.

[22] "The myth is true and cannot but be true, because it is the charter of a tribe's life, the foundation of a world, which cannot continue without that myth. On the other hand, the myth cannot continue without this world, of which it forms an organic part, as the 'explanation' of its beginnings, as its original *raison d'être*, its prologue in heaven. The life of myth, which is at the same time its 'truth', is the very life of its natal world of formation and incubation. Apart from this, the myth can indeed survive, but a surviving myth is no longer true, because no longer living; it has ceased to be a 'true' story and become a 'false' one". R. Pettazzoni, *o.c.*, p. 21.

[23] "Au lieu de traiter, comme leurs prédécesseurs, le mythe dans l'acceptation usuelle du terme, i.e. en tant que 'fable', 'invention', 'fiction', ils l'ont accepté tel qu'il était compris dans les sociétés archaïques, où le mythe désigne, au contraire, une 'his-

Bultmann

Bultmann with his program of demythologization occupies a special place in this new way of looking at myths.[24] Bultmann's aim is to bring to light the proper truth of the "affirmation" of God. This truth, he holds, has always made use of myths, and if these myths are not understood according to their own specific "truth", they falsify the "affirmation" of God.

In Bultmann's eyes, the atheist is right when he refuses to agree with the "affirmation" of God if this "affirmation" demands of him that he accept, as a truth of *historical science* or of *physical science*, something which cannot possibly be verified according to the normal procedures of the sciences of history or physics.[25] With respect to what Christianity preaches, in particular, the atheist will say : "That is only a myth".[26] Bultmann agrees with this kind of atheism. But he merely rejects myths insofar as they are falsely interpreted, i.e., held to be "true" in the sense of the sciences of history and physics, without being subject to the methods of verification accepted in these sciences. Accordingly, unlike Comte, Bultmann does not proclaim the "denial" of God, but only that the "affirmation" of God possesses a wholly distinct character.

For Comte, it was a contradiction to assume that the human mind could hold fast to primitive mythical thought and, at the same time, accept the scientific way of thinking, which is its exact opposite. That is why he opted for the rejection of myths. Bultmann proceeds from roughly the same premises as Comte, but arrives at an entirely different conclusion. He accepts that the pursuit of the physical and historical sciences requires a certain approach if one is to speak there of truth in the sense of physical or historical science. The truth of these sciences implies a specific way of asking and answering questions, specific laws and models, and a specific use of language. Without these, there can be no truth in the sense of physical or historical science.

In Bultmann's eyes, it is *unthinkable* that the pursuer of these sciences

---

toire vraie' et, qui plus est, hautement précieuse parce que sacrée, exemplaire et significative". Mircea Eliade, *Aspects du mythe*, Paris, 1963.

[24] R. Bultmann, *Neues Testament und Mythologie*, in : Kerygma und Mythos, I, 1960[4], pp. 15-48; R. Bultmann, *Zum Problem der Entmythologisierung*, in : Kerygma und Mythos, II, pp. 179-190; *Zum Problem der Entmythologisierung*, in : Kerygma und Mythos, VI-1, pp. 20-27.

[25] R. Bultmann, in : Kerygma und Mythos, VI-1, pp. 23-24.

[26] S. Ogden, *De christelijke verkondiging van God aan de mensheid van de zogenaamde "atheïstische tijd"*, in : Concilium, II (1966), p. 99.

imposes those demands on his scientific activity and the truths discovered by it and, at the same time, does not impose them. Now, myths constantly tell us that God interferes in the causality which is at work in nature and history,[27] while the narrated phenomena cannot be verified in the way this is customary and necessary in the sciences of nature and history. The man of science cannot grant that the domain of his discipline is governed by certain specific laws and, at the same time, grant that from time to time his domain is not governed by these laws. If the "affirmation" of God were to demand of him that he accept, as a truth of physical or historical science, something which cannot be verified by the physical or historical sciences, then the "affirmation" of God would be impossible for him. For Bultmann, this does not mean that myths which speak of God must be rejected, but only that they should not be understood in the sense of the physical or historical sciences.

All this is not yet the main reason why Bultmann does not wish to interpret the myths in the sense of historical or physical science. His ultimate reason is his conviction that anyone who accepts that God from time to time interferes in the causality at work in the world and history thereby conceives God as "world" and no longer as God.[28] Bultmann, then, really intends to make the "affirmation" of God reach its properly authentic level. To attain this, he does not reject the myths, but only their untenable interpretation as truth in the sense of physical or historical science. Myths, he holds, do not at all intend to establish truths in the sense of physical or historical science, but to speak about man as existence.[29] They should be interpreted existentially, he says.

For Bultmann, our thinking about man is not exhausted by the "objectifying" approach used in the physical and historical sciences. It

----

[27] "Wenn nun in unserer Auffassung Natur und Geschichte durch eine bestimmte Gesetzmässigkeit beherrscht sind, so können wir freilich nicht zu gleicher Zeit annehmen, dass sie es nicht seien, dass sie der Willkür überirdischer Mächte ausgeliefert sein können". Fr. Theunis, *Prolegomena zum Problem der Entmythologisierung*, in : Kerygma und Mythos, VI-1, p. 146.

[28] "Der gedankliche Inhalt des Mythos ist schlechthin undenkbar, eben weil in ihm von Gott Weltliches gedacht und ausgesagt wird; weil er nur bejaht werden kann, insofern Gott als Welt gedacht wird und nicht als Gott". Fr. Theunis, *a.c.*, p. 147.

[29] "Der eigentliche Sinn des Mythos ist nicht der, ein objektives Weltbild zu geben; vielmehr spricht sich in ihm aus, wie sich der Mensch selbst in seiner Welt versteht; der Mythos will nicht kosmologisch, sondern anthropologisch—besser : existential interpretiert werden". R. Bultmann, in : Kerygma und Mythos, I, p. 22; see also Kerygma und Mythos, II, p. 183 and VI-1, p. 24.

is *possible*, of course, to view man as an element of nature and of history, to study him as an "ingredient" of the sciences. But myths are not concerned with this, and that is why they are *true* in what they really intend to say. Their intention is to speak of "the proper reality of man", his "understanding of existence",[30] to express the idea that man's essence demands of him acknowledgment of the fact that the available world in which he lives does not have its ground and purpose within itself and that man is not his own master.[31] But disregarding their inmost intention, the myths "objectify" Other-worldly Reality in this-worldly reality, by representing the Transcendent as spatially distant and His power as exalted and surpassing that of man.[32] In Bultmann's view, myths use the name "God" precisely to speak about the dimension of man's "understanding of existence".

For one who is able and willing to understand Bultmann's sayings as he intends them, all this means the same as Bultmann's claim that asking questions and speaking about God is asking and speaking about man.[33] For Bultmann conceives man the way Heidegger taught him, viz., as existence, as a subject who is not what he is without that which he is not. This "what he is not" embraces, according to Heidegger, *at least* the world and the other, and according to Bultmann, *also* and *primarily* God. If, then, myths speak about the deepest dimension of man's self-understanding as existence, they speak, according to Bultmann, about God because man as a subject is not what he is, without God. Thus speaking about God is speaking about man.[34]

Reminding the reader that at present I merely intend to describe the actual situation with respect to the "affirmation" and the "negation" of God, let me add that the view which presents God as "puncturing"[35]

---

[30] R. Bultmann, in : Kerygma und Mythos, VI-1, pp. 24-25.

[31] "Im Mythos findet der Glaube Ausdruck, dass die bekannte und verfügbare Welt, in der der Mensch lebt, Grund und Ziel nicht in sich selber hat .... Und in eine damit gibt der Mythos dem Wissen Ausdruck, dass der Mensch nicht Herr seiner selbst ist, dass er nicht nur innerhalb den bekannten Welt abhängig ist, sondern dass er vor allem von jenen jenseits der bekannten waltenden Mächten abhängig ist, und dass er in dieser Abhängigkeit gerade von der bekannten Mächten frei werden kann". R. Bultmann, in : Kerygma und Mythos, I, pp. 22-23.

[32] R. Bultmann, in : Kerygma und Mythos, VI-1, p. 25 and I, p. 22, footnote 2.

[33] "Das Wissen um Gott ist zunächst ein Wissen des Menschen um sich selbst, um seine Begrenztheit, und Gott gilt als die Macht, die diese Begrenztheit des Menschen durchbricht und ihn dadurch zu seiner Eigentlichkeit emporhebt". R. Bultmann, *Glauben und Verstehen*, II, Tübingen, 1961³, p. 86.

[34] R. Bultmann, *Jesus Christ and Mythology*, London, 1966⁴, p. 5.

[35] R. Bultmann, *Glauben und Verstehen*, II, pp. 233-234.

the laws of nature and of history is also called the "supernaturalistic",[36] "metaphysical",[37] or "theistic"[38] view. But, as we shall soon see, these very terms, used in a different context, can have a broader sense than the one just indicated. At the same time, I must point out that if the use of these terms in the above-mentioned sense is proved to be rightly objectionable, one is not yet justified in rejecting these terms *in toto*. For it could very well be that the rejected meanings of those terms are degenerated forms of supernaturalism, metaphysics and theism. As a matter of fact, there are authors who continue to use these terms while rejecting the above-mentioned objectionable meanings.

Bultmann, we saw, does not reject the myths, but only their false interpretation. Nevertheless, mythical language is unintelligible to modern man, he thinks, because it is the language of a time, now past, which had not yet been shaped by scientific thought.[39] Our time, however, is. That is why Bultmann objects to the view that speaking about God must *necessarily* be mythical, as if mythical language were the only possible way of speaking about God in a relevant way.[40] Mythical language speaks with the aid of categories and models borrowed from a past worldview; that is why it has become unintelligible and antiquated for us.[41] Thus it follows that Bultmann cannot ascribe a distinct, specific and perhaps irreplaceable lucidity or function to mythical language. He does not wish to eliminate the myths, but to interpret them existentially.[42] For Bultmann, this means that everything the myths say "truthfully" *can* and, in our time, *must* be expressed differently. At most, mythical language is *provisionally* indispensable, i.e., as long as an adequate way has not yet been found.[43]

---

[36] John A.T. Robinson, *Honest to God*, London, 1963⁹, pp. 29-35; Heinz Zahrnt, *Die Sache mit Gott*, Die protestantische Theologie im 20. Jahrhundert, München, 1967, pp. 264-265.

[37] Paul van Buren, *The Secular Meaning of the Gospel*, London, 1966³, pp. 82, 167, 191, 198; C.A. van Peursen, *Hij is het weer!*, Beschouwingen over de betekenis van het woordje "God", Kampen, 1967, pp. 8, 33; Heinz Zahrnt, *o.c.*, pp. 266-269.

[38] J. Sperna Weiland, *Oriëntatie, Nieuwe wegen in de theologie*, Baarn, 1966, pp. 107-110.

[39] R. Bultmann, in : Kerygma und Mythos, I, pp. 16-21.

[40] "Oft freilich wird behauptet, dass die Sprache des Glaubens wie die der Religion überhaupt notwendig mythologische Rede sein müsse, da unserer Sprache andere Begriffe fehlten, um sachgemäss von Gott und seinem Handeln zu reden". R. Bultmann, in : Kerygma und Mythos, II, p. 185.

[41] Heinz Zahrnt, *o.c.*, pp. 279-280.

[42] R. Bultmann, in : Kerygma und Mythos, II, p. 184.

[43] "Sind die mythischen Vorstellungen und Begriffe wirklich unentbehrlich? Es

The question that immediately comes to mind is why Bultmann claims that the myths may not be eliminated. What he very generally calls "myths" is, after all, a "mode of human speech". If this mode is unintelligible and therefore has to be replaced, are not the myths eliminated when mythical language is *de facto* replaced by non-mythical language?

Although Bultmann refuses to admit it, he cannot escape eliminating the myths, for, in his view, mythical language is nothing but speaking in categories and models derived from the worldview of a past era.[44] That is why this language is unintelligible to us. What the myths *really* wish to say is true, also for us, but mythical language itself is finished. The question to be asked here is whether mythical language is indeed nothing but speaking in categories and models borrowed from a past worldview.

Antoine Vergote

Vergote occupies a special place among philosophical writers about myths. He, too, does not stop with what the positive sciences have said about myths, but tries to understand the essence of the mythical.[45]

The mythical story exercises an ontological function. It does not wish to offer any concrete explanations but, precisely as a story, it unfolds primordial time. This time is conceived as "all-encompassing"; the mythical story places "ordinary" human time within the framework of a beginning and an end, and primordial time makes itself felt in human time.[46]

The mythical events in mythical time offer a foundation and justification for human events and give them meaning. Thus the mythical story does not present a symbolic explanation of human events that are already whatever they are. On the contrary, the mythical story itself is the mani-

---

mag sein, dass sie es sind in einem vorläufigen Sinne, sofern in ihnen Wahrheiten intendiert sind, die sich in der Sprache der objektivierenden Wissenschaft nicht aussagen lassen. In mythologischer Sprache kommt dann zum vorläufigen Ausdruck, wofür die adaequate Sprache erst gefunden werden muss". R. Bultmann, in : Kerygma und Mythos, II, p. 186.

[44] "Pour Bultmann, le mythe se définit donc comme vision du monde. Et puisque toute son entreprise de démythisation s'appuie sur cette réduction du mythe à une vision du monde ...". A. Vergote, *Mythe, croyance aliénée et foi théologale*, in : Mythe et Foi, edited by E. Castelli, Paris, 1966, p. 163.

[45] "Je distingue donc le niveau ontologique du niveau psychologique". A. Vergote, *a.c.*, p. 191.

[46] A. Vergote, *a.c.*, p. 165.

festation of a primordial event which conditions the things in the world and man's actions.[47] The myth constitutes the "ontological difference" between the human world and the primordial reality on which the human world is founded.

Thus it is not surprising that the proper realm of the myth lies in the religious domain. The primordial reality is the domain of the "other", the sacred, the divine. This domain is distinct from the profane. The ritual separation, in space and time, between the sacred and the profane is secondary with respect to the primordial distinction, which is an "ontological difference". The primordial reality spoken of by the myth is the inexhaustible source of all beings and events, and these also return again to this source.[48]

Nevertheless, the world of the myth is not a subsistent, self-contained world. Such a view would conceive the mythical world by analogy with the human world and disregard their "ontological difference". The mythical story makes the human world be a manifestation of the primordial, the holy, the divine.[49] It discloses in the human world the primordial reality which encompasses and gives a foundation to human time and space, history, events and things.[50] Thus mythical language "clarifies" human reality in terms of primordial reality. But this does not mean that the primordial, the holy, the divine are adduced as the cause of the human world. Mythical language "clarifies" because and to the extent that it places the human world in the "clarity", the "light" of the primordial, the holy, the divine, thereby providing a foundation for the human world.

It stands to reason that the myth degenerates as soon as it is viewed in an objectivistic-realistic fashion. While mythical language places human history in the perspective of primordial reality and thus gives it a foundation, an objectivistic-realistic reading of myths puts the mystical events within the framework of the dubious certainty of human history.[51]

---

[47] "Au lieu d'être une interprétation imaginaire ou même symbolique des événements humains déjà constitués, le récit mythique, bien au contraire, est l'univers primordial de la manifestation qui conditionne les actes humains et les données du monde". A. Vergote, *a.c.*, pp. 165-166.

[48] A. Vergote, *a.c.*, p. 167.

[49] "Ainsi le discours mythique est-il une célébration du monde qui trouve son intégration dans l'univers sacral". A. Vergote, *a.c.*, p. 167.

[50] "Le mythe est pour l'homme, non pas une vision du monde, mais le discours de l'Autre qui manifeste le monde et révèle l'homme à lui-même". A. Vergote, *a.c.*, p. 164.

[51] A. Vergote, *a.c.*, p. 168.

The mythical content then becomes the object of an unjustifiable attitude of "holding to be true".[52] It becomes the object of an historical "belief" to which, on the one hand, historical reality is ascribed while, on the other, this object cannot be accepted as real because the criteria of history disallow it.[53] In this way mythical language degenerates into pseudo-scientific language.

If mythical language is conceived as disclosing and founding human existence, its origin cannot itself again become an object of a question.[54] "The myth is that which gives a foundation".[55] It constitutes man in his being-man, and as such is "first".[56] Thinking "about" the myth can exist only insofar as one enters into mythical discourse, allows oneself to be told, and recognizes what one is. Mythical speech is a discourse which precedes man and makes his objective discourse possible. It comes to man before he himself has spoken and makes it possible for him to speak about things.[57] Mythical speech is the appearance of the primordial light in which space and time, things and events can make their appearance and in which man dwells in the world. Because mythical speech is all-encompassing and foundational, it can never be explained by anything else. The myth's intelligibility is not derived from anything else, but every form of intelligibility and therefore also every explanation presupposes mythical speech as that which is all-encompassing and foundational.[58] Thus mythical speech itself is never the riddle to be solved.

The mythical story is, in a certain sense, "no one's" story, it does not

---

[52] "Il se fait, au sens fort de l'expression: objet de croyance. Le contenu du discours se détache de la forme du récit, et devient un objet historique hors d'atteinte". A. Vergote, a.c., p. 169.

[53] A. Vergote, a.c., p. 169.

[54] "Je ne peux pas dire d'où il nous vient, je dirai qu'on ne peut que le reconnaître dans sa présence. Je crois qu'ici la question du *Woher* est une question qui n'a plus d'application. En présence du mythe, nous sommes donc obligés de renoncer à la question de son origine pour reconnaître sa présence, et nous laisser investir par elle". A. Vergote, a.c., p. 186.

[55] A. Vergote, a.c., p. 186.

[56] "Il y a un discours premier qui fonde toute intelligibilité". A. Vergote, a.c., p. 173.

[57] "Le récit mythique est donc bien un univers de discours qui subsiste par lui-même. Il n'est pas la parole de l'homme sur les choses, mais le language premier qui advient à l'homme et lui permet de parler des choses". A. Vergote, a.c., p. 166.

[58] A. Vergote, a.c., p. 166.

have a subject.[59] Language obviously does not exist without a subject; hence in the myth there is a linguistic subject. But the subject is present in the myth as "blotted out".[60] In this respect the mythical story resembles the historical story, for there, too, facts and events present themselves as objective data and the author disappears behind the facts.[61]

However, the a-subjectivity of the mythical story is not entirely like that of its historical counterpart. First of all, the events presenting themselves in the myth are not ordinary happenings but primordial events. As a message from the origin, the myth cannot have any witness, any subject. Secondly, the myth presents itself as belonging to tradition and, as such, it excludes even the hidden presence of an author.[62]

It would be a typical misconception of modern man if he were to conclude that the a-subjectivity of the mythical story points to an anonymous or collective author. It is true, of course, that human beings tell, modify and expand the myths, but the myths' *distinct literary character* compels us to realize that the mythical message is a message from "no one" and comes from "nowhere". Vergote uses here Lévi-Strauss's formula : "Myths think themselves in man".[63]

To understand what mythical speaking essentially is, a "reversal" (Heidegger) is necessary in our traditional way of looking at speech.[64] We are used to view speech as the speaking of a subject who puts himself at a distance from an object and speaks *about* this object. Our speaking is the speaking *by* someone *about* something. Mythical speaking, however, is a speaking of no one, a self-saying discourse.[65] It precedes all philosophical reflection, all assuming of a position, all critique.[66] It is the discourse of no one, for "no one in particular" can be pointed to as its subject.[67] In mythical speech man is not intentionally orientated

---

[59] A. Vergote, *De mythe als manifestatie*, in : Tijdschrift voor Filosofie, 34 (1972), pp. 204-205.

[60] A. Vergote, *a.c.*, p. 204.

[61] A. Vergote, *a.c.*, pp. 201, 204.

[62] A. Vergote, *a.c.*, pp. 204-205.

[63] Cl. Lévi-Strauss, *Mythologiques*, Le cru et le cuit, Paris, 1964, p. 26.

[64] A. Vergote, *Mythe, croyance aliénée et foi théologale*, p. 179.

[65] "Le mythe n'est donc le langage de personne. Il est un discours qui se dit lui-même". A. Vergote, *a.c.*, p. 166.

[66] "Lorsque je dis 'langage de personne' j'entends le langage qui précède toute réflexion philosophique, toute prise de position, tout acte de se situer par rapport à ce discours ...". A. Vergote, *a.c.*, p. 178.

[67] "Dit par personne signifie: dit par personne de déterminé". A. Vergote, *a.c.*, p. 178.

to an object, but he is a listener who lets himself be spoken to by the mythical story and finds himself as existence.

Vergote objects to calling the mythical story "symbolic" in the accepted sense of this term. He objects to all interpretations which claim that myths express figuratively the things which their interpreters articulate and comprehend in deliberate and scientific concepts—concepts, moreover, which, according to these interpreters, offer a *better* expression of what the myths convey.[68] All they succeed in doing, says Vergote, is discovering in the myths their own thoughts. He tries to overcome this difficulty by objectively investigating the distinct literary character of the myth and to determine how the myth functions in its culture.[69]

This investigation leads him to the above-mentioned conclusion that mythical language may not be called "symbolic" in the accepted sense of the term. In the light of the preceding considerations the reason is not difficult to see. For symbolic language always implies a subject who uses signs with a specific intention. Now, in the myth such a subject is lacking; mythical speech is a-subjective. Moreover, contrary to what happens in symbolic speech, in mythical discourse no reality is referred to by the name of another reality.[70] Myths "think themselves in man", they do not symbolize something else but "speak" and "bring about" the disclosure of meaning.[71] One who wishes to call mythical discourse "symbolic" must determine what this word means in terms of the myth's own nature. The opposite approach, which interprets the myth in terms of other symbols, is, according to Vergote, a hermeneutical mistake.[72]

All this clearly shows that for Vergote the myth is much more than speaking in categories and models derived from a past worldview, as is claimed by Bultmann. In Vergote's eyes, the myth narrates and brings about man's constitution as existence.[73] This narration is essentially religious,[74] and man is not man without it.[75]

[68] A. Vergote, *De mythe als manifestatie*, p. 195.

[69] A. Vergote, *a.c.*, p. 196.

[70] A. Vergote, *a.c.*, p. 219.

[71] "Le mythe ne symbolise rien, mais il dit, et opère parce qu'il dit, l'avènement des choses au champ d'apparition". A. Vergote, *Mythe, croyance aliénée et foi théologale*, p. 166.

[72] A. Vergote, *De mythe als manifestatie*, p. 210.

[73] "Puisque le véritable mythe nous est apparu comme le discours qui révèle et fonde l'existence ...". A. Vergote, *Mythe, croyance aliénée et foi théologale*, p. 171.

[74] "Le discours mythique est donc par nature religieux". A. Vergote, *a.c.*, p. 167.

[75] "L'homme se définit par cette entrée, cette insertion dans un univers d'altérité que nous appelons religion ou mythe". A. Vergote, *a.c.*, p. 189.

Because it is possible for myths to degenerate, Vergote leaves room in his theory for demythologization. The myth degenerates as soon as it is read in an objectivistic-realistic way. The primordial reality disclosing itself in the myth is then reduced to a pseudo-scientific object and the myth becomes a pseudo-scientific story. Thus demythologization will consist in the attempt to overcome the illusions and alienations that occur in such a reifying way of thinking.[76] When the primordial is no longer thought of as the "other", it creates havoc.[77] Demythologization by psychoanalysis doesn't destroy mythical consciousness, but only those modes of expression which obscure the true sense of mythical discourse.[78]

According to Vergote, the Christian proclamation of God dwells in the religious openness brought about by the myth.[79] Thus this proclamation does not destroy the myth, religion and the sacred; it implies them and, if it didn't, then the proclamation would be "unintelligible".[80] Christian proclamation extends the religious openness and brings it to completion.[81]

This, however, does not mean that Christian proclamation "believes in myths", in the accepted sense of this term. No one can "believe in myths". As soon as anyone assumes a reflective attitude, he does not believe in the myth. But neither does one who does not reflect believe in it. No one "believes" in mythical discourse; we simply let it speak to us.[82] One who "believes in the myth" changes it into a pseudo-science.

According to Vergote, the philosophy of the later Heidegger must be understood as an attempt to take up again the essence of what the myth disclosed before man began to reflect on the myth and put himself at a distance from it.[83] Vergote does not develop this point, but a comparison of his ideas with those of Heidegger shows that he puts the

[76] "Etant une entreprise de vérité, la démythisation ne peut viser qu'à surmonter ce qu'il y a d'illusoire et d'aliénant dans les modes de pensée réifiants". A. Vergote, a.c., pp. 170-171.

[77] A. Vergote, a.c., pp. 169-172.

[78] A. Vergote, a.c., p. 171.

[79] A. Vergote, a.c., pp. 172, 175, 189.

[80] "Le Christianisme ne détruit pas les mythes, les vrais mythes; il se situe dans cette dimension ouverte par les mythes, par la religion". A. Vergote, a.c., p. 189.

[81] "Le kérygme chrétien prolonge et achève la manifestation mythique de la dimension éthico-religieuse du temps humain". A. Vergote, a.c., p. 169.

[82] A. Vergote, a.c., p. 191.

[83] "Dans la philosophie existentiale de Heidegger, cependant, on reprend l'essentiel de ce que le mythe nous révélait avant que l'homme n'y réfléchisse et ne prenne une distance par rapport à lui". A. Vergote, a.c., p. 191.

"ontological difference" between the myth's primordial reality and human reality on a par with Heidegger's "ontological difference" between Being (*Sein*) and be-ing (*Seiende*).[84] But the time for mythical discourse is gone. We can no longer place ourselves in the primordial light once spread by the myth. We now share in this light, says Vergote, in a different mode of speaking, that of ontology (in Heidegger's sense) or that of Christian proclamation.[85]

3. MYTHICAL SPEAKING AS AUTHENTIC SPEAKING "ABOUT" GOD

Despite their differences of opinion, the above-mentioned authors agree in their conviction that the era of the myth is definitively past, at least for us. There are other writers, however, who view the matter differently.

Gusdorf

Gusdorf claims that authentic human consciousness always implies a mythical "moment"; in other words, the mythical dimension is an essential element of man's authentic consciousness.[86] By an analysis of Lévy-Brühl's development, he shows how this famous anthropologist had come to the conclusion that human consciousness, even when it has reached the level of scientific rationality, continues to remain also mythical. Lévy-Brühl had started from the assumption that there is opposition between the primitive, mythical, prelogical consciousness and the consciousness of positive science. Later, however, he realized that scientific consciousness can never be the *only* heir of prelogical consciousness because the proximity of a rigorously constructed system of positive scientific concepts does not eliminate the prelogical consciousness.[87] Finally, he concluded that even the qualifier "prelogical" should be dropped because the "moment" which he had called "prelogical" and which he had been able to study most easily in "primitive men"

---

[84] A. Vergote, *a.c.*, p. 172.

[85] A. Vergote, *a.c.*, p. 191.

[86] "Il faut donc renoncer à toute ambiguïté en reconnaissant dans la conscience mythique une structure inaliénable de l'être humain. Elle apporte avec soi le sens premier de l'existence et ses orientations originaires". G. Gusdorf, *Mythe et métaphysique*, Paris, 1953, p. 188.

[87] "Le voisinage même d'un système de concepts rigoureusement ordonnés selon les lois logiques n'a sur elle que peu ou point d'action. Par suite, la pensée logique ne saurait jamais être l'héritière universelle de la mentalité prélogique". L. Lévy-Brühl, *Les fonctions mentales dans les sociétés inférieures*, Paris, 1922[6], p. 451.

disclosed itself to be essential for *every* authentic human consciousness.[88]

Gusdorf fully agrees with Lévy-Brühl. He describes human consciousness as exposed to a twofold possibility of alienation. The first is the claim that mythical consciousness suffices to let man dwell in an environment infinitely enlarged by science and technology. The second consists in the absolutism of the scientific consciousness, which sterilizes or eliminates fundamental human values.[89] But even when this happens, the resulting dislocation will show the "legitimacy" of the demands made by the mythical consciousness. Even the "myth of the twentieth century" is a myth, although it displays the lack of restraint that is typical of a collective psychical disturbance.[90]

Gusdorf follows the approach defended by van der Leeuw and Leenhardt in their reflections on myths. These two writers argued that, to understand myths, one should not focus on their contents but rather be sensitive to the fact that mythical consciousness is a structure of human existence, a style of life, a way of behaving. Mythical consciousness is *the spontaneous way of being-in-the-world.*[91]

It is not easy, however, to determine what exactly Gusdorf means by mythical consciousness. He objects to Comte's view and opposes to the latter's scheme of mental development—religious—metaphysical—scientific—one of his own : mythical—intellectual—existential. As soon as intellectual consciousness arises, says Gusdorf, "mythical innocence" is lost.[92] But what exactly is this good, mythical conscience, this mythical innocence?

It is a state of unity, indivision and harmony, in which the mythical man is taken up and in which he finds rest and happiness. Mythical consciousness is interwoven with everything, and the articulations which we introduce into our existence do not exist for it. There is no distinction between "I" and the world, "I" and the group, nature and supernature, science and religion, man and God, between present, past and future, nearby and far away, sacred and profane, real and possible. Time is taken up into timelessness, and space into infinity. For the mythical consciousness everything has already happened, and the everyday

---

[88] *Les Carnets de Lucien Lévy-Brühl*, Paris, 1949, pp. 131-132.

[89] G. Gusdorf, *o.c.*, p. 189.

[90] G. Gusdorf, *o.c.*, p. 190.

[91] "Retrouvé dans son contexte vécu, le mythe s'affirme donc comme la forme spontanée de l'être dans le monde". G. Gusdorf, *o.c.*, p. 16.

[92] G. Gusdorf. *o.c.*, pp. 133-134.

tasks of man cannot be anything but repetitions of what already "is". There is no need to ask questions, for all questions have already been answered before they are even raised. The absolute harmony present in the mythical consciousness means absolute petrifaction. The mythical man is the man who has not yet placed himself at a distance and who does not seek the focal point of his equilibrium in himself.[93]

In the light of all this it is clear why Gusdorf can say that mythical consciousness is the spontaneous form of man's being-in-the-world. But Gusdorf also says other things which make this statement rather problematic. He refers to the emergence of being-man as the rupture of harmony; the birth of humankind is a breach.[94] That is why man is threatened by anxiety and death.[95] Man has never known the innocence of a life without fissures.[96] Accordingly, the "spontaneous" form of being-in-the-world is a being uprooted.

That is why for Gusdorf the myth means an attempt to recover the lost integrity.[97] The myth is a protective garb allowing man to establish himself in the world and exorcise anxiety and death. It is a "formulary of re-integration",[98] a defense mechanism against the "spontaneous form of being-in-the-world". Obviously, however, the mythical consciousness cannot be called at the same time both the "spontaneous form of being-in-the-world" and a defense mechanism against the same.[99]

According to Gusdorf, the unity, indivision and harmony of the mythical consciousness are broken and dissolved by the emergence of the intellectual consciousness. The emergence of the personal "I" places the world in man's hands as an objective domain of personal possibilities. The world becomes the realm of his initiatives and potential self-realiza-

---

[93] "On peut même définir en général le primitif comme l'homme qui n'a pas encore pris ses distances, et dont l'équilibre ne se centre pas sur soi-même". G. Gusdorf, o.c., p. 88.

[94] "En fait, dès les origines humaines l'harmonie est déjà rompue. L'acte de naissance de l'humanité correspond à une rupture avec l'horizon immédiat". G. Gusdorf, o.c., p. 12.

[95] G. Gusdorf, o.c., pp. 12, 37.

[96] "L'homme n'a jamais connu l'innocence d'une vie sans fêlure". G. Gusdorf, o.c., p. 12.

[97] "Le mythe gardera toujours le sens d'une visée vers l'intégrité perdue". G. Gusdorf, o.c., p. 12.

[98] G. Gusdorf, o.c., p. 13.

[99] R.F. Beerling, Mythe—blijvend of voorbijgaand?, in : Wijsgerig Perspectief, III (1963), p. 191.

tion. Human existence then sees the rise of articulations, as well as distinctions between "I" and the world, "I" and the group, nature and supernature, the profane and the sacred, man and God, science and religion. The reign of disconnectedness, fancy and chimeras is ended,[100] and man is emancipated from a condition of inertia, paralysis, indolence and passivity.[101] Leaving behind prehistory, he enters history,[102] where reason takes over the stabilizing role of the myth.[103] "Progress" now becomes possible.

Gusdorf's way of speaking about intellectual consciousness makes his conception of mythical consciousness even more obscure. For he speaks of intellectual consciousness with "a backward looking sadness"[104] because the "enviable happiness",[105] the "good conscience" and the "innocence" of the mythical consciousne are destroyed by the intellectual consciousness. On the other hand, he also called the mythical consciousness fanciful, disconnected, filled with chimeras, indolent, inert and sterile. How can one who uses such qualifiers be, at the same time, saddened by the disappearance of the myths?

According to Gusdorf, however, mythical consciousness does not disappear entirely but, at most, can be pushed into the background for a short time.[106] For the degeneration of everything which violates and undermines the mythical consciousness is itself thoroughly mythical. The "myth of the twentieth century" also is a myth, one of which science, progress, Marxism, Fascism and Nazism are "moments".[107] It appears obvious that Gusdorf gives a new meaning to the term "mythical" here : it now covers also every absolutistic ideology.

Today, however, says Gusdorf, man's thinking is again on the road to recover the original wealth of mythical consciousness. The "I", the world and God are the object of a renewed understanding which over-

---

[100] "Le monde mythique était un monde d'incohérence et de passivité. A cette sagesse indolente se substitue une activité de conquête. L'homme historique réduit patiemment les mirages". G. Gusdorf, o.c., p. 151.

[101] "Le mythe entraîne donc une véritable paralysie des personnalités, captives du genre de vie. La conscience réfléchie apporte l'émancipation". G. Gusdorf, o.c., p. 138.

[102] G. Gusdorf, o.c., pp. 98-106.

[103] G. Gusdorf, o.c., p. 93.

[104] H.J. Pos, Terugtocht der Rede?, in : Algemeen Nederlands Tijdschrift voor wijsbegeerte en psychologie, 46 (1953-1954), p. 72.

[105] H.J. Pos, a.c., p. 71.

[106] "L'expulsion du mythe n'est donc pas définitive' ... l'élément censuré revient comme une mauvaise conscience ...". G. Gusdorf, o.c., p. 181.

[107] G. Gusdorf, o.c., p. 190.

comes the narrowness and the one-dimensionalism of intellectual consciousness manifesting themselves in scientism and rationalism. Existential consciousness, which recognizes the value and wealth of man's prereflective involvement in the life-world is the legitimate heir of the mythical consciousness.[108] Existential consciousness refuses to let the myths' main points of interest evaporate into logical operations of a deified Reason or become ingredients of the sciences. The myths spoke about concrete human existence with greater fidelity than did philosophy or science.[109] Mythical consciousness is familiar with birth and death, sexuality, lust, marriage, fatherhood, motherhood and children's love, with war, peace and revolution, home, hearth and bread, freedom, brotherhood and fatherland, with geniality, glory, despair and misfortune, with creation, sin, salvation, damnation and God.[110] These things are irreducible meanings of human existence.[111] These were the themes of mythical consciousness, and they are again the concern of existential consciousness. The subordination of any scientific worldview to the life-world, i.e., the restoration of the "horizon of all horizons" as the origin of scientific discourse, a restoration which is being performed by existential thinking, expresses the continuation of mythical consciousness in us, says Gusdorf.[112] Mythical consciousness is essential for the authenticity of human consciousness.[113]

In the preceding pages one can see that the term "mythical" has at least four senses for Gusdorf. It refers to 1) the spontaneous form of being-in-the-world; 2) the defense mechanism against this spontaneous form; 3) consciousness as a victim of absolutistic ideologies; 4) existential consciousness. But how can anyone claim all this at the same time?

Much of what Gusdorf says can, I think, be accepted by his readers.

---

[108] "Le retour à l'unité humaine en sa plénitude se réalise aujourd'hui dans les trois domaines de l'ontologie traditionelle ... L'être dans le monde avait perdu sa densité humaine à travers les atténuations, les stérilisations de l'intellectualisme. La pensée existentielle lui restitue toute sa richesse concrète". G. Gusdorf, o.c., p. 191.

[109] "Si la philosophie paraît ainsi aveugle à l'existence concrète, le mythe la transcrit beaucoup plus fidèlement". G. Gusdorf, o.c., p. 242.

[110] G. Gusdorf, o.c., pp. 241-244.

[111] "Or le propre du mythe apparaît, en somme, de manifester le sens de l'existence. A la lumière de son intelligibilité, il est clair que l'existence possède des significations irréductibles ...". G. Gusdorf, o.c., p. 219.

[112] G. Gusdorf, o.c., p. 219.

[113] "Or la saisie mythique du réel paraît bien devoir durer aussi longtemps que l'espèce humaine". G. Gusdorf, o.c., p. 213.

The difficulty lies in his use of the common denominator "mythical" for practically everything, including the absolute rejection of the mythical. On the other hand, what he really wishes to say seems clear. He strenuously objects to letting man's integral reality evaporate into logical operations of "Reason", as was done by rationalism, and he objects to the reduction of the same reality by scientism. He does not, however, reject reason itself and its critique of myths.[114] When H.J. Pos argues that Gusdorf makes this rejection,[115] he voices a reproach to which Gusdorf readily exposes himself : he simply speaks of "reason" where he intends to refer to degenerated forms of reason. Actually, Gusdorf also speaks of mythical consciousness as "reason", but in *the broadened and enriched sense*,[116] used by phenomenology. This reason is the store-house of the fundamental human values, spoken of in the mythical stories.[117] Such stories should be accepted only as "pointers" and "under benefice of inventory".[118] Critical reason, philosophy, must decipher their meanings.[119] Mythical consciousness is the human being himself, and the mythical stories develop all his possibilities, without distinguishing the valuable from the valueless. Indiscriminately and without offering any legitimation, the myths present values and non-values "in the raw".[120] Critical reason, however, cannot confirm every suggested value but exercises a purifying function. If it does not accept this task, the myths run wild.[121]

The preceding paragraph offers us an opportunity to indicate a second point of agreement between Gusdorf's mythical consciousness and phenomenology's enlarged reason, viz., the prereflective character of both. Phenomenology's enlarged reason is the "light" of existent subjectivity itself, the prereflective and spontaneous letting meaning appear, the "dwelling" in and being familiar with reality, the *Dasein*. According to phenomenology, herein lies the cradle of all explicit meanings assigned

---

[114] G. Gusdorf, *o.c.*, pp. 250-286.

[115] H.J. Pos, *a.c.*, p. 75-77.

[116] "La conscience mythique ne signifie donc nullement le renoncement à la raison. Bien plutôt, elle nous apparaît dans le sens d'un élargissement et d'un enrichissement de la raison". G. Gusdorf, *o.c.*, p. 281.

[117] "... le conservatoire des valeurs fondamentales". G. Gusdorf, *o.c.*, p. 278.

[118] "Les mythes ne doivent donc être acceptés qu'à titre indicatif et sous bénéfice d'inventaire". G. Gusdorf, *o.c.*, p. 282.

[119] G. Gusdorf, *o.c.*, p. 282.

[120] "... l'état sauvage ...". G. Gusdorf, *o.c.*, p. 284.

[121] G. Gusdorf, *o.c.*, p. 285.

to reality, a cradle which is a pre-understanding that is existence itself.[122] Gusdorf calls this the "mythical consciousness", which is not opposed to reason.[123]

Gusdorf places the "affirmation" of God within the framework briefly sketched above. In the room he has made for it, this "affirmation" is made almost inevitable. That is why he limits himself to a few quotations, mainly from Kierkegaard, Barth, Buber and Marcel,[124] while, on the other hand, he keeps up a running battle against all those who, misled by the degeneration of reason, have reduced the God of Christian revelation to "the God of philosophers".[125] Gusdorf refers to this reduction as "atheism".

For Gusdorf, the religious attitude consists in man's openness to the encounter with the living God. This encounter does not make him the adherent of a doctrine,[126] but a witness to "One who lives".[127] This conviction induces Gusdorf to deny *any* mediating function to reason, not only to degenerated reason but to reason as such. For reason can have not other aim than to make God subservient to itself.[128] And this is what metaphysics has always done.

4. RETROSPECT AND PROSPECT

According to Bultmann and Vergote, the time of myths is past. What the myths used to say can and must now be expressed differently. Gusdorf thinks that mythical consciousness needs the interpreting intervention of critical reason, for myths can run wild. Mythical stories can only be accepted as "pointers" and with reservation. Gusdorf conceives mythical consciousness as the implicit, enlarged reason spoken of by phenomeno-

---

[122] "Toute connaissance doit rejoindre une préintelligibilité, correspondant à la structure même de l'être humain". G. Gusdorf, *o.c.*, p. 264.

[123] "L'opposition entre la raison et le mythe n'est donc pas radicale. Une réconciliation s'avère possible, qui permet peut-être de pressentir la réalité d'une forme suprême de la connaissance humaine". G. Gusdorf, *o.c.*, p. 264.

[124] G. Gusdorf, *o.c.*, pp. 221-234.

[125] G. Gusdorf, *o.c.*, pp. 161-171.

[126] "La rencontre ne nous fait pas sectateur d'une doctrine, mais témoin d'un vivant". G. Gusdorf, *o.c.*, p. 230.

[127]. G. Gusdorf, *o.c.*, p. 231.

[128] "... l'entreprise de soumettre Dieu à l'obéissance de l'intellect". G. Gusdorf, *o.c.*, p. 232.

logy. That is why explicit, critical reason is not the enemy of mythical consciousness.

Strange to say, however, such an enmity does exist for Gusdorf when critical reason—philosophy—busies itself with the "affirmation" of God. There its intervention can only be disastrous. The question to be asked here is, of course, whether religious consciousness can never run amok. There is a kind of "religiousness" which drives man to sacrifice little children and burn surviving widows, but there is also a religiousness which contributes to the suppression of such violations of humanity. There is a kind of "religiousness" which leads to temple prostitution, but also one which invites to chastity. One kind of "religiousness" functions as an opiate of the people, another makes an authentic victory over despair possible. There is a "religiousness" that can be wrecked by the progress of physical science, but the same progress can also make it possible for man to give authentic expression to his religiousness. Some forms of "religiousness" simply collapse with the decline of a political system, others save man by wrecking a political system. Some forms of "religiousness' result in backwardness, ignorance, tyranny and psychical disturbance, others give man an opportunity to find authentic freedom. Gusdorf dwells extensively on the fatal consequences resulting from the interference of degenerate reason in the "affirmation" of God. But he says nothing about the disasters which "religiousness" can cause when critical reason is *not at all* allowed to function in this matter.[129]

The history of philosophy shows that "reason" has busied itself very much with the "affirmation" of God. In the following three chapters I shall attempt to survey the various contemporary standpoints with respect to the metaphysical "affirmation" of God. As was the case with mythical discourse, there are thinkers who reject metaphysical language in order to give a foundation to their "denial" of God, but there are also others who do the same for the purpose of making their "affirmation" of God authentic. The latter, then, do not reject *all* metaphysical discourse "about" God, but only an interpretation of metaphysical speech which they consider untenable. Finally, there are thinkers who hold that metaphysical discourse is the only possible way of speaking "about"

---

[129] "Il n'existe pas d'hérésie monstrueuse, d'orgie infernale, de cruauté religieuse, de folie, d'absurdité ou d'insanité magico-religieuse qui ne soit 'justifiée' dans son principe même, par une fausse—*parce que partiale, incomplète*—interprétation d'un grandiose symbolisme". Mircea Eliade, *Images et Symboles*, Essais sur le symbolisme magico-religieux, Paris, 1952, p. 18.

God. As in the case of mythical speaking, the actual meaning of these different standpoints depends again on the way one interprets metaphysical consciousness.

CHAPTER TWO

THE REJECTION OF METAPHYSICS AND
THE "NEGATION" OF GOD

When contemporary writers reflect on the claims of metaphysical thought, they usually intend to speak about the possibility or impossibility of affirming the "suprasensual" (Kant). Kant's use of this term was in keeping with what had become accepted in philosophy since Descartes; it refers to the universe, the soul or the "I", and God. Here, however, I will speak only about metaphysical reflection as thinking "about" God, even though the same term has also a broader usage.[1]

A restriction will again have to be made in the description of the way the "affirmation" of God is rejected. Strictly speaking, so-called postulatory atheism should also be included, that is to say, those ways of thinking which demand the "negation" of God in the name of the authenticity of human existence. According to Marx, Nietzsche, Freud, Sartre, Merleau-Ponty and many others, the "affirmation" of God makes authentic human existence impossible. These authors place full emphasis on the description of the demands imposed by this authenticity. They oppose to them an idea of God borrowed from *others* and then proceed to show that such an "idea" makes the authenticity which they defend impossible. This means that they reject the metaphysics of *others*, without *themselves* investigating the necessity, possibility or impossibility of metaphysical thought.[2] They reject the "affirmation" of God on other than epistemological grounds, but they reject this "affirmation" without reflecting on reflection "on" God.

In this chapter, however, I shall limit myself to the thought of those authors who, on the basis of explicit reflection on the necessity, possibility or impossibility of man's "saying"-of-*is*, have rejected metaphysics

---

[1] "Auf dem Gebiet der *Metaphysik* (einschliesslich aller Wertphilosophie und Normwissenschaft) ...". R. Carnap, *Überwindung der Metaphysik durch logische Analyse der Sprache*, in : Erkenntnis II (1931), p. 220.

[2] W. Luijpen, *Phenomenology and Atheism*, Pittsburgh 1964[2], pp. 92-337.

and the "affirmation" of God. It stands to reason that only specific ways of thinking will be considered and that there is no intention to present a complete list of names and representatives of those ways of thinking.

ANALYTIC PHILOSOPHY

In most of the older representatives of analytic philosophy the rejection of metaphysics is, as a matter of course, accompanied by the "denial" of God. It would go too far, however, to say that all of them reject metaphysics *in order to* find a basis for their "denial" of God. Most of them are not at all aiming at a rejection of God but view speaking "about" God simply as meaningless because there exists no cognitively meaningful language in which such a discourse can be made.[3] If, then, God is spoken of anyhow, so they hold, this is simply a misuse of language because one disregards what language can and cannot do.

These philosophers do not claim that statements "about" God are *not true*. The question whether a statement is true or not true presupposes that the statement is meaningful. One who says that "the table is teavy", that "Caesar is and" or that "Napoleon is a prime number"[4] cannot possibly demand that anyone investigate the truth or falsity of such statements. They do not satisfy the demands of cognitive meaningfulness which is inherent in language; that is why there is no basis for debating their truth or falsity. But a question can be asked about the statement, "the moon is square". This is a cognitively meaningful statement, but obviously not true.

The rejection of metaphysics by some representatives of analytic philosophy is the logical and consistent development of Hume's empiricism. It continues this empiricism by searching for a criterion of cognitive meaningfulness for language. When and on which conditions may a certain use of language be said to be cognitively meaningful? The answer to this question is given by the principle of verification, which says that the meaning of a statement is determined by the way the statement *can* be verified.[5] But what exactly does this mean?

---

[3] G. Nuchelmans, *Overzicht van de analytische wijsbegeerte*. Utrecht-Antwerpen, 1969, pp. 134-135.

[4] R. Carnap, *Überwindung der Metaphysik durch logische Analyse der Sprache*, in : Erkenntnis II (1931), pp. 219-228.

[5] "Kann auf keine Weise angegeben werden, wann ein Satz wahr ist, so hat der

Generally speaking, when can we be certain that the meaning of a question is clear? According to Moritz Schlick, this is the case if—and only if—we can exactly indicate the conditions on which the question must be answered with a "yes" or a "no".[6] The question, "does this bottle leak"? is clear because I know that it has to be answered with a "yes" if water poured into the bottle seeps out of it. If this does not happen, then the question must be answered with a "no". I know what the question means because I can indicate these conditions.

From this it follows that a statement is wholly *meaningless* if it is, in principle, impossible to indicate the conditions by which the statement can be made true or false,[7] for indicating these conditions is *the same* as understanding the meaning of the statement.[8] If a statement is to be meaningful, then, its truth or falsity must imply a difference that can be indicated. An assertion whose truth or falsity leaves the world exactly the same does not say anything and therefore is meaningless.[9] Similarly, a statement never says more than can be verified. For one who claims that it says more must show what he means by this "more". Now, this is possible only by indicating the conditions which decide about the truth or falsity of the statement he makes about this "more"—in other words, by indicating what would be different in the world if one denies this "more".[10] He who manages to do this thereby verifies this "more" and, at the same time, eliminates it. And one who does not succeed in doing this says nothing.

Among the older analytic philosophers the requirement that statements must be cognitively meaningful amounts, generally speaking, to the claim that this requirement is met by the analytic judgments of logic

---

Satz überhaupt keinen Sinn; denn der Sinn eines Satzes ist die Methode seiner Verifikation". Fr. Waismann, *Logische Analyse des Wahrscheinlichkeitsbegriffs*, in : Erkenntnis, I (1930-1931), p. 229.

[6] Moritz Schlick, *Gesammelte Aufsätze*, Hildesheim, 1969, p. 89.

[7] "Vermag ich einen Satz prinzipiell *nicht* zu verifizieren, d.h. weiss ich absolut nicht, wie ich es anstellen soll, was ich tun müsste, um seine Wahrheit oder Falschheit zu ermitteln, dann weiss ich offenbar gar nicht, was der Satz eigentlich behauptet". Moritz Schlick, *o.c.*, p. 90.

[8] "Die Angabe der Umstände, unter denen ein Satz wahr ist, ist dasselbe wie die Angabe seines Sinnes, und nichts anderes". Moritz Schlick, *o.c.*, p. 90.

[9] Moritz Schlick, *o.c.*, p. 91.

[10] "Jede Aussage ... besagt nur das, was verifiziert wird und schlechterdings *nichts* darüber hinaus. Behauptete jemand, dass sie doch mehr enthalte, so muss er sagen können, was denn dies Mehr sei, und dazu muss er wiederum sagen, was denn in der Welt anders sein würde, wenn er nicht recht hätte". Moritz Schlick, *o.c.*, p. 93.

and mathematics, the empirical judgments of the positive sciences, and the judgments of ordinary language insofar as they are approximations to empirical-scientific statements.[11]

Rudolf Carnap

The condemnation of metaphysics is implicit in all this. Metaphysical statements are not meaningful but a misuse of language. According to Carnap, metaphysics refuses to view its judgments as analytic—a view that would make them meaningful. Metaphysics assigns itself the task of discovering and stating knowledge which lies beyond the domain of the empirical sciences.[12] But, we saw, the meaning of a statement lies in the method of its verification; a statement asserts only as much as can be verified. Since, then, metaphysics does not wish to make analytic judgments and holds that its statements cannot be verified by the empirical sciences, it follows that its judgments are nothing but pseudo-judgments.[13]

The word "God" also is a pseudo-word. Used in a metaphysical sense, it refers to something transempirical; therefore it is meaningless.[14] Even the first demand of logic is disregarded in the use of the term "God". This first demand is that one indicate how the term occurs in elementary sentences. Such a sentence would assume here the form: "X is a God". But metaphysics absolutely rejects this form, without replacing it by any other; or else, if it accepts the form, it neglects to indicate the syntactic category for the variable "X". "God" means something like the term "teavy".[15]

Carnap stresses that his position differs from that of more ancient anti-metaphysicians. They called metaphysics a fairy-tale. But the statements in a fairy-tale are not meaningless because they do not violate the laws of logic; they merely go against experience and therefore are not true.[16] Metaphysics is not even meaningful.

According to Carnap, it is useless to appeal to the limitation of man's knowledge in an attempt to save the meaningfulness of metaphysics.

---

[11] G. Nuchelmans, o.c., p. 134.

[12] "Da die Metaphysik weder analytische Sätze sagen, noch ins Gebiet der empirischen Wissenschaft geraten will ...". R. Carnap, a.c., p. 236.

[13] R. Carnap, a.c., p. 236.

[14] R. Carnap, a.c., p. 226.

[15] R. Carnap, a.c., pp. 226-227.

[16] R. Carnap, a.c., p. 232.

Metaphysical statements, so it is sometimes said, are not verifiable, but nevertheless they are meaningful as conjectures and surmises of the answers which a perfectly knowing being would give to our questions. The trouble is that the questions themselves are meaningles if the meaning of a term cannot be specified or if a connection of words goes against syntax. Questions like, "is the table teavy?" and, "are even numbers darker than uneven numbers"? are meaningless, and not even an omniscient being could answer them. Animals could conceivably give us new knowledge, for instance, of a hitherto unknown law of nature. But this is possible only because we can verify such new knowledge. Statements which cannot be verified at all cannot be understood; thus they can never be considered as the communication of information.[17] They simply are meaningless chatter.[18]

Carnap finally had to ask himself how for so many centuries so many eminent thinkers could have busied themselves with meaningless juxtaposed words. Does metaphysics then have no contents at all? A negative answer must be given to this question, thinks Carnap. Although the pseudo-statements of metaphysics are not a "representation of a state of affairs",[19] they express a general and usually emotional attitude toward life. There is nothing special in this. One who has artistic talent expresses this attitude in a work of art. The metaphysician obviously lacks this talent; his thought is an inadequate way of expressing his fundamental attitude toward life. In principle, one can hardly object to the fact that some people express their attitude toward life in this way and that others do it that way. But the *way* chosen by the metaphysician is such that it gives rise to the suggestion that metaphysics is something which it is not at all, viz., a descriptive theory.

While metaphysics has no theoretical content whatsoever, the form of expression chosen by the metaphysician builds up the fiction that there is an objective content. The worst of it is that the metaphysician himself believes in this fiction and thinks that truth and untruth are at issue in his speaking.[20] His illusion does not arise from the fact that

[17] R. Carnap, *a.c.*, pp. 232-233.

[18] "Aber in Wirklichkeit liegt die Sache so, dass es keine sinnvollen metaphysischen Sätze geben kann. Das folgt aus der Aufgabe, die die Metaphysik sich stellt; sie will eine Erkenntnis finden und darstellen, die der empirischen Wissenschaft nicht zugänglich ist". R. Carnap, *a.c.*, p. 236.

[19] R. Carnap, *a.c.*, p. 238.

[20] "Der Metaphysiker glaubt sich im Gebiet zu bewegen, in dem es um wahr und falsch geht. In Wirklichkeit hat er jedoch nichts ausgesagt, sondern nur etwas zum Ausdruck gebracht, wie ein Künstler". R. Carnap, *a.c.*, p. 240.

he uses language to express himself, for lyrical poets also use it and they do not fall into the trap. They do not adduce arguments or argue with other poets. In other words, unlike metaphysicians, they understand their own speech.[21]

Music, says Carnap, is perhaps the purest way to express a fundamental attitude, for it does not at all refer to objects. The sense of harmony is perfectly expressed in Mozart's music. Lacking Mozart's talent, the metaphysician attempts to do the same but he does it inadequately, in a monistic system of concepts. Metaphysicians are musicians without musical talents. They have a tendency to form theories but do not put this tendency to work in the positive sciences; they have a need for self-expression but do not put it to work in an artistic endeavor; instead, they confuse the two and produce an edifice which is meaningless in the order of knowledge and inadequate as an expression of an attitude of life.[22]

Ayer

Similar considerations can be found in the work of A.J. Ayer.[23] The metaphysicians themselves, he says, do not wish their statements to be called *a priori* judgments, which would make them tautologies. But it is impossible to call metaphysical statements empirical judgments. For they claim to express a suprasensual reality. Now, there is no way in which such statements can be verified; therefore they are nonsensical.[24] All the work and trouble devoted to metaphysics is spent in the "production of nonsense".[25]

Speaking "about" God is thereby also condemned.[26] First of all, God's existence can never be *demonstrated*. For the possibility of such a demonstration presupposes that the premises leading to the affirmation of God's existence are *certain*. But even if it is assumed that such premises are verifiable, they would not be more than probable because

---

[21] R. Carnap, *a.c.*, p. 240.

[22] R. Carnap, *a.c.*, pp. 240-241.

[23] A.J. Ayer, *Demonstration of the impossibility of metaphysics*, in: Mind, 43 (1934), pp. 335-345.

[24] "And as tautologies and empirical hypotheses form the entire class of significant propositions, we are justified in concluding that all metaphysical assertions are nonsensical". A.J. Ayer, *Language, Truth and Logic*, London, 1953[9], p. 41.

[25] A.J. Ayer, *o.c.*, p. 34.

[26] "... this possibility has already been ruled out by our treatment of metaphysics". A.J. Ayer, *o.c.*, p. 114.

their truth could be taken away by further verification. The assertion, "God exists", then, is never certain, never demonstrated. Only *a priori* statements are certain because they are tautologies. But from tautologies one can only deduce another tautology, and not the existence of God.[27]

Secondly, the assertion, "God exists", is not even probable. It could be probable only if it were an empirically verifiable statement, such as one which follows from the regularity with which certain phenomena occur in nature. But then the assertion that God exists would merely mean that a certain regularity occurs in nature. As soon, however, as the assertion of God's existence is reduced to the affirmation of a certain regularity in nature, the religious man objects and claims that he wishes to affirm a transcendent being, a being which can be known on the basis of certain empirical manifestations but which cannot itself be defined in terms of these manifestations.[28] In that case, says Ayer, the term "God" is a metaphysical term and therefore nonsensical.[29] Thus, the assertion, "God exists", is neither true nor false, but simply meaningless, just as also the statement, "God does not exist", is meaningless.[30]

For Ayer this means that agnosticism also is untenable. The agnostic claims that he does not know how to decide which of the two propositions, "a transcendent God exists" and "there is no transcendent God", is true. He admits that one of the two assertions is true but does not know which one. What he should realize is that both are meaningless, that the question, "true or false"? cannot possibly be asked. Only if deities are identified with natural objects can meaningful statements be made about them. If, e.g., someone asserts that the occurrence of thunderstorms is necessary and sufficient to verify the truth of the statement that Yahweh is angry, his statement is meaningful because he does not affirm anything else than that there is a thunderstorm.[31] "Sophisticated religions", however, assume that a "Person" controls the empirical world without being localized in it. That "Person" is deemed to be "higher" than the empirical world and is placed outside this world; he becomes the bearer

---

[27] A.J. Ayer, *o.c.*, pp. 114-115.

[28] A.J. Ayer, *o.c.*, p. 115.

[29] "But in that case the term 'god' is a metaphysical term. And if 'god' is a metaphysical term, then it cannot be even probable that god exists. For to say that 'God exists' is to make a metaphysical utterance which cannot be either true or false". A.J. Ayer, *o.c.*, p. 115.

[30] A.J. Ayer, *o.c.*, pp. 115-116.

[31] A.J. Ayer, *o.c.*, p. 116.

of supra-empirical attributes. But in this way the term "God" becomes a metaphysical and therefore nonsensical word.[32]

The theists themselves, says Ayer, agree with him when you listen carefully. For they say that God's nature is a mystery which surpasses all human understanding. Now, one who makes such a claim asserts that what he is talking about is incomprehensible. But then he should also be willing to accept that his statements are incomprehensible when he describes the incomprehensible.[33]

The mystic, however, claims that his intuition reveals truth to him, even though he is unable to explain this truth to others. If others do not have this intuitive power, they have no basis on which they can deny that it is an intuition. Ayer replies to this objection that he does not intend to exclude any possibilities whatsoever to arrive at true statements. If the mystic's intuitive power makes certain discoveries, one cannot deny them by arguing that they have been made by means of an intuitive power. But we have to wait, of course, says Ayer, to see what statements the mystic is going to make in order to see whether these statements can be verified by empirical observations. And this does not happen. Intuition, therefore, does not disclose any facts at all to the mystic. And it does not make any sense to assert that he has observed facts but is unable to express them. One who really has obtained information about facts is able to express them. The assertion that the mystic cannot express what he knows means that his mystic intuition has no cognitive value. He merely supplies us with indirect information about his own mental condition.[34]

These considerations are also decisive with respect to religious experience in general. Some philosophers say that there is not any reason not to believe someone who claims to see God and to believe someone who asserts that he sees a yellow spot. Ayer answers that he is quite willing to believe someone who claims to see God as long as he means by this something like the assertion that he sees a yellow spot. However, people who claim to have a religious experience are not satisfied with such an assertion, but say that they experience a transcendent being. But such an assertion cannot be empirically verified, and that is why their state-

[32] "It is only when we enquire what God's attributes are that we discover that 'God', in this usage, is not a genuine name". A.J. Ayer, o.c., p. 116.

[33] A.J. Ayer, o.c., p. 118.

[34] A.J. Ayer, o.c., pp. 118-119.

ments are nonsensical.[35] The appeal to religious experience to demonstrate God's existence is simply fallacious.[36] The fact that there are people who have religious experiences is psychologically interesting, but philosophers who appeal to it merely gather materials for the psychoanalyst.[37]

What we have seen in the preceding pages is the general attitude of the older representatives of analytical philosophy with respect to metaphysics. A few details may be added here by discussing also the view of Flew, Hare and Findlay.

Indicating the conditions in which a statement is true or false is the same as understanding the sense of this statement; that is why Schlick emphasized that it must make a demonstrable difference whether a statement is true or false. A statement which leaves the world exactly the same, whether it is true or false, does not say anything and is therefore meaningless.[38]

This has led some thinkers to the conclusion that it is then perhaps better to replace the principle of verification by the principle of falsification. Karl Popper has made this claim,[39] not as a criterion for the meaningfulness of statement in general, but as a means to distinguish statements of the empirical sciences from statements of the non-empirical sciences, such as mathematics and logic, and from statements of "metaphysical" systems.[40] Popper, then, was looking for a "criterion of demarcation"[41] and thought that he could find this in the falsifiability of an empirical-scientific system.[42] It is not possible, says Popper, to verify a statement of empirical science in a decisive and definitive way, for a

[35] A.J. Ayer, o.c., p. 119.

[36] "... the argument from religious experience is altogether fallacious". A.J. Ayer, o.c., p. 119.

[37] A.J. Ayer, o.c., p. 120.

[38] Moritz Schlick, Gesammelte Aufsätze, Hildesheim, 1969, p. 89.

[39] K. Popper, Logik der Forschung, Zur Erkenntnistheorie der modernen Naturwissenschaft, Wien, 1935.

[40] "Die Aufgabe, ein solches Kriterium zu finden, durch das wir die empirische Wissenschaft gegenüber Mathematik und Logik, aber auch gegenüber 'metaphysischen' Systemen abgrenzen können, bezeichnen wir als Abgrenzungsproblem". K. Popper, o.c., p. 7.

[41] K. Popper, o.c., p. 12.

[42] "Diese Überlegung legt den Gedanken nahe, als Abgrenzungskriterium nicht die Verifizierbarkeit, sondern die Falsifizierbarkeit des Systems vorzuschlagen; mit anderen Worten : Wir fordern zwar nicht, dass das System auf empirisch-methodischem Wege endgültig positiv ausgezeichnet werden kann, aber wir fordern dass es die logische Form des Systems ermöglicht, dieses auf dem Wege der methodischen Nachprüfung negativ auszuzeichnen". K. Popper, o.c., pp. 12-13.

universal law always says more than can be justified on the basis of actually observed instances. It is possible, however, to falsify a statement of empirical science in a decisive and definitive fashion. A single well-established fact contradicting the statement suffices for this purpose. And if an empirical-scientific system *cannot* be made untrue by any observable fact, it does not have any empirical meaning at all.[43]

Anthony Flew went further by separating the falsification principle from Popper's original intention and applying it to man's speaking "about" God.

Flew

Let us begin with a parable, says Flew and he paraphrases a story borrowed from John Wisdom. Once upon a time there were two explorers, who deep in the jungle came upon a beautiful garden. The first explorer then says that a gardener must have been at work here, but his companion denies this. To settle the issue, they put electrically charged barbed wire around the garden and patrol it with blood hounds. But no gardener shows himself, no cry betrays anyone who got entangled in the barbed wire, the electric current is useless, and the blood hounds do not react. The "believing" explorer, however, fails to be convinced. He simply claims that the gardener is invisible because he has no body; that is why the charged wire and the barbs also are to no avail. And being odorless, there is nothing by which the blood hounds can smell him. Driven to despair, his sceptical companion exclaims, "But what remains in all this of your original claim? What is the difference between your invisible, incorporeal and odorless gardener and my 'no gardener'? "[44]

According to Flew, theology always speaks like the above-mentioned "believing" explorer. Statements such as "God intends", "God created the world" and "God loves us as a father loves his children" seem to be conceived by theologians as assertions.[45] Now, one who asserts that this or that is so must also deny that this or that is not so. Thus in doubt whether this or that is so, one will look for instances which could contradict his assertion. But in the preceding parable, as in theological discourse, it turns out to be impossible to conceive anything at all that

[43] "Ein empirisch-wissenschaftliches System muss an der Erfahrung scheitern können". K. Popper, *o.c.*, p. 13.

[44] A. Flew, *Theology and Falsification*, in : New essays in Philosophical Theology, ed. by A. Flew and A. MacIntyre, London, 1969[7], p. 96.

[45] A. Flew, *a.c.*, p. 97.

could falsify the above-mentioned assertions. When no gardener shows himself, he is called "invisible". When God's love does not take action when a beloved and innocent child is dying, his love is said to be "beyond human measurements" or "unfathomable". Statements, however, which simply *cannot* be falsified do not affirm anything and are not really assertions at all.[46] They die from the "thousand qualifications" added to them because with all these qualifications they ultimately no longer assert anything.[47] If *any* state of affairs can be harmonized with a certain affirmation, then this affirmation no longer says anything and is no longer a real affirmation.

Later, Flew recognized that he had not done justice to the theologian's discourse. He had presented matters as if the theologian did *not* conceive suffering as a fact arguing against the truth of the statement. "God loves man". But B. Mitchell pointed out to Flew that he was wrong on this score. The irreconcilability of suffering with God's love "generates the most intractable of theological problems".[48]

Flew now grants that he had disregarded the theologian's attempt to find an explanation of suffering which does not contradict the affirmation of God's love. But, he adds, the attributes which the theologian ascribes to God are of such a nature that every explanation becomes impossible. One cannot say that God would like to help the sufferer but is unable to do this, for "God is almighty"; or that he would help if only he knew, for "God knows everything"; or that God is not responsible for the evil of the others, for "God has created the others". The divine attributes make every explanation impossible; that is why the theologian is forced to take refuge in the "thousand qualifications" which completely wreck his original assertion.[49]

Hare

Richard M. Hare has replied to Flew by telling a parable of his own. A certain lunatic student, he relates, is convinced that all the dons

---

[46] "And if there is nothing which a putative assertion denies then there is nothing which it asserts either : and so it is not really an assertion". A. Flew, *a.c.*, p. 98.

[47] A. Flew, *a.c.*, p. 97.

[48] B. Mitchell, *Theology and Falsification*, in : New Essays ..., p. 103.

[49] "So though I entirely concede that Mitchell was absolutely right to insist against me that the theologian's first move is to look for an *explanation*, I still think that in the end, if relentlessly pursued, he will have to resort to the avoiding action of *qualification*. And there lies the danger of that death by a thousand qualifications". A. Flew, *o.c.*, p. 107.

intend to murder him. His friends introduce him to the most amiable and respectable dons in an effort to cure him from his illusion. They point out that so much friendliness surely indicates that he must be mistaken about their intentions to murder him. But to no avail; he cannot be convinced. All that friendliness, he says, simply is a part of their diabolical cunning.[50]

We say, argues Hare, that such a student is mentally deluded. But deluded with respect to what? The truth or the falsity of an affirmation? If Flew's view is applied to the student's assertion, his affirmation does not mean anything; it is not even an affirmation because it cannot be falsified. But from this it doesn't follow that there is no difference between what a mentally disturbed person thinks about the dons and what we think of them. Otherwise there would be no reason to call ourselves "healthy" and the student "sick", there would be no difference between "normal" and "abnormal".[51]

Hare calls this difference between "normal" and "abnormal" a difference in "blik", the way of looking at reality.[52] A normal "blik" also is a "blik", it is not "no blik". All Flew has done, says Hare, is show that a "blik" is not an affirmation or a system of affirmations. But even if a "blik" is not an affirmation, it remains extremely important to have the right "blik".

Flew's mistake, according to Hare, is that he conceives theological discourse as a kind of descriptive and explanatory way of speaking, in the sense scientists attach to these words.[53] However, this is not what theological discourse is. The speaking of the religious man and the theologian gives expression to a "blik", even as the presupposition that scientific explanations are possible is the expression of a "blik". Let us assume that someone asserts : everything that happens, happens by pure chance. According to Flew, his claim would not be an assertion since it could never be falsified and can be harmonized with whatever happens or does not happen. Such a claim is the expression of a "blik". Yet its consequences are enormous. It makes a great difference whether one holds this "blik" or another one. For one who claims that everything

---

[50] R.M. Hare, *Theology and Falsification*, in : New Essays ..., pp. 99-100.

[51] R.M. Hare, *a.c.*, p. 100.

[52] "Let us call that in which we differ from this lunatic, our respective *bliks*". R.M. Hare, *a.c.*, p. 100.

[53] "The mistake of the position which Flew selects for attack is to regard this kind of talk as some sort of *explanation*, as scientists are accustomed to use the word". R.M. Hare, *a.c.*, p. 101.

happens by chance can never explain or predict anything. This is the kind of difference that exists, says Hare, between people who believe in God and those who do not.[54]

Flew could offer only a weak reply to Hare's criticism. He claims that Hare should not call himself a genuine Christian if he does not admit that theological assertions really intend to be statements and views them only as expressions of a "blik".[55] According to Flew, theological assertions do intend to affirm that this or that is really the case. But since such affirmations can never be falsified, they have no meaning.

In the preceding pages we have seen examples in which all speaking "about" God is rejected on the ground that such speaking cannot be verified or falsified. Among the older representatives of analytic philosophy, however, there are also some who think that this philosophy can decisively and definitively *prove* the non-existence of God. J.N. Findlay offers us an example.[56]

Findlay

Findlay begins by pointing out that all arguments hitherto used to prove God's existence turn out to be indecisive. Religious people are resigned to this situation; some even like the idea that something which greatly transcends thinking in clear and distinct ideas also transcends the possibility of proving its existence. And non-religious people soften their rejection of God with a dose of agnosticism. But, according to Findlay, both are wrong and he promises to *prove* that God cannot exist.[57]

Who is the God whose non-existence Findlay wishes to prove? He is the "adequate object of religious attitudes".[58] Among these religious attitudes we find bending down and subjecting oneself, fully devoting oneself without asking any questions and kneeling down in adoration. But such attitudes are normal only if they are an answer to an object deserving these attitudes. What, then, ought such an object to be?

First of all, this object must show an evident superiority. It must transcend us human beings in greatness, power, wisdom or other quali-

---

[54] "This is the sort of difference that there is between those who really believe in God and those who really disbelieve in him". R.M. Hare, *a.c.*, p. 102.

[55] "If Hare's religion really is a *blik*, involving no cosmological assertions about the nature and activities of a supposed personal creator, then surely he is not a Christian at all". A. Flew, *a.c.*, p. 108.

[56] J.N. Findlay. *Can God's existence be disproved?*, in : New Essays ..., pp. 47-56.

[57] J.N. Findlay, *a.c.*, pp. 47-48.

[58] J.N. Findlay, *a.c.*, p. 48.

ties,[59] for otherwise it does not deserve our adoration. Secondly, its superiority must be an infinite superiority; otherwise another object, an infinitely superior object could conceivably demand our adoration, so that our attitude of adoration with respect to the first object would not be justified.[60] Thirdly, all other objects must be dependent on this infinitely superior object, and none of them may have any perfection which it could ascribe to itself without having derived it from the infinitely superior object. Finally, we must assume that the object of our religious attitude deserves our worship only if it does not merely *happen* to exist and the other objects do not merely *happen* to depend on that infinitely superior object. The object of our adoration must exist *of necessity* and the other objects must *of necessity* depend on it. Accordingly, it is necessary that no alternative be conceivable to the existence of a truly "divine" object. Essence and existence must coincide in it;[61] and all qualities ascribed to it must belong to it in a necessary way.[62]

We now have enough, says Findlay, to see that the existence of God can be disproved. The adequate object of our religious attitudes must be a Necessary Being; likewise, the statement, "God exists", must be a necessary proposition. Now, propositions are necessary only if they are tautological. But, as such, they say *nothing* about reality. The statement, "celibates are unmarried", is necessary, but its necessity merely reflects our usage of words, the conventions of our language.[63] Only synthetic statements could say something about the *reality* of God. But synthetic judgments can never be necessary, they can always be falsified by further experience; hence "reality" and "necessity" can never go together.

Accordingly, the affirmations that can be made in synthetic judgments about reality are insufficient for the "religious attitude", they are never about a "Necessary Existence", a "Necessary Goodness", a "Necessary Wisdom"; consequently, they are never affirmations of God. From this

---

[59] "To feel religiously is therefore to presume surpassing greatness in some object". J.N. Findlay, *o.c.*, p. 51.

[60] "And hence we are led on irresistibly to demand that our religious object should have an *unsurpassable* supremacy along all avenues, that it should tower *infinitely* above all other objects". J.N. Findlay, *a.c.*, p. 51.

[61] J.N. Findlay, *a.c.*, p. 52.

[62] "And so we are led on irresistibly ... to hold that an adequate object of our worship must possess its various qualities *in some necessary manner*". J.N. Findlay, *a.c.*, p. 53.

[63] "Necessity in propositions merely reflects our use of words, the arbitrary conventions of our language". J.N. Findlay, *a.c.*, p. 54.

it follows that it does not make sense to balance precariously in an agnostic attitude.[64] On the day when Anselm formulated his proof for God's existence, what he actually formulated was the proof for the non-existence of God.[65]

The ideas of the older representatives of analytic philosophy exemplify the trend of philosophy in which the "affirmation" of God is rejected together with metaphysics. I have endeavored to explain the essential points of this trend. My reference to the "older representatives" of analytic philosophy was not entirely correct, for I have spoken only of the logical positivism of the Vienna Circle and not about the logical atomism of Bertrand Russell and the early Wittgenstein, which preceded the Vienna Circle.

In logical positivism the rejection of metaphysics has the implication that God's existence is also "negated".[66] There exists, however also a trend of thought which rejects metaphysics in order to make the "affirmation" of God authentic.

---

[64] J.N. Findlay, a.c., p. 55.

[65] "Or 'non-significance', if this alternative is preferred". J.N. Findlay, a.c., p. 55, footnote.

[66] "Statements having to do with an invisible, ineffable God, a transcendent 'absolute', and the whole field of classical metaphysics in general could be neither proved nor disproved. Having no empirical function, they could not be called true or false, and they were consequently regarded as meaningless". Paul M. van Buren, *The Secular Meaning of the Gospel*, based on an analysis of its language, London, 1966³, pp. 14-15.

CHAPTER THREE

THE REJECTION OF METAPHYSICS AND
THE "AFFIRMATION" OF GOD

As was mentioned at the beginning of the preceding chapter, in the present context "metaphysical thought" exclusively refers to thinking "about" God. It should be obvious, then, that the rejection of metaphysics can be related to the "*affirmation*" of God only insofar as certain thinkers do not reject metaphysics *in toto* but only a certain interpretation of it which, in their eyes, is untenable. There are several ways in which this can be the case.

1. KANT'S SO-CALLED "AGNOSTICISM"

Immanual Kant had been educated in the rationalism of Christian von Wolff, but he had never been completely carried away by it.[1] For example, he always objected to the ontological proof for God's existence, so cherished by rationalism. Similarly, he had never been convinced that the views of Leibniz and Wolff about space were correct. Yet it was only slowly that he managed to detach himself from rationalism. He began to realize that necessity of thought should not unqualifiedly be identified with reality, that logico-conceptual operations do not say anything about reality. Metaphysicians became for him builders of thought worlds unrelated to reality.[2]

Kant then began to look for the relationship with reality, not in the innate concepts of rationalism, but in the concepts of empiricism, which are born from experience. Thus he replaced one form of dogmatism by another. According to his own testimony,[3] however, Hume's scepti-

---

[1] H.J. De Vleeschauwer, *Immanuel Kant*, Antwerpen-Nijmegen, 1931, p. 88.

[2] Wilhelm Windelband, *Lehrbuch der Geschichte der Philosophie*, herausgegeben von Heinz Heimsoeth, Tübingen, 1957, p. 461.

[3] "Ich gestehe frei : Die Erinnerung des David Hume war eben dasjenige, was mir vor vielen Jahren zuerst den dogmatischen Schlummer unterbrach, und meinen

cism awakened him from his slumber in empirical dogmatism.[4] If not even the principle of causality has any objective validity and is nothing but a subjective expectation, based on the mechanism of association, then not even the concepts which, according to empiricism, are given by experience offer any possibility of knowing reality.

Reading Hume, Kant became convinced that, if Hume were right in his view about human knowledge, he would have to conclude that no form of scientific knowledge whatsoever is possible. If man can know nothing but contingent and concrete impressions, than there is no room for the necessary and universal judgments of science. For the necessary and universal judgments of science imply that there is much more to the process of knowledge than Hume admits when he reduces the whole of knowledge to the registration of contingent and concrete impressions. In Kant's eyes, however, the fact of physical science cannot be denied; physical science does exist. Thus it does not make sense to talk about human knowledge as if physical science *cannot* exist as a science. Kant was unshakeably convinced that Newton's physics was valid.[5]

With respect to metaphysics, however, he thought, the situation was entirely different. This discipline had not yet found the secure road of science.[6] And if it ever was to find this road, an inquiry had to be made concerning the conditions which must be fulfilled if human knowledge in general is to be possible. Such an inquiry could not be impossible since, as a matter of fact, mathematics and physics already existed as sciences. In his CRITIQUE OF PURE REASON Kant himself undertook this investigation.

The aim of this CRITIQUE is to present a "theory of transcendental method". This theory is not itself metaphysics but explores, prior to metaphysics, the conditions underlying the possibility of all knowledge and therefore also of metaphysics.[7] This is what the term "transcenden-

---

Untersuchungen im Felde der spekulativen Philosophie eine ganz andere Richtung gab." I. Kant, *Prolegomena zu einer jeden künftigen Metaphysik*, Immanuel Kants Werke, ed. Cassirer, Berlin, 1913, Band IV, p. 8.

[4] "Der Dogmatismus, von dem also Kant durch Hume befreit worden zu sein erklärt, war der empiristische : den rationalistischen hatte er aus der Stimmung der zeitgenössischen Literatur schon vorher selbst überwunden". Wilhelm Windelband, *o.c.*, p. 461, footnote 7.

[5] H.J. De Vleeschauwer, *o.c.*, p. 61.

[6] I. Kant, *Kritik der reinen Vernunft*, Immanuel Kants Werke, ed. Cassirer, Berlin, 1913, Band III, p. 17.

[7] *Kr. d. r. V.*, p. 7.

tal" refers to. In Kantian language knowledge is called "transcendental" if it does not aim at objects but at the way in which we know objects. If we know objects in a certain way, then this knowledge must be *a priori* possible.[8] What must be accepted *a priori*, in order that knowledge *can* be what it is *de facto*?

Kant's transcendental method differs from Locke's psychological method. Locke thought that he could solve the problem of knowledge by analyzing it psychologically and explaining its genesis. Kant started from knowledge and its objects as they occur; he tried to investigate the conditions which make them possible and thus determine whether and in what sense metaphysical thinking is possible. Kant formulated this task for himself as the question about the possibility of synthetic *a priori* judgments,[9] for he held that the judgments used in the sciences are synthetic *a priori*.

Synthetic a Priori *Judgments*

According to Kant, a judgment can only claim to be "scientific" if it is synthetic *a priori*. It must be synthetic, for if it consisted exclusively in the analysis of the subject of a judgment, one could not claim that it is concerned with reality and increases our knowledge. In a synthetic *a priori* judgment a predicate is *added* to the subject of the judgment on the basis of experience—in other words, this predicate is no ctontained in the concept of the subject. A scientific concept, however, must also be *necessary* and *universal*. This is possible only if it does not wholly depend on experience, for the latter is *contingent* and *concrete*. Thus scientific judgments both presuppose and transcend experience.[10] The question, then, is, what must be necessarily presupposed and *a priori* accepted in order to make this possible? According to Kant, the only exclusion could be that the inquiry into the possibility of synthetic *a priori* judgments would have a negative result with respect to mathematics and physics, for these sciences are really given.[11] But the failure of metaphysics justifies doubt with respect to its possibility.[12]

[8] "Ich nenne alle Erkenntnis transzendental, die sich nicht sowohl mit Gegenständen, sondern mit unserer Erkenntnisart von Gegenständen, sofern diese a priori möglich sein soll, überhaupt beschäftigt". Kr. d. r. V., p. 49.

[9] It is striking that for Kant "knowledge" is identical with "judgmental knowledge".

[10] *Kr. d. r. V.*, pp. 34-45.

[11] *Kr. d. r. V.*, p. 46.

[12] "Was aber Metaphysik betrifft, so muss ihr bisheriger schlechter Vorgang, und weil man von keiner einzigen bisher vorgetragenen, was ihren wesentlichen

Space and Time as a Priori *Sense Forms*

How, Kant asks himself, do the objects of our knowledge, whether inside or outside us, appear to us?[13] They appear to us as juxtaposed in space, i.e., as outside us and outside and alongside each other. The inner states of our feelings appear to us as ordered in time, as "before" or "after", as preceding or following one another. Let us now ask which conditions must be fulfilled of necessity in order that the objects of our knowledge *can* appear as they do—as ordered in space and time. To Kant, it is obvious that this would be wholly *impossible* if the *empiricist conception* of sense experience were true.

According to empiricism, sense knowledge is a purely passive picturing of objects isolated from the knower in a kind of conscious mirror. Kant allows that the objects "affect" and "touch" our senses. He uses the term "experience" (*Empfindung*) to indicate that the senses are affected by the influence of the objects. The matter of sense knowledge offered by "experiences", then, is given *a posteriori*.

Unlike empiricism, however, Kant was unable to accept that *nothing but* a "passive mirroring" occurs in sense knowledge. One who holds that there is nothing else there can no longer account for the conception of time, the "before" and "after" schema. To show this, let us assume that three successive light signals from the external world are received by the conscious mirror. If the mirror reflects the external world in a purely passive way, one cannot possibly account for the fact that the second signal is experienced as *after* the first, and the third as *after* the second. For when the second signal arrives, the first exists no longer; and, since sense knowledge is conceived as a purely passive kind of mirroring, one is forced to say that, after the disappearance of the first signal, nothing remains of it in the conscious mirror. But if nothing of it remains there, how could one say that the second signal is received *after* the first? For at the moment the second is received, the first is simply *nothing*. In the empiricist view of sense experience, "after the first signal" simply means "after nothing"; it is not a real "after".

Similar remarks apply to the representation of space, the "alongside" and "outside" schema. Three points alongside and outside one another in space cannot be experienced as such if sense experience is nothing

---

Zweck angeht, sagen kann, sie sei wirklich vorhanden, einen jeden mit Grunde an ihrer Möglichkeit zweifeln lassen". *K. d. r. V.*, *p.* 46.

[13] *Kr. d. r. V.*, pp. 55-58.

but a passive mirroring. A passive mirroring of three points alongside and outside one another contains no more than the impression of "one point", "one point" and "one point". The realization that they lie alongside and outside one another implies more than a passive mirroring; it implies that these points are *brought* into relation with one another, and this is more than being passive, even as *bringing* one light signal to relate to another by *holding fast* to the first is more than mere passivity.[14]

Kant had this empiricist theory of knowledge in mind when he claimed that the space and time forms themselves cannot again be called results of sense experience and thus are not *a posteriori* representations. They are *a priori*. This must necessarily be presupposed and accepted *a priori* if the objects of our knowledge are to be able to appear as they do appear.

Justification of the Possibility of Mathematics

The possibility of mathematics is very easily explained when one recognizes the importance of the *a priori* forms of intuition (*Anschauung*). Mathematics is a science which determines the properties of space in synthetic *a priori* judgments.[15] But this determination cannot be made by mere analysis of concepts. That two sides of a triangle together are longer than the third side cannot be deduced from the concepts "line" and "triangle";[16] mathematical judgments are synthetic. On the other hand, mathematical judgments are necessary and universal; hence they are *a priori*. But how can this be? Necessity and universality cannot be produced by the contingent and concrete data of experience; they point to an *a priori* element in the mathematical judgment.

This *a priori* element is the spatial principle of order. As *a priori*, it orders *of necessity* and therefore orders also *all* experience, thus giving rise to the necessity and universality which finds expression in the mathematical judgment.[17] A great light arose for the man who first constructed an isosceles triangle and realized that his determination of its properties did not consist of what he *saw* in this figure but of what he himself had put into it.[18] Only when this had been seen did it become possible for mathematics to enter the royal road of science.

---

[14] A. De Sopper, *Wat is philosophie?*, Haarlem, 1950, pp. 42-50.

[15] *Kr. d. r. V.*, p. 59.

[16] *Kr. d. r. V.*, p. 59.

[17] "Also macht allein unsere Erklärung die Möglichkeit der Geometrie als einer synthetischen Erkenntnis a priori begreiflich". *Kr. d. r. V.*, p. 60.

[18] *Kr. d. r. V.*, p. 15.

The Objective Validity of the a Priori *Forms of Sense Experience and the "in Itself"*

From all this it should be evident that, according to Kant, space should not be conceived as a property of the "things in themselves". It is wrong, therefore, to think that space is inherent in the "things in themselves" and continues to be inherent in them even if the *a priori* froms of sense experience are thought away.[19] The same is true for time.[20]

Space and time are impressed on things insofar as these appear; thus they are only objectively valid for the "phenomena".[21] Kant, then, teaches the "reality" (the objective validity) of space and time with respect to the "phenomena" and, at the same time, their "ideality" in reference to "things in themselves".[22] The "thing in itself", then, is never known and can never be known, but experience does not even look for it.[23]

The assertion that the *a priori* forms of sense experience possess objective validity only for the "phenomena" does not mean that, according to Kant, we merely know things as they *seem* to be. Things do not *seem* to be outside but *appear* as outside me. As far as concerns things which do *not* appear, I cannot say that they are "in themselves" outside me.[24]

Sense Experience and Thought

The objects of our knowledge, however, do not merely reveal themselves as "spatially and temporally ordered". They reveal themselves as "house", "tree", "animal", "man", etc. Objects are *given* in intuition, i.e., by the synthesis of experiences and *a priori* sense forms. But our

---

[19] "Der Raum stellet gar keine Eigenschaft irgendeiner Dinge an sich oder sie in ihrem Verhältnis aufeinander vor, d.i. keine Bestimmung derselben, die an Gegenständen selbst haftete, und welche bliebe, wenn man auch von allen subjektiven Bedingungen der Anschauung abstrahierte". *Kr. d. r. V.*, p. 60.

[20] *Kr. d. r. V.*, p. 65.

[21] *Kr. d. r. V.*, p. 61.

[22] *Kr. d. r. V.*, pp. 61-62.

[23] *Kr. d. r. V.*, p. 62.

[24] "So sage ich nicht, die Körper scheinen bloss ausser mir zu sein, oder meine Seele scheint nur in meinem Selbstbewusstsein gegeben zu sein, wenn ich behaupte, dass die Qualität des Raumes und der Zeit, welcher als Bedingung ihrers Daseins gemäss ich beide setze, in meiner Anschauungsart nicht in diesen Objekten an sich liege". *Kr. d. r. V.*, pp. 76-77.

intellect also seizes them as intelligible essences.[25] Which conditions, then, must necessarily be presupposed and accepted *a priori* in order to make it possible for the intellect to seize them? This question must be answered if the possibility of physical science is to be established. For physical science also uses necessary and universal propositions in which it speaks about these objects with the aid of necessary and universal predicates, such as "caused", "cause", "one" and "many". How, then, is this possible?

Kant thinks that this question can be answered by accepting the existence of *a priori* forms of thinking or concepts. By means of *a priori* forms, reason lays down the law for nature.[26] It is, moreover, wholly to be excluded that the opposite would be the case, that nature would lay down the law for reason. Necessary and universal knowledge can never arise from experience, in the sense intended by empiricism—i.e., as purely passive mirroring—for such experience offers only the contingent and the concrete. It is only through the *a priori* character of the forms of thinking that the universal and necessary judgments of physical science are possible.[27]

The sensitive aspect of human knowledge is distinguished from thinking by its receptivity, while reason is characterized by spontaneity. But we should never forget that *both* elements *together* give us human knowledge as it exists. Without the receptivity of the senses, no cognitive objects are given, so that the concepts are "empty", i.e., they "are concerned with nothing". Without concepts, on the other hand, sense experiences are blind,[28] i.e., they have no conceivable object. Concepts, then, must receive their object from sense experience, and the data of sense experience must be put into concepts.[29] Sence experience and concept together are the elements of our knowledge; neither concepts

---

[25] *Kr. d. r. V.*, pp. 79-80.

[26] "Kategorien sind Begriffe, welche den Erscheinungen, mithin der Natur als dem Inbegriffe aller Erscheinungen (natura materialiter spectata) Gesetze a priori vorschreiben". *Kr. d. r. V.*, p. 133.

[27] "Die empirische Ableitung aber, worauf beide (Locke and Hume) verfielen, lässt sich mit der Wirklichkeit der wissenschaftlichen Erkenntnisse a priori, die wir haben, nämlich der reinen Mathematik und allgemeinen Naturwissenschaft, nicht vereinigen, und wird also durch das Faktum widerlegt". *Kr. d. r. V.*, p. 112.

[28] "Gedanken ohne Inhalt sind leer, Anschauungen ohne Begriffe sind blind". *Kr. d. r. V.*, p. 80.

[29] "Daher ist es ebenso notwendig, seine Begriffe sinnlich zu machen (d.i. ihnen den Gegenstand in der Anschauung beizufügen), als seine Anschauungen sich verständlich zu machen (d.i. sie unter Begriffe zu bringen)". *Kr. d. r. V.*, p. 80.

without sense experience nor sense experience without concepts results in knowledge.[30] Kant calls these *a priori* forms of reason or concepts "categories".[31]

From all this it should be evident that reason cannot make a transcendental but only an empirical use of its concepts.[32] This means that its concepts never refer to the 'things in themselves" but only to the "phenomena". For the object of a concept can only be given in a sense experience; hence concepts without sense experience do not have any really given object, no objective validity.[33] But sense experience only puts us into contact with "appearances". Thus the use of concepts which bypass sense experience is nothing but a game.[34] The pure "thinking" of "things in themselves" by the intellect, equipped with categories, is not real *knowledge* of real objects.

Condemnation of Metaphysics

These considerations, Kant holds, as a matter of principle, decide the fate of metaphysics. Traditional metaphysics, which speaks of the universe (cosmology), the soul (rational psychology) and God (natural theology), is impossible as a science, for it deals with "objects" which cannot be given in sense experience. It is "empty" thinking about the "suprasensual", which does not refer to any given object.

Nevertheless, this "empty" thinking is *necessary*. The concepts "universe", "ego" and "God"—which Kant usually calls "ideas" conceived by reason [35]—bring about the highest synthesis in our knowledge and must *necessarily* be thought. For we cannot escape conceiving all "phenomena" in nature within the all-encompassing connection of the universe; we cannot escape conceiving all "phenomena" in our consciousness as referring to the soul, the always self-identical "ego";

[30] "Anschauung und Begriffe machen also die Elemente aller Erkenntnis aus, so dass weder Begriffe, ohne ihnen auf einige Art korrespondierende Anschauung, noch Anschauung ohne Begriffe ein Erkenntnis abgeben können". *Kr. d. r. V.*, p. 79.

[31] *Kr. d. r. V.*, p. 98.

[32] *Kr. d. r. V.*, p. 214.

[33] "Nun kann der Gegenstand einem Begriffe nicht anders gegeben werden als in der Anschauung, und wenn eine reine Anschauung noch vor dem Gegenstande a priori möglich ist, so kann doch auch diese selbst ihren Gegenstand, mithin die objektive Gültigkeit nur durch die empirische Anschauung bekommen, wovon sie die blosse Form ist". *Kr. d. r. V.*, p. 214.

[34] "Ohne dieses haben sie gar keine objektive Gültigkeit, sondern sind ein blosses Spiel". *Kr. d. r. V.*, p. 214.

[35] *Kr. d. r. V.*, p. 269.

and we cannot escape conceiving everything as the result of an absolute cause or God. How Kant arrived at this division or enumeration need not concern us here.[36]

It is extremely important, however, to see that the ideas of reason should not be conceived as referring to given objects. The "ego", the universe and God are not really known but must of necessity be *thought*. They are not *given* in and by knowledge, but are *imposed* on us as tasks.[37] We *conceive* the reduction of all intellectual knowledge to the ultimate "unconditioned" as an *accomplished* task.

The mistake of traditional metaphysics, says Kant, consists in the fact that it "ontologized" the ideas of reason. It conceived the "ego", the world and God as given realities and as objects of knowledge. In this way metaphysics got entangled in "transcendental semblance" and self-deception.[38] Thus the "affirmation" of God is *per se* empty. Although the idea of God is indispensable and even inevitable as ideal of knowledge,[39] it is not objectively applicable to any *ens realissimum*, regardless of how one wishes to define this *ens*.[40] After showing how the idea of God originates or rather necessarily *must* originate,[41] Kant proceeds to demolish the proofs traditionally offered to demonstrate the *reality* of what is contained in the idea of God. Kant, we should not forget, recognizes that

---

[36] Cf. H. v. Oyen, *Philosophia*, II, 1949, pp. 169-177; W. Windelband, *Lehrbuch der Geschichte der Philosophie*, Tübingen, 1957, pp. 471-473; J. Maréchal, *Le point de départ de la Métaphysique*, Cahier III, La Critique de Kant, Bruxelles-Paris, 1944, pp. 220-225.

[37] "Daher sind die reinen Vernunftbegriffe von der Totalität in der Synthesis der Bedingungen wenigstens als Aufgaben, um die Einheit des Verstands wo möglich bis zum Unbedingten fortzusetzen, notwendig, und in der Natur der menschlichen Vernunft gegründet, es mag auch übrigens diesen transzendentalen Begriffen an einem ihnen angemessenen Gebrauch *in concreto* fehlen, und sie mithin keinen andern Nutzen haben, als den Verstand in die Richtung zu bringen, darin sein Gebrauch, indem er aufs äusserste erweitert, zugleich mit sich selbst durchgehends einstimmig gemacht wird". *Kr. d. r. V.*, p. 262.

[38] *Kr. d. r. V.*, pp. 244-247.

[39] *Kr. d. r. V.*, p. 400.

[40] "Daher wird der bloss in der Vernunft befindliche Gegenstand ihres Ideals auch das Urwesen (*ens originarium*), sofern es keines über sich hat : das höchste Wesen (*ens summum*), und sofern alles als bedingt unter ihm steht : das Wesen aller Wesen (*ens entium*) genannt. Alles dieses aber bedeutet nicht das objektive Verhältnis eines wirklichen Gegenstandes zu andern Dingen, sondern der Idee zu Begriffen, und lässt uns wegen der Existenz eines Wesens von so ausnehmendem Vorzuge in völliger Unwissenheit". *Kr. d. r. V.*, p. 402.

[41] *Kr. d. r. V.*, pp. 395-404.

all things traditional metaphysics ascribed to the *reality* of God are implied in the *idea* of God as ideal of human knowledge.

Interlude

Did Kant, we may ask, reject metaphysics, *tout court*, metaphysical speaking "about" God pure and simple? It should be evident that this is not the case. Kant showed that the "affirmation" of God may not be conceived as the affirmation of an object given in sense experience. To "affirm" God is not on a par with affirming a house, a horse or a cause. Who could object to this? Kant, moreover, explicitly also observed that if the "affirmation" of God, in the sense he indicated, is impossible, the same must be said of the "negation" of God. This "negation", he held, went just as much beyond the possiblities of a *real* negation as the "affirmation" exceeded the possibilities of a *real* affirmation.[42] Once again, who could object to this?

What, then, did Kant want? He himself has answered this question : he wanted to "obtain room for faith".[43] But what does this mean? What is this "faith" with respect to God? Is it still a way of "affirming"? If so, what kind of "affirmation" is it since it cannot be conceived as the affirmation of an object given in sense experience?

"Rational Faith"

In his first CRITIQUE Kant had asked himself what had to be unconditionally accepted to make it possible for human knowledge to be what it is and for the objects to appear as they do appear. In his CRITIQUE OF PRACTICAL REASON, Kant raises a similar question : what must be unconditionally accepted to make it possible for morality to be what it undeniably is?

Morality, we should recall, is for Kant a *fact* even as physical science is a *fact*. This fact is concerned with a specific way of being "good or evil" which refers to the will. Truly good is only the good will, the puremindedness which acts in a certain way for *no other reason* than that it is good, that it has been commanded this way, that it is a duty. Morality is what it is by virtue of "Thou shalt". It is a specific way of being "obli-

---

[42] "Das höchste Wesen bleibt also für den bloss spekulativen Gebrauch der Vernunft ein blosses, aber doch fehlerfreies Ideal, ein Begriff, welcher die ganze menschliche Erkenntnis schliesst und krönet, dessen objektive Realität auf diesem Wege zwar nicht bewiesen, aber auch nicht widerlegt werden kann". *Kr. d. r. V.*, p. 440.

[43] *Kr. d. r. V.*, p. 25.

ged", which is universal and necessary. Even as the universality and necessity of the judgments made by physical science find their explanation in the *a priori* forms of reason, so the universality and necessity of the ethical obligation find their explanation in the existence of an *a priori* form of practical reason, which Kant calls the "categorical imperative". This imperative imposes itself on all human actions and implies the absolute being-obliged, not based on experience, that is proper to morality.

The fact of morality with its categorical imperative contains, according to Kant, certain postulates. First that of freedom. If morality demands that an action be done out of duty, then it postulates freedom, for duty without freedom is meaningless. The entire domain of phenomena, however, lies in the grip of determinism; our life of consciousness runs its course according to the causal laws of psychology. That is why freedom cannot be affirmed in this realm. But freedom is postulated in the realm of the "in itself".[44] The "ego" or soul must be a free substance.

Morality also postulates the immortality of the ego or soul. For Kant, this follows from the fact that virtuousness is always imperfect. Wholly virtuous is only he who acts out of *sheer* duty, i.e., without being motivated by the hope of certain results or the desire to be happy. Yet this kind of motivations constantly affects man's virtuousness and see to it that his deeds are not done out of *sheer* duty. Virtuousness can only be realized "in a progressive way stretching out to infinity".[45] This "progressing to infinity" of virtuousness postulates the immortality of the ego or soul, as a free substance.[46]

Finally, morality postulates the existence of God. For Kant, this follows from the fact that the virtuous man acquires a "dignity", on the basis of which he may lay claim to a destiny in keeping with his virtuousness. This destiny is happiness. Happiness may never be the

---

[44] "Folglich wenn man sie noch retten will, so bleibt kein Weg übrig, als das Dasein eines Dinges, sofern es in der Zeit bestimmbar ist, folglich auch die Kausalität nach dem Gesetze der Naturnotwendigkeit bloss der Erscheinung, die Freiheit aber eben demselben Wesen als Dinge an sich selbst beizulegen". Immanuel Kant, *Kritik der praktischen Vernunft*, ed. Cassirer, Berlin, 1914, Band V, p. 104.

[45] *Kr. d. pr. V.*, pp. 132-133.

[46] "Dieser unendliche Progressus ist aber nur unter Voraussetzung einer ins Unendliche fortdaurenden Existenz und Persönlichkeit desselben vernünftigen Wesens (welche man die Unsterblichkeit der Seele nennt) möglich ... ein *Postulat* der reinen praktischen Vernunft." *Kr. d. pr. V.*, pp. 132-133.

motivation of virtuous actions. The motive is duty, but when a man acts out of duty and thus is virtuous, his moral "dignity" entitles him to happiness.

The virtuous man is worthy of happiness, but in actual fact he often does not receive it. Happiness, according to Kant, is the state of a rational being in the world for whom everything goes in accordance with his will and desires.[47] But man cannot exercise causality in the world in such a way that virtuousness and happiness converge. Yet morality demands that they do; hence it *must* be possible. Now this convergence is possible only if outside nature there is a Supreme Cause of nature which also brings about the harmony between virtuousness and happiness. This Supreme Cause is God.[48]

Accordingly, morality simply cannot be what it undeniably is unless freedom, the immortality of the soul, and the existence of God are "affirmed". Theoretical reason—which states what *is*—is unable to affirm the existence of realities corresponding to these three ideas. But the undeniable existence of moral duty forces practical reason— which states what *ought to be*—to accept that realities correspond to these three ideas, for without freedom, immortality and the existence of God morality cannot be what it undeniably is.[49] Certain "affirmations", then, which are not justified for theoretical reason are legitimate for practical reason.[50]

---

[47] *Kr. d. pr. V.*, p. 135.

[48] "Also ist das höchste Gut in der Welt nur möglich, sofern eine oberste Ursache der Natur angenommen wird, die eine der moralischen Gesinnung gemässe Kausalität hat ... ein Wesen das durch Verstand und Willen die Ursache ... der Natur ist, d.i. *Gott*". *Kr. d. pr. V.*, p. 136.

[49] "Das moralische Gesetz führete in der vorhergehenden Zergliederung zur praktischen Aufgabe, welche ohne allen Beitritt sinnlicher Triebfedern, bloss durch reine Vernunft vorgeschrieben wird, nämlich der notwendigen Vollständigkeit des ersten und vornehmsten Teils des höchsten Guts, der Sittlichkeit, und da diese nur in einer Ewigkeit völlig aufgelöset werden kann, zum Postulat der Unsterblichkeit. Eben dieser Gesetz muss auch zur Möglichkeit des zweiten Elements des höchsten Guts, nämlich der jener Sittlichkeit angemessenen Glückseligkeit, ebenso uneigennützig wie vorher, aus blosser unparteiischer Vernunft, nämlich auf die Voraussetzung des Daseins einer dieser Wirkung adäquaten Ursache führen, d.i. die Existenz Gottes, als zur Möglichkeit des höchsten Guts ... notwendig gehörig, postulieren". *Kr. d. pr. V.*, p. 135.

[50] "Also wird durchs praktische Gesetz, welches die Existenz des höchsten in einer Welt möglichen Guts gebietet, die Möglichkeit jener Objekte der reinen spekulativen Vernunft, die objektive Realität, welche dies ihnen nicht sichern konnte, postuliert; wodurch denn die theoretische Erkenntnis der reinen Vernunft allerdings einen Zuwachs

Kant, however, emphatically speaks of *postulates*. Freedom, the immortality of the soul and the existence of God are not objects of *knowledge*; nevertheless, they must be "affirmed" as existing realities. That is why, according to Kant, they are objects of "faith".[51] The ideas of theoretical reason are merely regulatory principles which perfect and complete our experiential knowledge. What the ideas of freedom, immortality and the existence of God express is never given in sense experience and therefore can never be affirmed by theoretical reason. But practical reason can do it. This, however, does not mean that the thinking of practical reason is raised to the level of knowledge.[52] The categorical imperative of practical reason gives to the ideas of theoretical reason the corresponding objects; these are not "reached" in an act of knowledge, but in an act of faith.[53]

Retrospect

Detouring by way of morality, then, Kant tries to answer the questions which really concern man.[54] His intention is not to eliminate metaphysics, the speaking "about" God, pure and simple. According to Kant, here always has been and always will be metaphysics, not as a science about a given object, but as a "natural disposition", a necessity implied in man's nature, to raise certain questions.[55] The act by which these questions are answered is not an act of knowledge but an act of faith. What exactly does this mean?

Evidently, the "affirmation" of God, which Kant by way of morality wishes to view as an act of faith, gives to metaphysics precisely the form which many thinkers today reject, not in order to deny the "affirmation" of God but to make it truly authentic.

---

bekommt, der aber bloss darin besteht, dass jene für sie sonst problematische (bloss denkbare) Begriffe jetzt assertorisch für solche erklärt werden, denen wirkliche Objekte zukommen". *Kr. d. pr. V.*, pp. 145-146.

[51] *Kr. d. pr. V.*, p. 137.

[52] *Kr. d. pr. V.*, pp. 145-148.

[53] "Die obige drei Ideen der spekulativen Vernunft sind an sich noch keine Erkenntnisse; doch sind es (transzendente) Gedanken, in denen nichts Unmögliches ist. Nun bekommen sie durch ein apodiktisches praktisches Gesetz, als notwendige Bedingungen der Möglichkeit dessen, was dieses sich zum Objekte zu machen gebietet, objektive Realität, d.i. wir werden durch jenes angewiesen, dass sie Objekte haben, ohne doch, wie sich ihr Begriff auf ein Objekt bezieht, anzeigen zu können, und das ist auch noch nicht Erkenntnis dieser Objekte". *Kr. d. pr. V.*, p. 146.

[54] *Kr. d. r. V.*, Vorrede, p. 5.

[55] *Kr. d. r. V.*, Einleitung, p. 47.

Faith, as conceived by Kant, is an act of holding "to be true". It is not knowledge or affirmation of God as an object given in sense experience, for otherwise God would be put in the realm of sense perceptible objects and no longer be God.[56] Nevertheless, man possesses the idea of "God". Faith, then is the act by which man accepts that an "object" in itself (*sic*), God, corresponds to the idea of "God" and therefore really exists. Faith is the act by which man accepts that the judgment "God exists" is *true*, i.e., it agrees with the reality-in-itself of God. Theoretical reason does not possess an objectively sufficient foundation for such a judgment of truth, but practical reason has a subjectively sufficient foundation.[57]

In this way Kant positions himself within an age-old tradition. It is the tradition that had always been defended by Christian thinkers and that is based on Aristotle and Plato. But this tradition is rejected by many contemporaries who wish to give an authentic character to the "affirmation" of God.

2. THE INTELLECTUALISM AND OBJECTIVISM OF CHRISTIAN THOUGHT

Speaking about Bultmann, I have pointed out that the views representing God as a factor which sometimes "punctures" the laws of nature and of history is not only called "mythical" but also "supernaturalistic", "theistic" and "metaphysical". The last three of these qualifiers, however, are also used in reference to the intellectualistic and objectivistic character of Christian thinking "about" God,[58] with or without the "mythical" signification of these three qualifiers.

---

[56] *Kr. d. r. V.*, pp. 433-477.

[57] H. de Vos, *Kant als theoloog*, Baarn, 1968, pp. 61-69.

[58] Carl Michalson, *Is de Amerikaanse theologie bezig volwassen te worden?*, in : Wending 21 (1966), p. 95; S. Ogden, *De christelijke verkondiging van God aan de mensheid van de zogenaamde "atheïstische tijd"*, in : Concilium, II (1966), no. 6, pp. 98-103. "Subjectivistic-objectivistic thinking is the thinking of metaphysics and science, which in the essential sense precisely does not 'think'. 'Overcoming metaphysics' in the area of theology does not take place by defining all thinking as basically objectifying in nature, and then distinguishing from this thinking the contingent act of believing existence itself. Rather, it takes place by understanding thinking otherwise than as subjectivistic and objectifying thinking in the sense of metaphysics and science, namely, as experimental thinking". Heinrich Ott, *What is systematic theology?*, in : The Later Heidegger and Theology, New York, 1963, p. 109; John A.T. Robinson, *Exploration into God*, London, 1967, *passim*.

The Core of the Intellectualistic and Objectivistic Conception of Faith

I call a view intellectualistic and objectivistic if it "defines" faith as a "yes" to a judgment taken to be in agreement with the divine reality in itself. The term "to define" needs some explanation. It does not primarily refer to an explicit determination of the essence of faith but rather to something that is *not* explicitly mentioned in speaking about faith, something that is an "unspoken", "unquestioned" presupposition.[59] That which is not explicitly mentioned in philosophizing as well as theologizing is what determines the essence of a philosophy or theology; thus it is what "defines" them. In other words, I am not claiming that any philosophy or theology has ever explicitly stated that faith is a "yes" to a judgment which is in "agreement" with a divine reality in itself. As soon as one realizes that "reality in it self" means "reality that is not judged", it is obvious that nothing can be said about it in a judgment. But it is not obvious that everyone who speaks about the relationship between judgment and reality explicitly knows which ontological status he ascribes to what he calls "reality". Nevertheless, he cannot escape presupposing a certain ontological view of reality; that is why it can subsequently become obvious that this view is not tenable. What is simply presupposed remains unquestioned, but the presupposition gives an answer to this unspoken question, an answer that remains "a hidden option".[60]

The Temptation of Christian Thought to be Objectivistic and Intellectualistic

There is a special reason, I think, why Christian thought is very much exposed to the temptation of intellectualism and objectivism. The reason is that Christian thought has always defended God's transcendence, it has always refused to call God a be-ing just as that which is not God is called a be-ing. Of a be-ing one can say that it *is*. But if God is not a be-ing, how can one say that God ...? Wouldn't it be wiser to say that God is *not*?

Thomas Aquinas clearly saw this difficulty : "We cannot know what God is", he said.[61] Yet, he did not want to say *unconditionally* that God

[59] A. Dondeyne, *La différence ontologique chez M. Heidegger*, in : Revue philosophique de Louvain, 56 (1958), pp. 38, 44-45.

[60] A. De Waehlens, *Signification de la phénoménologie* in : Diogène, 5 (1954), p. 64.

[61] "Ergo dicendum quod licet de Deo non possumus scire quid est ...". *S. Th.*, I, q. 1, a. 7, *ad* 1.

is *not*.[62] His endeavor to overcome this dilemma unwittingly fostered the intellectualistic and objectivistic conception of faith.

The term "is", says Thomas can be used in two ways : to affirm the being of reality and as a verbal copula. As a verbal copula, it connects the subject and the predicate of a judgment or proposition. According to Thomas, "is" cannot be used in the first way with respect to God, for such a usage would deny his transcendence; it can only be used in the second way. One who says that God "is" intends to affirm that the statement which says that God "is" is true.[63]

Thomas is obviously concerned with God's transcendence. But the way he secures this transcendence in his thought is so fraught with danger that only a small step is needed to arrive at the view that faith is a "yes" to propositions which are assumed to mirror God-in-himself. Leslie Dewart thinks that Thomas himself already took this step.[64] I do not intend to judge this issue, but it is beyond doubt that others did take this fatal step.[65]

The Objectivism of Scholastic Thought

Christian thought, I said, is particularly exposed to the temptation of objectivism because it has always defended God's transcendence. This temptation became a kind of fatal exposure when Christian thought accepted the imprint of Greek thinking, for objectivism was an unspoken presupposition of Greek philosophy.

This option had already been made by Plato when he thought that he should assume the existence of a separate world of necessary and universal ideas. For he was the heir of the thought of Heraclitus, for whom the world contained nothing but contingent and individual beings. To Plato it was evident that no necessary and universal ideas could ever originate in such a world; yet, undeniably, man has universal and necessary ideas. Since these cannot originate in the real world, they must come from the contemplation of an ideal world, in which these essences have an independent, ideal existence.

---

[62] *Summa contra Gentiles*, I, 14.

[63] "Scimus enim, quod haec propositio, quam formamus de Deo, cum dicimus Deus est, vera est". *S. Th.*, I, q. 3, a. 4, *ad* 2.

[64] Leslie Dewart, *The Future of Belief*, Theism in a world come of age, London, 1967, p. 167.

[65] "Verbum *Credo* significat : firmiter assentior, propter auctoritatem Dei revelantis, veritatibus quae in Symbolo continentur". P. Gasparri, *Catechismus Catholicus*, Typis Polyglottis Vaticanis, 1933[10], p. 95.

Plato conceived the *being* of ideas as the only "really real" being and depreciated the *being* of worldly meaning. According to Plato, worldly meaning, strictly speaking, "is" not because of the fact that in matter the idea, the "pure appearance", is mis-shaped.[66] Thus ideas became prototypes of worldly realities. They were conceived as necessary and universal norms by which worldly realities, as shadows of the ideas, could be measured and on the basis of which one could determine whether a being had this or that particular essence.[67] For example, in the world of ideas there existed for Plato the pure essence of the state, the work of art, man, virtues, and the horse. The ideas were conceived as the norm for the truth of things. Things themselves were not "really" true. "Really" true were the ideas, and for this reason all things occurring in worldly reality had to be guided by the ideas as their prototypes.[68] Concrete living man also had no other task than to realize his necessary, universal, immutable and eternal essence in the mutability of time.[69]

Plato conceived the world of pure ideas as a world of pure "light". What is pure idea is pure "light". The meaning spoken of by phenomenology is not pure "light" but an admixture of "light" and "darkness", of unconcealedness and concealedness.[70] The unconcealedness of meaning presupposes the "letting be" of meaning by the subject-as-*cogito*. The moment of the subject-as-*cogito*'s emergence is the "moment of vision" at which truth as unconcealedness issues forth. This moment is the beginning of a never-finished history of dis-closure. Meaning is never *pure* "light".

---

[66] "Das Sein als ἰδέα wird jetzt zum eigentlich Seienden hinaufgesteigert, und das Seiende selbst, das vormals Waltende, sinkt herab zu dem, was von Plato μὴ ὄν genannt wird, was eigentlich nicht sein sollte und eigentlich auch nicht ist, weil es die Idee, das reine Aussehen, in der Verwirklichung doch immer verunstaltet, indem es dieses in den Stoff hineinbildet". M. Heidegger, *Einführung in die Metaphysik*, Tübingen, 1953, p. 140.

[67] "Die ἰδέα ihrerseits wird zum παράδειγμα, zum Musterbild. Die Idee wird zugleich und notwendig zum Ideal. Das nachgebildete 'ist' eigentlich nicht, sondern hat nur Teil am Sein, μέθεξις. Der χωρισμός, die Kluft zwischen der Idee als dem eigentlich Seienden, dem Vor- und Urbild, und dem eigentlich Nichtseienden, dem Nach- und Abbild, ist aufgerissen". M. Heidegger, *o.c.*, pp. 140-141.

[68] M. Heidegger, *o.c.*, p. 141.

[69] "So ist von vornherein festgelegt und erblickt, was der Mensch sein soll und sein muss. Ihm bleibt nichts anderes übrig als Verwirklicher seines eigenen ewigen Wesens zu sein, seine unveränderliche, ihn ermöglichende innere Möglichkeit ins Dasein überzuführen". M. Müller, *Existenzphilosophie im geistigen Leben der Gegenwart*, Heidelberg, 1949, p. 17.

[70] "Die Unverborgenheit braucht die Verborgenheit". M. Heidegger, *Vorträge*

The fact that phenomenology conceives meaning as the chiaroscuro of unconcealedness and concealedness makes it possible to call meaning the *real* terminus of the cognitive encounter. *Real* termini of man's cognitive encounter are a mixture of "light" and "darkness." When Plato represents meaning as pure idea, i.e., as pure "light", he has already ceased to conceive meaning as a real *terminus of encounter*. The Platonic idea, conceived as pure "light", actually is meaning whose "moment of vision"—of dis-closure—is "forgotten", and whose history of dis-closure is considered finished. But for such a finished result there is no room within knowledge as an authentic *encounter*, for in the *real* encounter with meaning the latter reveals itself as the chiaroscuro of unconcealedness and concealedness and, consequently, as a never-ending invitation to dis-closure by the subject-as-*cogito*. Plato, then, had to cut meaning loose from the encounter in order to place it as an "in itself" of a purely ideal kind in a world of pure essence.[71]

Aristotle's philosophy no longer conceived essences as lying in an ideal world, but placed them in the real world. Plato's essences were ideal "in themselves", not termini of encounter. But because Aristotle limited himself to "realizing" the essences, i.e., placing them in "reality", he also implicitly conceived the "reality" of the essences as "in themselves". Aristotle "relocated" the "in itself" from the ideal world to the real world, but he did not restore it to the encounter. Just as the Platonic essences, the Aristotelian essences were conceived as an absolute "light", albeit of a real, and not an ideal, character. His essences were represented as in themselves necessarily, universally, immutably and eternally "true" because, as absolute and real "light", they were held to be the norm of truth for judgmental knowledge. In this way there arose a picture of reality as a collection of essences, stored in a land of supposedly absolute "light", while the history of the birth of "light" failed to receive any attention.

This view underlies the realistic philosophy of order known as Scho-

---

und Aufsätze, Pfullingen, 1954, p. 221.

[71] "Jetzt treten ὄν und φαινόμενον auseinander". M. Heidegger, *Einführung in die Metaphysik*, p. 141.

[72] "L'objectivisme naturaliste ... regarde ... l'omnitudo realitatis, assigne à l'homme son rang... dans le spectacle qu'elle s'offre et néglige totalement de retenir que l'origine de cette hiérarchie réside dans l'activité législatrice du 'regard' de l'étant illuminateur du spectacle et qui le 'constitue' tel". A. De Waelhens, *La philosophie et les expériences naturelles*, The Hague, 1961, pp. 190-191.

[73] M. Müller, *o.c.*, pp. 19-20.

lasticism, in which every essence is assigned a place of its own in "brute" reality. Man also, with his own essence, was assumed to have his own place in that order :[72] below God, but above animals, plants and things. The holy also ranked above the beautiful, the beautiful above the useful, and the useful above the agreeable; the common good outranked the individual good, and the soul the body.[73] Similarly, the essences of human acts were located as pieces of rocks in the "totality of reality"; they were assumed to be in their essences what they are : necessarily, universally, immutably and eternally "true" "in themselves". The essence of the marriage act, for example, was conceived as in itself necessarily, univerally and immutably orientated to reproduction. This orientation was the "truth in itself" of the marriage act, the norm for every judgment about this act. Natural rights and natural duties also were placed as hills and valleys in the "totality of reality"—as necessarily, universally, immutably and eternally "true in themselves", and, consequently, as the norm of all statements about rights and duties.

This view logically led to a specific theory of ethical deeds. If immutable and eternal essences are stored in the "totality of reality"; if immutable and eternal relations constitute an immutable and eternal hierarchical order of essences; and if man and his actions occupy an immutable and eternal place in this complex of "truths in themselves", then, the concrete and living man will do ethically good if he "reads" the essences and their essential order and conforms his actions to what he reads.[74] By doing this, he fulfills God's will. For Scholasticism did not merely transfer the Platonic ideas to the "real" world, but also located them, as exemplars of the real essences, in God's intellect : by a command of his will, God realized these exemplars in his act of creation. Scholasticism, then, ascribed a "truth in itself" to the essences, which was measured by, and derived from their being "true" in God's intellect : "every being is true".[75] Insofar as man's true knowledge mirrored the "truth in itself" of the essences, man possessed God's view of things. In this way the essentialism, objectivism and realism of Scholastic philosophy reached its peak in the claim to speak about things in God's name.[76]

---

[74] "Für die Handlungen gibt es keine anderen Maxime als die : Beobachte den unveränderlichen *Ordo*, schütze ihn, wo er bedroht ist, stelle ihn her, wo er gestört ist, verwirkliche ihn dort, wo sein Gegenteil Wirklichkeit geworden und in die Möglichkeit zurückgesunken ist. Zu diesem *Ordo* gehört auch dass du den Platz einnimmt, der dir auf Grund deines Wesens zukommt". M. Müller, *o.c.*, p. 20.

[75] L. Landgrebe, *Philosophie der Gegenwart*, Bonn, 1962, p. 157.

[76] "... comme si la conscience humaine pouvait en quelque sorte se survoler elle-

An objectivistic philosophy emphasizes, more than any other type of thought, that man is held by *bonds* in his speaking about reality. This point, however, is exaggerated so much that truth is conceived as an absolute "initiative" of "objective" reality. The subject "humbly withdraws" as an "unprejudiced" witness, in the sense that he thinks that he can isolate himself from the "coming to pass" of truth. But in this way, the "objective" reality is "objective"-for-no-one, so that no one can say anything whatsoever. This conclusion, however, is not acceptable to the objectivist : he *does* speak, the "humble" subject *does* claim to express "objectivity" in spite of everything. But his "humility" turns into absolutism here, for what the subject says he ascribes to the absolute "initiative" of "objectivity". "God's created truth" is assumed to have the "initiative", but the subject *cannot avoid* thinking that he represents this "initiative" if he is to say anything at all about "objective" reality.

It is not difficult to see that an objectivistic philosophy is dangerous because it eliminates all risks from man's search—his "origination" and "letting come to pass" of truth. The existent subject-as-*cogito* lets truth as unconcealedness "come to pass", and no subject whosoever has any guarantees at all in this matter. He may think that he expresses his "standing-in-unconcealedness" while actually he gives voice to his "standing-in-semblance". Objectivism buries this risk under verbiage. It does not lapse into scepticism but elevates itself to the absolutism of God's created "truth-in-itself". It thereby declares that all those who merely have their own searching and groping for truth-for-man at their disposal can be judged to be wrong from its lofty standpoint. "In God's name" they are wrong. There is not even any need for a dialogue,[77] for the objectivist is "one who knows".[78] But who does not see that the objectivist does not have God's "view" of truth at his disposal but only his own searching and groping subjectivity?[79]

This is the objectivism which arose in ancient Greece and penetrated

---

même et son monde, et contempler l'univers du point de vue de Dieu". A. Dondeyne, *La différence ontologique chez M. Heidegger*, in : Revue philosophique de Louvain, 56 (1958), p. 57.

[77] "Qui se réclame de l'absolu ne voudra écouter personne; il doit se persuader que toute contestation est un crime de lèse-majesté envers l'autorité qui cautionne son attitude". G. Gusdorf, *Traité de Métaphysique*, Paris, 1956, p. 131.

[78] "Comment y aurait-il véritable échange entre celui qui sait et celui qui ne sait pas"? M. Merleau-Ponty, *L'homme et l'adversité*, in : La connaissance de l'homme au XXe siècle, Rencontres internationales de Genève, 1950, p. 74.

[79] M. Merleau-Ponty, *Sens et non-sens*, Paris, 1948, p. 189.

Christian thought "about" God. God also was conceived as God-in-himself, and the attributes ascribed to him were likewise viewed as belonging to God-in-himself. Because a God-in-himself had to be "conceived" as wholly separated and isolated from man—a conception which cannot *really* be made—God's revelation could only be presented as a reception from God of secret information about his divine essence. Thus faith had to be "defined" as accepting such information, as affirming propositions of faith to be true, i.e., "agreeing" with the reality of God-in-himself. In this way it was also easy to give a simple definition of the difference between "theists" and "atheists" : the former affirm that the proposition "God exists" is true in the sense that the reality of God-in-himself agrees with this proposition, while the latter deny this.[80]

Feuerbach and Nietzsche were the philosophers who launched the most strenuous attacks on this objectivism in Christian thought. Objectivism became the target of Schleiermacher's critique also and led to his subjectivism. However, it is striking that in contemporary Christian thought "about" God there is an "antimetaphysical" tendency while, at the same time, the positions of Feuerbach, Nietzsche and Schleiermacher are not assumed.[81] This antimetaphysical tendency does not consist in the *total* rejection of metaphysics—except in a purely verbal way—but only in the critique of the intellectualism and objectivism which permeate metaphysics as a "hidden option". Thus one can see how certain representatives of the *so-called* antimetaphysical trend of thinking "about" God *seemingly* reject all traditional attributes of God, but do not *really* do so. For example, following Tillich, John Robinson does not wish to allow the term "person" to be used for God. But it quickly becomes apparent that what he objects to is not this term itself but the objectivism which is traditionally attached to it.[82] The same applies to his rejection of such terms as Providence, Goodness, Omnipotence, Wisdom, Creator and Lawgiver.

One can understand, I said, that certain representatives of the so-called antimetaphysical trend of thinking "about" God *seemingly* reject all traditional attributes of God, but do *not really* do so. While this may

---

[80] "For, to the ordinary way of thinking, to believe in God means to be convinced of the existence of such a supreme and separate Being. 'Theists' are those who believe that such a Being exists, 'atheists' those who deny that he does". John A.T. Robinson, *Honest to God*, London, 1963⁹, p. 17.

[81] H.M. Kuitert, *De realiteit van het geloof*, Over de anti-metafysische tendens in de huidige theologische ontwikkeling, Kampen, 1966.

[82] John A.T. Robinson, *o.c.*, pp. 39-42, 48-49.

be true, it is also very confusing, and it does not make sense. By what right should the use of a particular term be considered to have a *necessary* connection with the untenable presuppositions that have crept into this use? In chemistry water is called H_2O, and for a long time people thought that this is what water was "in itself". If this presupposition is now untenable, does it follow that therefore water should no longer be called chemically H_2O?

3. THE "OVERCOMING OF METAPHYSICS" IN HEIDEGGER

Heidegger also thinks that it is necessary to abandon the Western interpretation of metaphysics if the "affirmation" of God is again to recover its authentic character. Western metaphysics, he says, has sunk into "forgetfulness of Being", so that the approach to God and gods is blocked. Heidegger is not directly concerned with the question "about" God; his thought is primarily a groping search for the meaning of Being.

The Approach to Being

Everyone, says Heidegger, thinks that he knows what Being is. But people think that they know this without really having asked the question about the meaning of Being.[83] Thus all kinds of unquestioned elements and prejudices could creep into our concept of Being, so that we do not really know what Being is. We must therefore ask again the question about Being; for Heidegger, this means that we must "first develop the question itself sufficiently".[84] Asking about the meaning of Being is primarily a matter of asking about the possibility of raising this question.

The approach to our understanding of Being must be found in questioning an exemplary be-ing. Being is that which determines be-ing as be-ing and is not itself a be-ing.[85] But which be-ing should be questioned? Is there a be-ing which has priority with respect to the question about Being? Heidegger answers in the affirmative. For asking about Being itself is a mode-of-Being of a particular be-ing[86]—the be-ing which the questioning man himself is. The question about the meaning of Being presupposes that the Being of man asking about Being—*Dasein*—is

---

[83] M. Heidegger, *Sein und Zeit*, Tübingen, 1949[6], p. 2.

[84] M. Heidegger, *o.c.*, p. 4.

[85] "Das Gefragte der auszuarbeitenden Frage ist das Sein, das, was Seiendes als Seiendes bestimmt ... Das Sein des Seienden 'ist' nicht selbst ein Seiendes". M. Heidegger, *o.c.*, p. 6.

[86] M. Heidegger, *o.c.*, p. 7.

first clarified.[87] This is possible because man is the only be-ing which, in its Being, is concerned with its Being.[88] Man is the be-ing which is capable of reflection upon its own Being, and the question about Being in general is a mode of that "own Being".[89] The "fundamental ontology of *Dasein*"[90] can give thought access to Being.

"Forgetfulness of Being"

What is the "forgetfulness of Being" which Heidegger ascribes to traditional metaphysics? Did this metaphysics really fail to speak about Being?[91]

No one could seriously make such a claim. At the same time, no one could seriously assert that traditional metaphysics was very attentive to what Heidegger calls Being.[92] According to Heidegger, metaphysics spoke only about be-ing but paid no attention to the wonder of Being.[93] It talked about be-ing but neglected the wonder that "be-ing *is*".[94] It did not pause in gratitude to marvel at the "coming about", the "event" of the Being of be-ing. The "coming about", the "event", the "Being" of be-ing is the "appearing", the "coming to presence", the "becoming manifest", the "self-giving", the "light" of be-ing. This "appearing" is not itself a be-ing, the appearing is not that which appears,[95] the "coming to

---

[87] "Das Fragen dieser Frage ist als Seinsmodus eines Seienden selbst von dem her wesenhalf bestimmt, wonach in ihm gefragt ist—vom Sein". M. Heidegger, *o.c.*, p. 7.

[88] M. Heidegger, *o.c.*, p. 12.

[89] "Wenn die Interpretation des Sinnes von Sein Aufgabe wird, ist das Dasein nicht nur das primär zu befragende Seiende, es ist überdies das Seiende, das sich je schon in seinem Sein zu dem verhält, wonach in dieser Frage gefragt wird. Die Seinsfrage ist dann aber nichts anderes als die Radikalisierung einer zum Dasein selbst gehörigen wesenhaften Seinstendenz, des vorontologischen Seinsverständnisses". M. Heidegger, *o.c.*, p. 15.

[90] M. Heidegger, *o.c.*, p. 41.

[91] "Nach dem vorhin über Thomas van Aquin Gesagten blieb wenigstens bei ihm die Frage nach dem Sein nicht ungedacht, weshalb die Metaphysik wenigstens für ihn jene Frage nicht nur mitumfasst, sondern letztlich zum Kern alles Fragens erhebt". J. Lotz, *Denken und Sein nach den jüngsten Veröffentlichungen von M. Heidegger*, in : Scholastik, XXXIII (1958), p. 83.

[92] Lotz disregards this.

[93] "Weil die Metaphysik das Seiende als das Seiende befragt, bleibt sie beim Seienden und kehrt sich nicht an das Sein als Sein". M. Heidegger, *Was ist Metaphysik?*, Frankfurt a. M. 1955[7], p. 8.

[94] M. Heidegger, *Was ist Metaphysik?*, pp. 46-47.

[95] E. Fink, *Sein, Wahrheit, Welt*, The Hague, 1958, p. 51.

presence" is not that which comes to presence,[96] the "self-giving" is not that which is given,[97] the "presentness" not that which is present.[98] He calls the appearing of the thing the "thinging" of the thing,[99] and speaks of the appearing of the world as the "worlding" of the world.[100] But "thinging" is not the thing and "worlding" is not the world. In the same way Heidegger says that Being is not be-ing. By the "event" of appearing, which Being is, be-ing has a "face", man has something to say, and be-ing is "given". Without this "event", nothing at all would be given. Metaphysics has never thought about this "event".

Traditional metaphysics has represented, explained and calculated Being, using such categories as cause, effect, subject, object, essence and substance. But it paid no attention to that which remained "unspoken" and "unthought" in metaphysical thinking, viz., that this thinking was and is possible only on the basis of an "event", the "event" by which be-ing appeared and still appears as representable, explainable and calculable. Metaphysics took, and still takes for granted that be-ing appeared and still appears as cause, effect, subject, object, substance, etc.

A similar presupposition also exists in thinking. When metaphysics represents, explains and calculates be-ing, it takes for granted that thinking has already "sprung up" as representing, explaining and calculating. But this also is an "event", a "coming about" that should be considered. Metaphysics has not done this.

Heidegger views his own thought as an attempt to dwell on that which remained and still is hidden in be-ing[101] and in thinking—namely, the "event" that happens when be-ing is and thinking thinks. Asking the question about Being means, for Heidegger, asking why be-ing appeared as it appeared and appears as it appears, asking also why thinking thought as it thought and thinks as it thinks.[102] Because traditional metaphysics

[96] M. Heidegger, *Holzwege*, Frankfurt a. M., 1963⁴, pp. 335-336.

[97] O. Pöggeler, *Sein als Ereignis*, in : Zeitschrift für philosophische Forschung, XIII (1959), p. 621.

[98] A. De Waelhens, *La philosophie et les expériences naturelles*, p. 198.

[99] M. Heidegger, *Vorträge und Aufsätze*, p. 172.

[100] M. Heidegger, *Holzwege*, p. 33.

[101] "Die Metaphysik achtet jedoch dessen nie, was sich in eben diesem ὄν, insofern es unverborgen wurde, auch schon verborgen hat". M. Heidegger, *Was ist Metaphysik?*, p. 20.

[102] S. IJsseling, *Het zijn en de zijnden*, in : Tijdschrift voor Filosofie, 28 (1966), pp. 24, 29, 51.

thought and still thinks only as representing, explaining and calculating, it neither could nor can ask the question about Being. All it would do would be merely asking about Being as a representable, explainable and calculable be-ing.[103] But Being is not a be-ing but rather "nothing".[104] There is an "ontological difference" between Being and be-ing. From its beginning in Greek thought, metaphysical thinking has moved about in the "event" of Being, without, however, reflecting on this "event". It speaks of "Being" but means "the totality of be-ings";[105] or it means the Supreme Be-ing, God.[106] Because it speaks of "Being" but in actual fact only talks about be-ings, traditional metaphysics has neglected the "ontological difference"; it has always confused Being and be-ing.[107] This neglect has caused metaphysics to lapse into "forgetfulness of Being".[108]

Back to the Ground of Metaphysics

Because metaphysics has not spoken about the "event" in which it exists and has never dwelled on that which is hidden in be-ing, it has, strictly speaking, no foundation. For metaphysics lives on what remains "unthought" and "unspoken" in it. That's why metaphysics must be transcended. This requires a "step back", not in history,[109] but toward the ground of metaphysics.[110] This "step back" is made by leaving "representing",[111] "explaining"[112] and "calculating"[113] thinking, and entering

---

[103] "Alles wird dem Vorstellen zu Seiendem". M. Heidegger, *Vorträge and Aufsätze*, p. 240. "Die Metaphysik denkt, insofern sie stets nur das Seiende als das Seiende vorstellt, nicht an das Sein selbst". M. Heidegger, *Was ist Metaphysik?*, p. 8.

[104] M. Heidegger, *Was ist Metaphysik?*, pp. 23-42; M. Heidegger, *Zur Seinsfrage*, Frankfurt a. M., 1956, pp. 37-40.

[105] M. Heidegger, *Was ist Metaphysik?*, p. 11.

[106] M. Heidegger, *o.c.*, p. 19.

[107] "Das Aussagen der Metaphysik bewegt sich von ihrem Beginn bis in ihre Vollendung auf eine seltsame Weise in einer durchgängigen Verwechslung von Seiendem und Sein". M. Heidegger, *o.c.*, p. 11.

[108] "Wir bewegen uns mit dem ganzen Bestand noch innerhalb der Zone des Nihilismus, gesetzt freilich, das Wesen des Nihilismus beruhe in der Seinsvergessenheit". M. Heidegger, *Zur Seinsfrage*, p. 40. "Die Seinsvergessenheit ist die Vergessenheit des Unterschiedes des Seins zum Seienden". M. Heidegger, *Holzwege*, p. 336.

[109] M. Heidegger, *Identität und Differenz*, Pfullingen, 1957, p. 48.

[110] M. Heidegger, *Was ist Metaphysik?*, p. 7.

[111] M. Heidegger, *o.c.*, p. 7.

[112] M. Heidegger, *Vorträge und Aufsätze*, p. 180.

[113] M. Heidegger, *Gelassenheit*, Pfullingen, 1959, pp. 14-15.

foundational,[114] authentic,[115] re-collective,[116] thoughtful[117] originating[118] and "cordial"[119] thinking. The most worrisome aspect of our worrisome time is that we do not think, not yet genuinely think.[120] Thinking must become "more thoughtful".[121] What does this mean?

Thinking does not become "more thoughtful" by making a greater effort but by replacing the "representing of be-ing" by a thinking in which the truth of Being is seen in relation to the essence (*Wesen*) of man,[122] and in which truth itself is thought of as unconcealedness in its essence.[123] According to Heidegger, this is *not* done by metaphysics in its "representing of be-ing". It does not see the truth of Being in relation to man's essence nor truth itself as unconcealedness in its essence.

The crucial question here is what Heidegger means by "essence" (*Wesen*). This term has for him the meaning of a verb : it means "coming about", "coming to pass".[124] Man as a thinking be-ing "comes about"; truth as unconcealedness "comes about". Man "and" truth, thinking "and" truth belong together, they stand in a relationship of reciprocal implication[125] and "come to pass". Man's "coming to pass", his emergence in the cosmos, is a breaking-through the density of things. This breakthrough makes man the be-ing which in its Being is concerned with its Being, the be-ing which is characterized by "understanding of Being", the be-ing which is a "light" unto itself. But, as such, man is equiprimordially the "letting be" of the other than self, so that truth

---

[114] M. Heidegger, *Was ist Metaphysik?*, p. 49.

[115] M. Heidegger, *Vorträge und Aufsätze*, p. 143.

[116] M. Heidegger, *o.c.*, p. 180.

[117] M. Heidegger, *Der Satz vom Grund*, Pfullingen, 1957, p. 199.

[118] M. Heidegger, *Was ist Metaphysik?*, p. 49.

[119] M. Heidegger, *Gelassenheit*, p. 27.

[120] M. Heidegger, *Was heisst Denken?*, Tübingen, 1954, p. 3.

[121] M. Heidegger, *Was ist Metaphysik?*, p. 13.

[122] "Das Denken auf einen Weg zu bringen, durch den es in den Bezug der Wahrheit des Seins zum Wesen des Menschen gelangt, dem Denken einen Pfad zu öffnen damit es das Sein selbst in seiner Wahrheit eigens bedenke, dahin ist das in 'Sein und Zeit' versuchte Denken 'unterwegs' ". M. Heidegger, *o.c.*, p. 13.

[123] "Aber die Metaphysik bringt das Sein selbst nicht zur Sprache, weil sie das Sein nicht in seiner Wahrheit und die Wahrheit nicht als die Unverborgenheit und diese nicht in ihrem Wesen bedenkt". M. Heidegger, *o.c.*, p. 10.

[124] M. Heidegger, *Vorträge und Aufsätze*, p. 38.

[125] M. Heidegger, *Identität und Differenz*, pp. 22-23; M. Heidegger, *Vorträge und Aufsätze*, pp. 193, 248-249.

as unconcealedness also "comes to pass".[126] Man as thinking "and" truth as unconcealedness belong together.

Metaphysics, says Heidegger, never dwelled in the wonder of all wonders that thinking "and" truth "come to pass". It "represented" be-ing but "forgot" Being, the "coming to pass" of be-ing. Precisely because metaphysics did not stop to consider Being as the "coming about" of be-ing, all kinds of presuppositions and unquestioned assumptions could permeate man's thinking. Thus metaphysics did not realize that its "representing" way of thinking contained an implicit ontology of the represented object and the representing subject.[127] The represented object was implicitly conceived as a "be-ing that is always 'already' there",[128] as existing in itself,[129] as be-ing in itself,[130] and the subject was conceived as an isolated subject. Heidegger objects to the implicit ontology of "subject", "object" and their mutual "relationship" that has crept into "representative" thinking.[131] Subject and object are not isolated entities which from time to time deal with each other.[132] Even in his early work BEING AND TIME Heidegger unmasked this false ontology and replaced it by the ontology of *Dasein* as "Being in the world". He points out there that he can reject the false conceptions of "Being-in"

---

[126] M. Heidegger, *Vom Wesen der Wahrheit*, Frankfurt a. M., 1954³, pp. 14-17. "Mit dem Sein des Daseins und seiner Erschlossenheit ist gleichursprünglich Entdecktheit des innerweltlichen Seienden". M. Heidegger, *Sein und Zeit*, p. 221.

[127] M. Heidegger, *Vorträge und Aufsätze*, pp. 75, 84-85.

[128] "In der metaphysischen Verbindung von Sein und Wahrheit ist das Sein als stete Anwesenheit, die Wahrheit ebenso als das stets für die Erkenntnis Anwesende oder, vom Erkennen her, als Anmessung an das stets Anwesende gedacht". O. Pöggeler, *Der Denkweg Martin Heideggers*, Pfullingen, 1963, pp. 88-89.

[129] "Wie gelangt die Gegenständigkeit in den Charakter, das Wesen des Seienden als solchen auszumachen? Man denkt 'Sein' als Gegenständigkeit und müht sich dann von da aus um das 'Seiende an sich', wobei man nur vergisst zu fragen und zu sagen, was man hier mit 'seiend' und mit 'an sich' meint". M. Heidegger, *Vorträge und Aufsätze*, p. 84.

[130] A. Dondeyne, *La différence ontologique chez M. Heidegger*, in : Revue philosophique de Louvain, 56 (1958), p. 57.

[131] "Vorausgesetzt wird immer ein vorhandenes Subjekt und ein vorhandenes Objekt. Zwischen beiden entsteht oder besteht eine Beziehung. Heidegger nennt die Ontologie, die dem Ansatz der Beziehung eines Subjektes auf ein Objekt in dieser Weise zugrundeliegt, die Ontologie der Vorhandenheit. Aus ihr entspringt die neuzeitliche Erkenntnistheorie. In dieser entsteht die Frage : Wie kommt ein Subjekt hinaus zu seinem Objekt? Begründet ist diese Ontologie der Vorhandenheit in der Philosophie Descartes". G. Noller, *Sein und Existenz*, München, 1962, p. 45.

[132] M. Heidegger, *Sein und Zeit*, p. 57.

only because in every *Dasein* the true character of "Being-in" is "seen" to some extent.[133] This is so because *Dasein* is characterized by "understanding of Being", and this "understanding" is essential for *Dasein*.[134] But the nature of this "Being-in" is fundamentally misunderstood or insufficiently explicitated.[135] Although the "Being-in" was pre-phenomenologically "experienced" and "known", it became *invisible* on the road of an ontologically unsuitable explicitation.[136] Thus, says Heidegger, everything we know about "Being-in" now bears the seal of that false interpretation, and this as something that is simply taken for granted.[137] This false interpretation thereby became the "self-evident" starting point for the theory of knowledge."For what is more self-evident than that a subject refers to an object, and vice versa? The subject-object relationship must be presupposed". But, says Heidegger, if the ontological significance of this presupposition is left in darkness, then the presupposition itself is fatal.[138] For in that case a false ontology of the "subject", the "object" and their "relationship" becomes something that is taken for granted, while in reality that ontology is nothing but a "hidden option". It is this false ontology that Heidegger has in mind when he demands that "representing" thinking be replaced by "foundational" thinking.[139]

When Heidegger makes the "step back" from metaphysics to the foundation of metaphysics, when he expresses the "unspoken" and "un-

---

[133] "Der phänomenologische Aufweis des In-der-Welt-Seins hat den Charakter der Zurückweisung von Vorstellungen und Verdeckungen, weil dieses Phänomen immer schon in jedem Dasein in gewisser Weise selbst 'gesehen' wird". M. Heidegger, *o.c.*, p. 58.

[134] M. Heidegger, *o.c.*, p. 58.

[135] "Das Phänomen ist aber auch zumeist immer schon ebenso gründlich missdeutet oder ontologisch ungenügend ausgelegt". M. Heidegger, *o.c.*, p. 58.

[136] "Das In-der-Welt-sein wird—obzwar vorphänomenologisch erfahren und gekannt—auf dem Wege einer ontologisch unangemessenen Auslegung unsichtbar". M. Heidegger, *o.c.*, p. 59.

[137] M. Heidegger, *o.c.*, p. 59.

[138] "Man kennt die Daseinsverfassung jetzt nur noch—und zwar als etwas Selbstverständliches—in der Prägung durch die unangemessene Auslegung. Dergestalt wird sie dann zum 'evidenten' Ausgangspunkt für die Probleme der Erkenntnistheorie oder 'Metaphysik der Erkenntnis'. Denn was ist selbstverständlicher als dass sich ein 'Subjekt' auf ein 'Objekt' bezieht und umgekehrt? Diese 'Subjekt-Objekt-Beziehung' muss vorausgesetzt werden. Das bleibt aber eine—obzwar in ihrer Faktizität unantastbare—doch gerade deshalb recht verhängnisvolle Voraussetzung, wenn ihre ontologische Notwendigkeit und vor allem ihr ontologischer Sinn im Dunkel gelassen wird". M. Heidegger, *o.c.*, p. 59.

[139] G. Noller, *o.c.*, pp. 47-48.

thought" assumption of traditional metaphysics, this means for him also—but not only and exclusively—that he wishes to rethink the steps which tradition has made in its thinking and which have made it lose its way.[140] That which in the history of thought remained "unthought" and "unspoken" *de facto* decided our thinking. Heidegger wants to put these decisions up again "for decision".[141] IJsseling compares Heidegger's work in this respect to that of the psychoanalyst. Even as the psycho-analyst wants to let the forgotten and repressed history of the individual man find expression, so Heidegger wants to do the same for the history of thought, in order to put decisions made in the course of history up again "for decision".[142]

Being as "Initiative" and "Mittence" (Geschick)

The preceding considerations could give rise to the conclusion that Heidegger intends to think and say that which remained unthought and unspoken in the history of thought. But such a conclusion would only be partly true. It is valid for the implicit ontologies which, because they were presupposed as self-evident, led to an "unsuitable explana-tion",[143] a "dissembling" and "disarranging" of reality.[144] They derailed man's thinking and made him lapse into "forgetfulness of Being". The decisions to which they gave rise must be put up again for decision.[145] On a more profound level, however, it is not true that Heidegger wishes to think and say that which remained unthought and unspoken. On a more profound level the unthought remains in principle unthought, and the unspoken stays in principle unspoken. The reason for this

---

[140] O. Pöggeler, *o.c.*, p. 75.

[141] "Durch ein Thema wie 'Augustinus und der Neuplatonismus' (oder auch 'Kier-kegaard und Hegel') werden jene Entscheidungen wieder neu zur Entscheidung gestellt, die das abendländische Denken geformt haben". O. Pöggeler, *o.c.*, pp. 44-45.

[142] S. IJsseling, *a.c.*, pp. 48-49.

[143] M. Heidegger, *Sein und Zeit*, p. 59.

[144] M. Heidegger, *o.c.*, p. 58.

[145] "Was von der Metaphysik gedacht worden ist, wird durch den Rückgang in den Grund der Metaphysik neu zur Entscheidung gestellt und kann auf diese Weise ursprünglich angeeignet werden. Durch eine seinsgeschichtliche Besinnung denkt Heidegger die Bestimmungen des Sinnes von Sein nach, die für die verschiedenen Phasen der Metaphysik leitend, aber nicht eigens zur Frage gemacht worden waren. So sucht Heidegger das metaphysische Denken zurückzustellen auf den ungedacht gebliebenen Grund und das eigene Denken einzufügen in das Wahrheitsgeschehen, wie es uns aus unserer Überlieferung entgegenkommmt". O. Pöggeler, *Sein als Ereignis*, in : Zeitschrift für philosophische Forschung, XIII (1959), p. 622.

becomes a little clearer as soon as one notices that there is a gradual shift of emphasis in Heidegger's works. Where at first he ascribed a certain priority to *Dasein*, to thinking, later he assigns a priority to Being itself, a priority which he calls a certain "initiative" and "mittence". In this way the "forgetfulness of Being" acquires a new dimension.

"When Being remains unthought", Heidegger says, "the reason seems to lie in thinking",[146] but this is not true. If Being remains unthought, this must be ascribed to the "dallying of Being itself".[147] That Being remains unthought is "forgetfulness of Being", but this forgetfulness itself also is a form of Being's own "coming about".[148]

Thus metaphysics' "forgetfulness of Being" is, according to Heidegger, not an "unfortunate" project of man himself but rather a "project" of Being, which, as "mittence", is in a certain sense a "resort dominating man",[149] an "initiative".[150] Heidegger's groping thought is a questioning as to why be-ing appears as it appears and has appeared in history. But this questioning may not be understood as the search for an explanatory cause of the "coming to pass" of Being "and" thinking.[151] One who looks here for an explanatory cause disregards the wonder of the "coming to pass" of Being, for what matters here is precisely to "understand" why be-ing has appeared in history as explainable and why thinking has developed as explanatory thinking.[152] Be-ing is explainable and thinking is explanatory "on the ground of" the "coming to pass" of Being.[153] In the same way we must say, according to Heidegger, that

[146] M. Heidegger, *Nietzsche*, Pfullingen, 1961, II, p. 352.

[147] M. Heidegger, *o.c.*, p. 353.

[148] M. Heidegger, *Die Technik und die Kehre*, Pfullingen, 1962, p. 43.

[149] J. v.d. Wiele, *Zijnswaarheid en onverborgenheid*, Een vergelijkende studie over de ontologische waarheid in het Thomisme en bij Heidegger, Leuven, 1964, p. 282.

[150] J. Richardson, *Heidegger, Through phenomenology to thought*, The Hague, 1962, p. 435.

[151] "Wir können den Satz vom Grund auf eine zweifache Weise hören : einmal als obersten Grundsatz über das Seiende, zum anderen als Satz vom Sein. In dem zweiten Fall sind wir dahin gewiesen, den Grund als Sein und Sein als Grund zu denken. In solchem Falle beginnen wir mit dem Versuch : Sein als Sein zu denken. Dies sagt : *Sein nicht mehr durch etwas Seiendes erklären*". M. Heidegger, *Der Satz vom Grund*, pp. 118-119.

[152] S. IJsseling, *Het zijn en de zijnden*, pp. 32-33.

[153] "Der Satz vom Grund sagt : *Zum Sein gehört dergleichen wie Grund. Das Sein ist grundartig, grundhaft*. Der Satz : 'Sein ist grundhaft', spricht ganz anders als die Aussage : Das Seiende hat einen Grund. Sein ist grundhaft', meint also keineswegs : 'Sein hat einen Grund', sondern sagt : *Sein west in sich als gründendes*. Der Satz vom

be-ing is representable and that thinking is representing "on the ground of" the "coming to pass" of Being.[154] The idea that be-ing has appeared as explainable and representable calls for a reflection that is concerned with the history of Being. This reflection should be understood as an attempt to dwell in the neighborhood of Being as "history", by again taking in thought the "steps" which thought has already made.[155] This is an attempt to raise again the questions concerning the explicitations of be-ing which characterized the various periods of metaphysical thought, while focusing on that which could not yet be spoken of then, viz., the "coming to pass" and the "reigning" of Being as that *of which man is not the lord and master*, the "coming to pass" and the "reigning" of Being itself as "mittence".

The "forgetfulness of Being" in which formerly Being "came to pass" and through which metaphysics is what it is should not be ascribed to man's negligence; rather, it is "no go" with Being; Being itself fails to appear.[156] The "forgetfulness of Being" belongs to the concealed "coming to pass" of Being,[157] and the history of Being necessarily begins with "forgetfulness of Being".[158] Metaphysics, in its "coming about", belongs to the unthought mystery of Being itself.[159] This "coming about" is

---

Grund sagt dies freilich nicht aus. Was er sagt, lässt der unmittelbar vernehmliche Satzinhalt ungesagt. Das, *wovon* der Satz vom Grund sagt, kommt nicht zur Sprache, nämlich nicht zu jener Sprache, die *dem* entspricht, *wovon* der Satz vom Grund sagt. *Der Satz vom Grund ist ein Sagen vom Sein.* Er ist dies, aber verborgenerweise. Verborgen bleibt nicht nur, wovon er sagt, verborgen bleibt auch *dass* er vom Sein sagt". M. Heidegger, *Der Satz vom Grund*, p. 90.

[154] "Worauf beruht das Nichterscheinen des Dinges als Ding? Hat lediglich der Mensch es versäumt, das Ding als Ding vorzustellen? Der Mensch kann nur das versäumen, was ihm bereits zugewiesen ist. Vorstellen kann der Mensch, gleichviel in welcher Weise, nur solches, was erst zuvor von sich her sich gelichtet und in seinem dabei mitgebrachten Licht ihm gezeigt hat". M. Heidegger, *Vorträge und Aufsätze*, p. 169.

[155] See footnote 145, p. 69 of this volume.

[156] "Aus dem Geschick des Seins gedacht, bedeutet das nihil des Nihilismus, dass es mit dem Sein nichts ist. Das Sein kommt nicht an das Licht seines eigenen Wesens. Im Erscheinen des Seienden als solchen bleibt das Sein selbst aus". M. Heidegger, *Holzwege*, p. 244.

[157] "Die Vergessenheit des Seins gehört in das durch sie selbst verhüllte Wesen des Seins. Sie gehört so wesentlich in das Geschick des Seins, dass ...". M. Heidegger, *o.c.*, p. 336.

[158] "Die Geschichte des Seins beginnt und zwar notwendig mit der Vergessenheit des Seins". M. Heidegger, *o.c.*, p. 243.

[159] M. Heidegger, *o.c.*, p. 244.

not accessible to metaphysics because metaphysics itself is a "moment" of this "coming about".

Clearly, while Heidegger at first ascribed a certain priority or primacy to *Dasein*, later he attributed to Being itself a certain "initiative" or "mittence".[160] This does not mean that Being is conceived "separately" from be-ing[161] and "separately" from man. Be-ing and Being belong to the essence of man.[162] To think "foundationally" is to accomplish the relationship of Being to man's essence. "Foundational" thinking does not "make" or "establish" this relationship, but finds itself in this relationship.[163] The term "essence" here has again the value of a verb : man's essence is the "coming about" of man's truth, and the essence of be-ing is the "coming about" of the truth of be-ing. These two belong together.[164] Being's "claim" gives man his essence.[165]

When Heidegger in his later works calls Being "mittence", he intends to say that *man* does not "decide" how be-ing apears and how thought thinks.[166] When he asks, "What is (*heisst*) thinking"? he does not simply wonder what "thinking" really is, but looks for what "calls" (*heisst*) us to think, i.e., "orders" us to think.[167] And it is Being that does this.[168]

---

[160] "Während in 'Sein und Zeit' gesagt wird, dass die Seinsfrage nur geschichtlich gestellt werden könne, weil das fragende *Dasein* des Menschen von geschichtlicher Art ist, heisst es in der Humanismusschrift umgekehrt, das Denken des Seins sei geschichtlich, weil es die Geschichte des *Seins* gebe, in die das Denken als Andenken dieser Geschichte, von ihr selbst ereignet, gehört". K. Löwith, *Heidegger*, Denker in dürftiger Zeit, Göttingen, 1960², p. 52.

[161] "... dass das Sein nie west ohne das Seiende, dass niemals ein Seiendes ist ohne das Sein". M. Heidegger, *Was ist Metaphysik?*, p. 46.

[162] "Aber — sobald ich denkend sage 'Menschenwesen', habe ich darin schon den Bezug zum Sein gesagt. Insgleichen, sobald ich denkend sage : Sein des Seienden, ist darin schon den Bezug zum Menschenwesen genannt". M. Heidegger, *Was heisst Denken?*, p. 74,

[163] M. Heidegger, *Über den Humanismus*, Frankfurt a. M., 1947, p. 5.

[164] M. Heidegger, *Was heisst Denken?*, p. 74.

[165] "Der Anspruch des Seins räumt den Menschen erst in sein Wesen ein". M. Heidegger, *Der Satz vom Grund*, p. 119.

[166] "Der Mensch ist vielmehr vom Sein selbst in die Wahrheit des Seins 'geworfen', dass er, dergestalt ek-sistierend, die Wahrheit des Seins hüte, damit im Lichte des Seins das Seiende als das Seiende, das es ist, erscheine. Ob es und wie es erscheint, ob und wie der Gott und die Götter, die Geschichte und die Natur in die Lichtung des Seins hereinkommen, an- und abwesen, entscheidet nicht der Mensch. Die Ankunft des Seienden beruht im Geschick des Seins". M. Heidegger, *Über den Humanismus*, p. 19.

[167] M. Heidegger, *Was heisst Denken?*, p. 79.

[168] M. Heidegger, *o.c.*, p. 149; *Was ist Metaphysik*, p. 49; *Nietzsche*, II, p. 29, 359, 372; *Über den Humanismus*, pp. 13, 16.

In BEING AND TIME Heidegger characterizes *Dasein* as "natural light" and therefore calls it *logos*. Because *Dasein* is a kind of "ex-plaining" and "col-lecting", the world is not a chaos for man but a meaningful whole. Man can speak meaningfully because *Dasein* is a certain "light". But in Heidegger's later works it is no longer *Dasein* but Being which "ex-plains" and "collects". [169] Not *Dasein* is called "*logos*", "light" and "lan-uage" there, but Being is.[170] The fact that Being was not spoken of as "initiative" is the "forgetfulness of Being" committed by Western meta-physics and even of the West's entire history, but even this was an "ini-tiative", a "mittence" of Being.[171]

The "Reversal"

This shift of accent in Heidegger's thought obviously has consequences also for the way he conceives the victory over the "forgetfulness of Being". This victory is now more than a matter of giving expression to the implicit ontologies which decided about man's thinking, in order to put these decisions up again for decision. For such a thing would still be left to the "initiative" of man himself as a thinker. But if Being itself is a kind of "initiative", if the "forgetfulness of Being" is really an "abandonment by Being",[172] the situation becomes different.

If the history of the West lies immersed in "forgetfulness of Being", asks Heidegger, what are we to do? But he adds at once that this is not the right question. The problem is not, what must we do? but, how must we think?[173] Authentic thinking is attentive to the "coming to pass" of Being. Thinking must prepare for the "coming to pass" of Being the "place" where man is sensitive to the "call of Being". Man must first and foremost recover the breadth of his own essence. This will not happen as long as man limits himself to explaining the metaphysical order in which he lives in a morphological, psychological and historical way,

---

[169] "Das Sein ist das Seiende. Hierbei spricht 'ist' transitiv und besagt soviel wie 'versammelt'. Das Sein versammelt das Seiende darin, dass es Seiendes ist". M. Heidegger, *Was ist das — die Philosophie?*, Pfullingen, 1960, p. 22.

[170] M. Heidegger, *Unterwegs zur Sprache*, Pfullingen, 1961, pp.185.

[171] "Die Vergessenheit des Seins gehört in das durch sie selbst verhüllte Wesen des Seins. Sie gehört so wesentlich in das Geschick des Seins, dass ...". M. Heidegger, *Holzwege*, p. 336.

[172] M. Heidegger, *Was ist Metaphysik?*, p. 46.

[173] M. Heidegger, *Die Technik und die Kehre*, p. 40.

as long as he tries to represent his own situation as an "effect" of "causes", as long as he works with an apparatus for adding explanatory symptoms to explanatory symptoms. For in this way he remains encompassed by calculating representations.[174] The metaphysical order can only be understood as a phase in the history of Being "in this sense that Being sends itself".[175] But because metaphysical thinking itself belongs to the "mittence" of Being, it is not certain that man will ever find the breadth of his own essence, in which there is room for the authentic truth of Being.[176] Whether man will succeed in letting the truth of Being "come to pass" in his own essence is something that is not decided by man, but depends on the "mittence" of Being.[177] The sway of metaphysics is the "danger", but because man does not decide autonomously about metaphysics, Being itself is the "danger".[178] The danger of metaphysics cannot be overcome by an autonomous decision of man because he is not the "lord of Being".[179]

"But where there is danger, there salvation also grows".[180] When danger *as* danger "is", then danger itself is salvation. For when danger *as* danger "is", then, together with the "reversal" of "forgetfulness", the truth of Being "comes to pass". In the "coming to pass" of danger

---

[174] M. Heidegger, o.c., pp. 45-46.

[175] M. Heidegger, o.c., p. 38.

[176] "Niemand kann wissen, ob und wann und wie dieser Schritt des Denkens zu einem eigentlichen ... Weg und Gang und Wegebau sich entfaltet. Es könnte sein, dass die Herrschaft der Metaphysik sich eher verfestigt und zwar in der Gestalt der modernen Technik und deren unabsehbaren rasenden Entwicklungen. Es könnte auch sein, dass alles, was sich auf dem Weg des Schrittes zurück ergibt, von der fortbestehenden Metaphysik auf ihre Weise als Ergebnis eines vorstellenden Denkens nur genützt und verarbeitet wird". M. Heidegger, *Identität und Differenz*, p. 71.

[177] "Überdies aber ist der Entwurf wesenhaft ein geworfener. Das Werfende im Entwerfen ist nicht der Mensch, sondern das Sein selbst, das den Menschen in die Ek-sistenz des Da-seins als Sein Wesen schickt. Dieses Geschick ereignet sich als die Lichtung des Seins, als welche es ist. Sie gewährt die Nähe zum Sein. In dieser Nähe, in der Lichtung des 'Da' wohnt der Mensch als der Ek-sistierende, ohne dass er es heute schon vermag, dieses Wohnen eigens zu erfahren und zu übernehmen". M. Heidegger, *Über den Humanismus*, p. 25.

[178] "Insofern die Gefahr das Sein selber ist ...". M. Heidegger, *Die Technik und die Kehre*, p. 41.

[179] "Wenn das Wesen der Technik, das Gestell als die Gefahr im Sein, das Sein selbst ist, dann lässt sich die Technik niemals durch ein bloss auf sich gestelltes menschliches Tun meistern, weder positiv noch negativ. Die Technik, deren Wesen das Sein selbst ist, lässt sich durch den Mensch niemals überwinden. Das hiesse doch : der Mensch sei der Herr des Seins". M. Heidegger, o.c., p. 38.

[180] M. Heidegger, o.c., p. 41.

a favor "comes to pass" and "dwells"—the favor of the "reversal" from the "forgetfulness of Being" to the truth of Being.[181] This reversal takes place without any intermediary whatsoever, for the reversal is Being itself, which does not belong to any causal interconnection.[182] Thus the coming of Being is not guaranteed. This coming is not accomplished without man, yet it is not achieved by man's absolute initiative.[183] In the past Being's self-giving in the West assumed the form of metaphysics. This meant that "the truth of Being was delayed". However, it does not necessarily have to remain thus.[184] Perhaps we are already living in the shadow cast ahead by the "reversal".[185] Whether and when the "reversal" will take place, nobody knows. But it isn't necessary to know this. It would even be pernicious because it belongs to the very essence of man to be "awaiting". Man must await the "coming to pass" of Being by thoughtfully shepherding it,[186] and not by calculatingly trying to master it.[187] Thus the "mittence" of Being is also, and primordially, the "mittence" of thinking.[188]

The God of Metaphysics

From its very beginning among the Greeks, says Heidegger, metaphysics has always developed in two phases.[189] On the one hand, metaphysics thought about be-ing as be-ing or be-ing in general. As such, meta-

---

[181] "Wenn die Gefahr als die Gefahr ist, ereignet sich mit der Kehre der Vergessenheit die Wahrnis des Seins". M. Heidegger, o.c., p. 42.

[182] M. Heidegger, o.c., pp. 42-43.

[183] M. Heidegger, Über den Humanismus, p. 19.

[184] "Geschick aber ist wesenhalf Geschick des Seins, so zwar, dass das Sein selber sich schickt und je als ein Geschick west und demgemäss sich geschicklich wandelt". M. Heidegger, Die Technik und die Kehre, p. 38.

[185] M. Heidegger, o.c., pp. 40-41.

[186] "Wann und wie sie sich geschicklich ereignet, weiss niemand. Es ist auch nicht nötig, solches zu wissen. Ein Wissen dieser Art wäre sogar das Verderblichste für den Menschen, weil sein Wesen ist, der Wartende zu sein, der des Wesens des Seins wartet, indem er es denkend hütet. Nur wenn der Mensch als der Hirt des Seins der Wahrheit des Seins wartet, kann er eine Ankunft des Seinsgeschickes erwarten, ohne in das blosse Wissenwollen zu verfallen". M. Heidegger, o.c., p. 41.

[187] M. Heidegger, o.c., p. 46.

[188] M. Heidegger, Über den Humanismus, p. 46.

[189] "Aber die Metaphysik stellt die Seiendheit des Seienden in zweifacher Weise vor : einmal das Ganze des Seienden als solchen im Sinne seiner allgemeinsten Züge (ὄν καθολόν, κοινόν); zugleich aber das Ganze des Seienden als solchen im Sinne des höchsten und darum göttlichen Seienden (ὄν καθολόν ἀκρότατον, θεῖον)". M. Heidegger, Was ist Metaphysik?, p. 19.

physics is ontology. On the other hand, metaphysics spoke of be-ing
in its highest realization, i.e., about the divine be-ing.[190] As such, metaphysics is theology. The "first philosophy", then, is as ontology at the
same time also theology of the highest be-ing. But this highest be-ing
was, in an increasingly confusing and ambiguous way, also called Being.[191]

What was the character of this ontology and theology? According
to Heidegger, they were conceived in the same fashion as psychology,
biology, cosmology and archeology were conceived[192]—in other words,
as sciences. As a -logy, onto-theology shared not only the "logical"
aspect, the inner connection and coherence of any science, but also,
like the sciences, searched for the "ground", i.e., the cause of what it
spoke about, of be-ing as be-ing.[193] The highest be-ing was conceived
as First Cause.[194] This, says Heidegger, was to be expected. For in
metaphysics the actuality of be-ing was conceived as causality because
every cause exercises its causal influence by virtue of its actuality. The
highest be-ing, God, is highest precisely because it is pure actuality, it contains no potentiality at all but is "pure act". That is why the highest
be-ing is also to the highest degree cause.[195] The highest be-ing, i.e.,
the first cause, functioned in metaphysics as the answer to the question,
"Why is there something rather than nothing"?

According to Heidegger, the question of the "why" of be-ing had an
entirely different meaning in ancient Greece than in the metaphysics
of later times.[196] The reason is that "reality" (*Wirklichkeit*) in ancient
Greece was still understood in its original sense : "the real (*wirkliche*)

---

[190] "Die Metaphysik ist in sich, und zwar weil sie das Seiende als das Seiende zur
Vorstellung bringt, zweifach-einig die Wahrheit des Seienden im Allgemeinen und
im Höchsten. Sie ist ihrem Wesen nach zugleich Ontologie im engeren Sinne und
Theologie". M. Heidegger, *o.c.*, p. 19.

[191] "Dieses Seiende, τό θεῖον, das Göttliche, wird in einer seltsamen Zweideutigkeit
auch 'das Sein' genannt". M. Heidegger, *Holzwege*, p. 179.

[192] M. Heidegger, *Identität und Differenz*, p. 55.

[193] M. Heidegger, *o.c.*, pp. 56-57.

[194] "Die ursprüngliche Sache des Denkens stellt sich als die Ursache dar, als die
causa prima, die dem begründenden Rückgang auf die ultima ratio, die letzte Rechen-
schaft, entspricht". M. Heidegger, *o.c.*, p. 57.

[195] "Die actualitas aber ist causalitas. Der Ursachecharakter des Seins als Wirklichkeit zeigt sich in aller Reinheit an jenem Seienden, das im höchsten Sinne das Wesen
des Seins erfüllt, da es das Seiende ist, das nie nicht sein kann! 'Theologisch' gedacht,
heisst dieses Seiende 'Gott' .... Das höchste Seiende ist reine, stets erfüllte Verwirklichung, actus purus". M. Heidegger, *Nietzsche*, II, p. 415.

[196] M. Heidegger, *Was ist Metaphysik?*, p. 22.

is that which works or has been worked",[197] and this expression meant "brought to presence".[198] The term "to work", then, did not express "to bring about" or "brought about", but the fact that something comes to stand in unconcealedness.[199] When the Greeks spoke of that which the Romans were to call "efficient cause", they never intended to refer to the production of an effect.[200] The Greeks spoke of *energeia*, but it did not mean what our term "energy" (said of an efficient cause) implies. The Greek *energeia* meant "coming to presence", and this may be translated as reality (*Wirklichkeit*) only if "to work" is understood as the Greeks did : "to bring 'out'—into unconcealedness, forth—into presence".[201] What follows from "work" is the real (*wirkliche*), not conceived as the effect of an efficient cause, but as that which comes forth from concealedness, the present.[202] Because the real (*wirkliche*) was no longer understood as the unconcealed but as the caused, metaphysics omitted all questions about the unconcealedness of reality and at once set out to look for the cause. That is why it got stuck in "forgetfulness of Being".

The fact that metaphysics called the first cause—the highest be-ing— "God" means, according to Heidegger, that it has presented us with an ungodly "God". "What kind of a 'God' is this?, he asks." Certainly not a 'God' to whom man can pray, bring a sacrifice, a 'God' for whom he can fall on his knees, play music or dance". One who rejects the "God-Cause", he says is closer to the godly God than is he who accepts this "God-Cause".[203] Thinking that has become "god-less" is not a kind of atheism.[204]

---

[197] M. Heidegger, *Vorträge und Aufsätze*, p. 49.

[198] " 'Wirklichkeit' meint dann, weit genug gedacht : das ins Anwesen hervorgebrachte Vorliegen, das in sich vollendete Anwesen von Sichhervorbringendem". M. Heidegger *o.c.*, p. 49.

[199] M. Heidegger, *o.c.*, p. 49.

[200] M. Heidegger, *o.c.*, pp. 49-50.

[201] M. Heidegger, *o.c.*, p. 50.

[202] "Das Her- und Vor-gebrachte erscheint jetzt als das, was sich aus einer operatio er-gibt. Das Ergebnis ist das, was auf einer und aus einer actio folgt : der Er-folg. Das wirkliche ist jetzt das Erfolgte. Der Erfolg wird durch eine Sache erbracht, die ihm voraufgeht, durch die Ursache (causa). Das Wirkliche erscheint jetzt im Lichte der Kausalität der causa efficiens". M. Heidegger, *o.c.*, p. 50.

[203] "Dies ist die Ursache als die Causa sui. So lautet der sachgerechte Name für den Gott in der Philosophie. Zu diesem Gott kann der Mensch weder beten, noch kann er ihm opfern. Vor der Causa sui kann der Mensch weder aus Scheu ins Knie fallen, noch kann er vor diesem Gott musizieren und tanzen. Demgemäss ist das gottlose Denken, das den Gott der Philosophie, den Gott als Causa sui preisgeben muss, dem göttlichen Gott vielleicht näher. Dies sagt hier nur : Es ist freier für ihn, als

Heidegger also has serious objections to traditional Christian theology, for the idea of creation occupies the center of it.[205] To develop this idea, Christian theology took over philosophical elements from Plato[206] and Aristotle[207] : it called God the Supreme Be-ing and the First Cause of all other be-ings. Accordingly, God did not enter philosophy by way of theology. He was already there because of *the very character of metaphysics* itself. Precisely because of this character, because of the fact that metaphysics had a certain way of thinking, the metaphysical representation of God "fitted in" with Christian theology, metaphysical elements of Plato and Aristotle could be assimilated by this theology,[208] and the great philosophers of Greece could be viewed as Christian theologians who had not yet attained full growth.[209]

We have here a destructive attack on Christian theology. On the basis of metaphysics' *own* character, the God of metaphysics "fitted in" very well with Christian theology, says Heidegger. But metaphysics' "own character" is "forgetfulness of Being". Thus the ease with which theology could take over the God of metaphysics means that, in Heidegger's eyes, theology also is imbued with "forgetfulness of Being". If Heidegger wishes to keep Christian theology away from his philosophy, the reason is not only that philosophy is philosophy but also and especially that Christian theology lives in "forgetfulness of Being". Christian theological thought does not move in the climate, the dimension of "foundational thinking",[210] because it has never asked an ontological question about the Being of *Dasein*.[211]

---

es die Onto-Theo-Logik wahrhaben möchte". M. Heidegger, *Identität und Differenz*, pp. 70-71.

[204] M. Heidegger, *o.c.*, p. 71.

[205] M. Heidegger, *Einführung in die Metaphysik*, p. 5.

[206] M. Heidegger, *Platons Lehre von der Wahrheit*, Bern, 1947, p. 48.

[207] M. Heidegger, *Was ist Metaphysik?*, p. 19.

[208] "Der theologische Charakter der Ontologie beruht somit nicht darauf, dass die griechische Metaphysik später von der kirchlichen Theologie des Christentums aufgenommen und durch diese umgebildet wurde. Er beruht vielmehr in der Art, wie sich von früh an das Seiende als das Seiende entborgen hat. Diese Unverborgenheit des Seienden gab erst die Möglichkeit, dass sich die christliche Theologie der griechischen Philosophie bemächtigte". M. Heidegger, *o.c.*, pp. 19-20.

[209] M. Heidegger, *Einführung in die Metaphysik*, p. 97.

[210] "Eine weltanschauliche, d.h. immer populär ontische Stellungnahme und erst recht jede theologische kommt als solche — sie mag zustimmen oder ablehnen — überhaupt nicht in die Dimension des Problems einer Metaphysik des Daseins". M. Heidegger, *Kant und das Problem der Metaphysik*, Frankfurt a. M., 1951, p. 214.

[211] "Die Idee der 'Transzendenz', dass der Mensch etwas sei, das über sich hinaus-

All kinds of accusations addressed to theology, scattered through Heidegger's works, now become clear. He reproaches theology for having tried to be a "world view" to its adherents[212] and for putting itself into the rank of the "sciences".[213] In Heidegger's eyes, all this is a manifestation of the fact that Christian theology also lives in "forgetfulness of Being". He wishes to say, then, that, like metaphysics, Christian theology, by its inmost nature, is unable to arrive at an authentic "affirmation" of God.

Heidegger's rejection of the God of metaphysics finds its strongest expression in his agreement with Nietzsche's statement that "God is dead". Heidegger has paid great attention to Nietzsche's work, not because he thought that Nietzche began to give expression to certain things which he himself wished to express, but because the absolute necessity of the "other thinking" becomes visible in Nietzsche. Heidegger does not find any attempt in Nietzsche to think the truth of Being itself[214]—which is the only point Heidegger is interested in. But the absolute necessity of the "other thinking" is evident to Heidegger from the fact that Nietzsche brought metaphysics to its finish. Nietzsche is for him the last metaphysician. Nietzsche's philosophy finished what Plato started, viz., the foundation of the truth of be-ing as be-ing in the supreme be-ing.[215] For Nietzsche be-ing is "will to power", and Superman is the highest form of "will to power", the highest form of the only value.[216] Superman is the one who brings about the "transvaluation of all former values",[217] all of which are of Platonic origin. But this means that Nietzsche's philosophy must be called a metaphysics just as much as that of Plato. Nietzsche's metaphysics is an inverted Platonism, in which the sensual is represented as the true world, and the suprasensual as the world of semblance.[218] But since Nietzsche merely puts Platonism upside down,

---

langt, hat ihre Wurzeln in der christlichen Dogmatik, von der man nicht wird sagen wollen, dass sie das Sein des Menschen je ontologisch zum Problem gemacht hätte". *Sein und Zeit*, p. 49.

[212] M. Heidegger, *Holzwege*, p. 70.

[213] M. Heidegger, *Sein und Zeit*, pp. 10, 248.

[214] "Nirgends begegnet uns ein Denken, dass die Wahrheit des Seins selbst und damit die Wahrheit selbst als das Sein denkt". M. Heidegger, *Holzwege*, p. 243.

[215] O. Pöggeler, *Der Denkweg Martin Heideggers*, p. 105.

[216] M. Heidegger, *Nietzsche*, II, p. 39.

[217] M. Heidegger, *o.c.*, p. 40.

[218] "Denn Nietzsches Vollendung der Metaphysik ist *zunächst* Umkehrung des Platonismus (das Sinnliche wird zur wahren, das Übersinnliche zu scheinbaren Welt)". M. Heidegger, *o.c.*, p. 22.

he thereby testifies that he most decidedly is a metaphysician. His thinking is not the "other thinking" which Heidegger deems necessary.[219] Nietzsche drives Platonism to its extremes, puts it upside down, and thereby exhausts the ultimate possibilities of metaphysics.[220] Thus he confronts us with the highest decision—the decision between the primacy of be-ing and the sway of Being.[221]

Nietzsche's claim that God is dead, says Heidegger, means that the suprasensual world has become powerless. If God as the suprasensual cause and the suprasensual purpose of all reality is dead, if the suprasensual world of ideas has lost its binding and inspiring character, then nothing remains that can serve as an anchor and a beacon for man. The claim, "God is dead", implies that "nothingness" is expanding.[222] "Nothingness" here means the absence of a suprasensual, binding world.[223] "Nihilism stands before the door".[224]

When, however, the unadulterated faith of the Churches in a suprasensual world of ideals which in a certain sense determines life from above disappears, this does not mean the simultaneous disappearance of the fundamental structure according to which earthly life is dominated by a goal that functions as the suprasensual.[225] As a matter of fact, there has been no such disappearance. The place of the vanished authority of God and the magisterium of the Church was first taken by that of conscience, then by reason, progress, the happiness of the majority, culture and civilization.[226] Nihilism has remained incomplete. Incomplete nihilism substitutes new values for the old, but assigns to them the "old place".[227] Nihilism will not be complete until it removes the

---

[219] M. Heidegger, o.c., p. 23.

[220] "Was meint aber dann 'Ende der Metaphysik?" Antwort : den geschicklichen Augenblick, in dem die *Wesensmöglichkeiten* der Metaphysik erschöpft sind. Die letzte dieser Möglichkeiten muss diejenige Form der Metaphysik sein, in der ihr Wesen umgekehrt wird". M. Heidegger, o.c., p. 201.

[221] "Die höchste Entscheidung, die fallen kann und die jeweils zum Grund aller Geschichte wird, ist diejenige zwischen der Vormacht des Seienden und der Herrschaft des Seins". M. Heidegger, *Nietzsche*, Pfullingen, 1961, I, p. 476.

[222] M. Heidegger, *Holzwege*, p. 200.

[223] "Nichts bedeutet hier : Abwesenheit einer übersinnlichen, verbindlichen Welt". M. Heidegger, o.c., p. 200.

[224] M. Heidegger, o.c., p. 200.

[225] M. Heidegger, o.c., p. 203.

[226] M. Heidegger, o.c., p. 203.

[227] "Der unvollständige Nihilismus ersetzt zwar die bisherige Werte durch andere, aber er setzt sie immer noch an die alte Stelle, die als der ideale Bereich des Übersinnlichen gleichsam freigehalten wird". M. Heidegger, o.c., p. 208.

"place" of values, the suprasensual, as a distant domain, and then assigns a different place to the values.[228]

"We have killed him", says Nietzsche when he realizes that God is dead. What does this killing mean? According to Heidegger, it means the destruction of the suprasensual world-in-itself by man.[229] But by this very fact man himself becomes different. He raises himself as subject, as "will to power" and kills off every other be-ing-in-itself.[230] God is dead.

According to Heidegger, the God declared dead by Nietzsche is really dead. This God is the God of metaphysics, and the place God occupied in metaphysics can stay empty.[231] But, in Heidegger's eyes, all this still leaves the main point unspoken. Nietzsche, he holds, merely remained on the surface of nihilism. He wrecked metaphysics and declared God dead, but as an antimetaphysicist Nietzsche himself was no less a metaphysicist. Nietzsche did not realize that both metaphysics and his own antimetaphysics were nihilistic in an entirely different sense than the one he proposed.[232] Like the metaphysics before him, Nietzsche did not recognize the "essence" (*Wesen*), i.e., the "coming to pass", the "event" of nihilism.[233] Viewed from the "mittence of Being", the *nihil* of nihilism means that "it is 'no go' with Being", Being "dallies" and "fails to appear".[234]

When our eyes are open to this, it strikes us that the fool in Nietzsche's parable kept shouting : "I am looking for God. I am looking for God". The fool is a fool insofar as he is "disturbed" : he has nothing in common with the crowd of people standing around him "who do not believe in God". They are not unbelievers because God has become unbelievable to them, but because they have given up even the possibility of belief since they are no longer able to look for God. And they can no longer look for him because they no longer *think*. The fool, however, looks for God because he cries out for him. "Perhaps a thinker has

---

[228] M. Heidegger, *o.c.*, p. 208.

[229] "Das Töten meint die Beseitigung der an sich seienden übersinnlichen Welt durch den Menschen". M. Heidegger, *o.c.*, p. 241,

[230] "Das Wertsetzen hat alles an sich Seiende unter sich und damit als für sich Seiendes umgebracht, getötet". M. Heidegger, *o.c.*, p. 242.

[231] M. Heidegger, *o.c.*, p. 235.

[232] M. Heidegger, *o.c.*, p. 244.

[233] "Nietzsche hat jedoch das *Wesen* des Nihilismus nie erkannt, so wenig wie je eine Metaphysik vor ihm". M. Heidegger, *o.c.*, p. 244.

[234] M. Heidegger, *o.c.*, p. 244.

really cried there *de profundis*".[235] And what about our own thinking? Has it any "ear"? Does it still not hear the cry? This cry cannot be heard by one who doesn't begin to *think*.[236]

The Godly God

Even as the sway of metaphysics is not, according to Heidegger, an unfortunate project of man himself, but lies in Being as "mittence", so also is God's absence not an omission by man. He who becomes aware of God's absence, likewise, should not ask : "What must we do about it"? but, "What must we think"? As long as we do not thoughtfully experience that which is, we cannot listen to what will be. It does not depend on man, however, whether he will again find a road to God, but on Being as "mittence".[237]

Traditional metaphysics, which lived in "forgetfulness of Being", not merely made the interpretation of Being very difficult, but also defended atheism. For, despite of the fact that it was always talking about "God", it was concerned with a pseudo-God. But if it is very difficult to rise above metaphysics by the "step back" and to go forward to the essence of metaphysics, the best one can do, says Heidegger, is provisionally to remain silent about God.[238] Because traditional thinking about God is metaphysics, and metaphysics must be transcended, our thinking is provisionally not yet in a position to say what "God" means. "We must often remain silent for lack of holy names" (Hölderlin).

Accordingly, Heidegger does not assert that the road to God is wholly inaccessible. It is impossible for traditional metaphysics and very difficult for "foundational thinking". The road will only be found when man's thinking recovers its proper dimension, i.e., unfolds as re-collecting

---

[235] M. Heidegger, *o.c.*, p. 246.

[236] M. Heidegger, *o.c.*, pp. 246-247.

[237] "Ob der Gott lebt oder tot bleibt, entscheidet sich nicht durch die Religiosität der Menschen und noch weniger durch theologische Aspirationen der Philosophie und der Naturwissenschaft. Ob Gott Gott ist, ereignet sich aus der Konstellation des Seins und innerhalb ihrer. Solange wir nicht denkend erfahren, was ist, können wir nie dem gehören, was sein wird". M. Heidegger, *Die Technik und die Kehre*, p. 46.

[238] "Wer die Theologie, sowohl diejenige des christlichen Glaubens als auch diejenige der Philosophie, aus gewachsener Herkunft erfahren hat, zieht es heute vor, im Bereich des Denkens von Gott zu schweigen. Denn der onto-theologische Charakter der Metaphysik ist für das Denken fragwürdig geworden, nicht auf Grund irgendeines Atheismus, sondern aus der Erfahrung eines Denkens, dem sich in der Onto-Theologie die noch *ungedachte* Einheit des Wesens der Metaphysik gezeigt hat". M. Heidegger, *Identität und Differenz*, p. 51.

the truth of Being. But even then this thinking will not be directly a form of theistic thought; it will be neither theistic nor atheistic. Heidegger doesn't want to say that he is indifferent to the theistic or atheistic character of his thinking, but merely expresses his reverence for the boundaries set to man's thought.[239]

Even as thinking must prepare for the "coming to pass" of Being a "place where man is sensitive to the "call of Being"—i.e., even as man must first recover the breadth of his own essence if the truth of Being can "come to pass"—so also must man first dwell in the dimension of the "coming to pass" of the holy before he can expect to be able to think and say what the term "God" means.[240]

Heidegger's "holy" has nothing to do with virtues in the traditional sense of the term. It is primarily nature that is called "holy." "Nature 'educates' the poets,"[241] and they are called to express the holy.[242] Poets are wholly seized by powerful, divinely beautiful, omnipresent nature,[243] and recall that which most of all "concerns" the sons of the earth if they are to be able to "dwell". Poets express the holy which rules gods and men. They make the gods feel like gods and willing to appear in the abode of men on earth. Poets stand as "pointers" between the gods and men.[244] The blossom on a tree contains the gratuitous grant of the fruit—the saving holy which favors the mortals. The openness of the holy is the "wholeness", the integrity of authentic "dwelling".

The fundamental feature of dwelling is sparing (*Schonen*), keeping in order, saving.[245] This characteristic shows us that being-man is based

[239] M. Heidegger, *Über den Humanismus*, p. 37.

[240] "Erst aus der Wahrheit des Seins lässt sich das Wesen des Heiligen denken. Erst aus dem Wesen des Heiligen ist das Wesen von Gottheit zu denken. Erst im Lichte des Wesens von Gottheit kann gedacht und gesagt werden, was das Wort 'Gott' nennen soll". M. Heidegger, *o.c.*, pp. 36-37.

[241] M. Heidegger, *Erläuterungen zu Hölderlins Dichtung*, Frankfurt a. M., 1963³, p. 51.

[242] "Der Dichter denkt das Heilige". *Was ist Metaphysik?*, p. 51.

[243] M. Heidegger, *Erläuterungen zu Hölderlins Dichtung*, p. 53.

[244] "Aber soll der Dichter nicht gerade das Heilige denken, das über den Göttern und den Menschen ist? Gewiss. Doch muss er das Heilige darstellen, damit durch sein Sagen die Götter sich selbst fühlen und so sich selbst zum Erscheinen bringen in der Wohnstatt der Menschen auf dieser Erde. Der Dichter muss an das denken, was die Erdensöhne zuerst angeht, wenn sie sollen wohnen können in ihrem Heimischen .... Der Dichter steht als der Zeigende zwischen den Menschen und den Göttern". M. Heidegger, *o.c.*, p. 116.

[245] M. Heidegger, *Vorträge und Aufsätze*, p. 149.

on dwelling, in the sense of the mortals' sojourning on earth. But "on earth" implies "under heaven". Earth and heaven point to the godly, and to the "togetherness"of the mortals. Earth, heaven, the godly and mortals belong together in a primordial unity.[246] Earth serves and supports, blooms and produces fruit, extends into water and rock, expands into plants and animals. Heaven is the arching course of the sun and the moon, the sparkle of the stars, the seasons, the dawn and dusk of the day, the darkness and light of the night, the pleasant and unpleasant character of the weather, the passing of clouds, the deep blue of the sky. The godly are the beckoning messengers of the godhead. The mortals are men, called "mortals" because they are capable of death *as* death. Heidegger calls the primordial togetherness of these four— earth and heaven, the godly and mortals—the "foursome" (*das Geviert*).[247]

Thus dwelling contains four aspects. Mortals "dwell" insofar as they spare the earth, not overpowering and subjecting it; mortals "dwell" insofar as they receive heaven as heaven, leaving the sun and the moon their course, the stars their paths, the seasons their blessings and their rigors, not changing night into day, and not making the day into a restless race; mortals "dwell" insofar as they expect the godly, hoping for the unhoped-for, even in calamity waiting for the salvation that has fled; the mortals "dwell" insofar as they accompany mortals in order that death may be a good death. In the sparing of the earth, the receiving of heaven, the expectation of the godly, and the accompanying of mortals "dwelling" comes about as the sparing of "the foursome". To spare means to shepherd "the foursome" in its "coming about".[248]

Man, however, has wholly lost the ability to dwell authentically. He has let the "wholeness" of his *Dasein* shrivel away. "The true habitational distress does not just lie in a housing shortage",[249] but in man's "homelessness". This homelessness does not merely keep the holy as pointing to the Godhead hidden; it also dislocates "wholeness" and thus seems to wipe away even the reference to the holy.[250] The godly

---

[246] "Doch 'auf der Erde' heisst schon 'unter dem Himmel'. Beides meint mit 'Bleiben vor den Göttlichen' und schliesst ein 'gehörend in das Miteinander der Menschen'. Aus einer *ursprünglichen* Einheit gehören die Vier : Erde und Himmel, die Göttlichen und die Sterblichen in eins". M. Heidegger, o.c., p. 149.

[247] M. Heidegger, *o.c.*, p. 150.

[248] M. Heidegger, *o.c.*, pp. 150-151.

[249] M. Heidegger, *o.c.*, p. 162.

[250] "Das Heile entzieht sich. Die Welt wird heil-los. Dadurch bleibt nicht nur das

have fled. Only when he again becomes sensitive to the "coming to pass" of the holy, may man hope that he can again think and say what the term "God" means.

Heidegger views Hölderlin as the poet *par excellence* of God's absence.[251] But the poets are called to give voice again to the holy and prepare for the coming of God. In his poetical calling the poet lets the High One himself appear.[252] God's appearing comes about in a dis-closure which lets us see what is hidden. However, it does not show the hidden by tearing it out of its concealedness, but by reverencing it in its self-concealment. The unknown God[253] appears as the Unknown.[254]

Heilige als die Spur zur Gottheit verborgen, sondern sogar die Spur zum Heiligen, das Heile, scheint ausgelöscht zu sein". M. Heidegger, *Holzwege*, p. 272.

[251] "Indem Hölderlin das Wesen der Dichtung neu stiftet, bestimmt er erst eine neue Zeit. Es ist die Zeit der entflohenen Götter und des kommenden Gottes. Das ist die dürftige Zeit, weil sie in einem gedoppelten Mangel und Nicht steht : im Nichtmehr der entflohenen Götter und im Nochnicht des Kommenden". M. Heidegger, *Erläuterungen zu Hölderlins Dichtung*, p. 47.

[252] "Dichtend nennen bedeutet : im Wort den Hohen selbst erscheinen lassen". M. Heidegger, *o.c.*, p. 26.

[253] M. Heidegger, *Vorträge und Aufsätze*, p. 197.

[254] "So erscheint der unbekannte Gott als der Unbekannte durch die Offenbarkeit des Himmels". M. Heidegger, *o.c.*, p. 197.

CHAPTER FOUR

THE ACCEPTANCE OF METAPHYSICS AND
THE "AFFIRMATION" OF GOD

The acceptance of metaphysics and of the ' affirmation" of God as a possibility of metaphysical thinking also has assumed various forms in the history of thought, forms which continue to exist even today. Let us examine them here.

1. THE OBJECTIVISTIC TRADITION : LAKEBRINK

First of all, there is the objectivistic tradition of 'orthodox" scholasticism, spoken of in the preceding chapter. It was mentioned there as being rejected by others who hold the view that this rejection is necessary in order to give an authentic character to the "affirmation" of God. There are, however, authors who view the objectivistic conception of metaphysical thought as the only authentic standpoint and who claim that objectivism is an essential condition for making the metaphysical "affirmation" of God possible. One of the leading proponents of this trend is B. Lakebrink.[1]

Lakebrink rejects as an intolerable form of subjectivism the very point that existential thinkers regard as essential for any form of human thought, viz., that the subject is beyond dispute because all speaking about reality presupposes the subject as the "letting be" of reality.[2] Lakebrink interprets this "letting be" as an arbitrary "positing" of being and rejects it as wholly unacceptable to modern science.[3]

---

[1] B. Lakebrink, *Klassische Metaphysik*, Eine Auseinandersetzung mit der existentialen Anthropozentrik, Freiburg i.Br., 1967.

[2] B. Lakebrink, *o.c.*, p. 58.

[3] "Welt und Natur als das Ergebnis menschlichen Setzens zu begreifen, das sie erst als solche sein lässt, das sie ausserdem zu blossen Momenten existentiellen Selbstvollzuges aufhebt, ist für die moderne Wissenschaft völlig unannehmbar". B. Lakebrink, *o.c.*, pp. 58-59.

The consequences of Lakebrink's view are rather obvious. If the subject is not given any place as the "letting be" of reality, one can hardly escape conceiving reality as in-itself, as brute reality. Knowledge then becomes a passive mirroring of reality-in-itself in the subject. As a matter of fact, this is what Lakebrink claims.[4] "Reality"-in-itself is related to our knowledge as cause to effect.[5] Whether man knows it or not, makes no difference to "reality"-in-itself.[6] The thing does not refer to science, but science refers to the thing.[7] Because existentialism holds that reality is related to the knowing subject, this trend of thought is, according to Lakebrink, a form of idealism and subjectivism. The only true being is for him the "act of being" of be-ing-in-itself. And Thomas Aquinas—not Heidegger —saw what this really means.[8]

Because the subject as the "letting be" of reality is called "historical", all truth says Lakebrink, must evaporate with history.[9] Thus there are no longer any immutable and eternal truths, and obviously, Lakebrink adds, this "modernistic" way of thinking therefore also denies the immutable and eternal ideas in God's mind.[10] The exemplars of everything are taken away from God; he is no longer the ultimate ground of all perfections; the lights of eternal truth, goodness and beauty in him are extinguished.[11]

Here also lies the reason why, according to Lakebrink, subjectivity as freedom can no longer find anywhere a fixed norm. "Modern subjectivism" thus becomes allied with voluntarism. This voluntarism, with the freedom worship unchained by it, has just exhausted itself in the political domain. But now it is penetrating a resort which has hitherto

---

[4] "Weil dieses innergeistige Sein die Wirklichkeit der Dinge reflektiert und dieser intellektuelle Widerschein der Welt von ihr selbst bestimmt und bemessen wird, sachlich von ihr abhängt, erweist sich dieses ideale Sein der Dinge als weniger in sich beschlossen und perfekt denn ihre in sich ständige Realität an sich". B. Lakebrink, *o.c.*, p. 16.

[5] B. Lakebrink, *o.c.*, p. 18.

[6] B. Lakebrink, *o.c.*, pp. 17, 20-21.

[7] "Denn das Ding bezieht sich nicht auf die Wissenschaft, wohl aber umgekehrt". B. Lakebrink, *o.c.*, p. 21.

[8] B. Lakebrink, *o.c.*, p. 57.

[9] "Alles das, was als Wesenheit und Wahrheit immer schon war, wird in die Geschichtlichkeit menschlichen Daseins hineingerissen, das sich ohne übergeschichtliches Mass und ewige Norm rein aus sich selbst vollbringt". B. Lakebrink, *o.c.*, p. 209.

[10] B. Lakebrink, *o.c.*, pp. 145-167.

[11] "Die Urbilder der Dinge selbst sind aus ihm verbannt; er gilt nicht mehr als Urgrund der existentiellen und essentiellen Vollkommenheiten dieser Welt, die Lichter des ewigen Wahr-Gut-Schön sind in ihm erloschen". B. Lakebrink, *o.c.*, p. 177.

always stood firm against all wild raging and all existential storms and stresses—viz., the realm of Catholic theology.[12] Lakebrink's black sheep here is Karl Rahner.

Because, according to Lakebrink, existential thinking does not have an authentic conception of Being and delivers the meaning of be-ing to the arbitrariness of the subject, it leaves no room for an authentic "affirmation" of God. Lakebrink argues that in existential thinking all traditional attributes of God are ascribed to man. This position cannot be harmonized with the traditional doctrine of the world's creation by God.[13] Existential thinking makes man "once more" the measure and origin of all things and their reality.[14] In such an atmosphere of thought there is no possibility of developing a theology in the traditional sense of the term.[15]

Although the objectivistic tradition of metaphysical thought had already been extensively discussed in the preceding chapter, it had to be mentioned here again because I wanted to present a catalogue of the various standpoints taken with respect to metaphysics and the "affirmation" of God. In the preceding chapter we saw that some people reject an objectivistic metaphysics in order to make room for an authentic "affirmation" of God. I insinuated there that I agreed with this rejection of what is sometimes called "metaphysics" *tout court*. But the intention of cataloguing these various standpoints now forces me to return to this rejection of "metaphysics" *tout court* because it would be wrong to think that this interpretation of metaphysics is nowadays universally rejected. This is certainly not the case; Lakebrink is not a lone hold-out. Unlike Lakebrink, some people try to "differentiate" and "soften" the fundamental objectivistic thesis, but the thesis itself is maintained. This happens, for instance, when a distinction is made between immutable "truth in itself" and mutable "truth as a human possession". But an immutable "truth in itself" is a truth-for-no one, and as such can be found only in the objectivistic tradition of metaphysics.

[12] B. Lakebrink, *o.c.*, p. 213.

[13] "Denn Gott hat eine Welt voll der glühenden Wirklichkeiten, aber nicht ein anämisches Phainomenon geschaffen, das sein gegenständliches An-sich-Sein dem Setzen beziehungsweise dem Seins-zuspruch unseres Verstandes danken müsste". B. Lakebrink, *o.c.*, p. 17.

[14] "Der existential-dialektische Anthropozentrismus macht den Menschen wieder einmal zum Mass und Ursprung aller Dinge und ihrer Wirklichkeit". B. Lakebrink, *o.c.*, p. 260.

[15] B. Lakebrink, *o.c.*, pp. 65, 260.

Lakebrink's work clearly demonstrates how difficult the dialogue is between those who reject and those who accept metaphysics *tout court*. As soon as existential thought emphasizes that the knowing subject is not a purely passive mirror but a "letting be" of reality, Lakebrink and others interpret this as a "positing" of reality, an autonomous and arbitrary decision about the meaning of reality. Lakebrink, however, arbitrarily escalates the subject's activity, ascribes this view to Heidegger and Rahner and does not realize that these very authors emphatically resist such an escalation. But I can understand that in Lakebrink's view their resistance is unsuccessful. For Heidegger and Rahner do not start from what for Lakebrink is an unspoken and unquestioned assumption, viz., the idea that knowledge is nothing but the passive mirroring-in-the-subject of reality-in-itself.[16] By now it should be evident what I think of such an assumption.

2. THE SPIRITUALISTIC-MONISTIC TRADITION

The spiritualistic trend of the post-Kantian era needs to be briefly mentioned in connection with the acceptance of metaphysics and the possibility of metaphysically "affirming" God's existence. Here, again, I shall try to present the core of this trend without entering into too many details.

The term "trend" is appropriate. Spiritualistic monism is a trend rather than a system. It is a trend of thought which exploits and absolutizes the weak point of materialism. It is a trend that *begins* by emphasizing the relative priority of the subject but *ends* by retaining nothing but the Absolute Subject.

The subject's relative priority discloses itself when one realizes that materialism, despite its identification of be-ing and thing, "speaks" of things. This means, it "says" that things are and what they are. But how is this possible? What is this primordial "saying"-of-*is* which is presupposed by all explicit "speaking"? It is *man* who speaks of things and of himself. No matter, then, how "thinglike" man is, it will never be possible to think away the "resort" by which he is able to speak of things and of himself. But this "resort" is not the "thinglike" element of man—at least not if we accept, as all materialists do, that geological strata and rainstorms cannot speak of anything. Man is distinct from mere things by his ability to "speak about things", to "say"-*is*. That's

---

[16] B. Lakebrink, *o.c.*, pp. 16, 70, 79-80, 233.

why he transcends the "thinglike" aspect in his essence,[17] and all non-materialists refer to this as subjectivity.

Thus it is man's subjectivity that is simply set aside by the materialist.[18] The being of man, on the proper level of being-human, is a being-conscious, by which man exists for himself[19] and can assign a name to himself. He calls himself "I." Thanks to the light of subjectivity, of the conscious *I* which man is, man exists for himself and is a "light" in the world of things; things now appear with meaning to man, are-for-man, are "spoken" of.

The subject's relative priority can also be explicitated as follows. The world of things always and of necessity reveals itself as the *non-I*. Not-being-I belongs to the *reality* of the world of things. Things in the world of things which are not distinct from the *I*, which do not reveal themselves as non-I, are not real things. One who wishes to express the *reality* of things, then, will always be obliged to affirm their non-identity with the subject. This, however, means that it is impossible to eliminate the *I* when speaking about the *reality* of things because otherwise the world of things as the *non-I* cannot be expressed either. But the not-being-I belongs to the *reality* of things.

Thus a relative priority of the *I* must be accepted, and this means that it is impossible to consider the *I* as the result of cosmic forces and processes. For without the *I* these processes and forces are not in the cosmos what they *really* are, viz., not-*I*. How, then, could that which without the *I* simply is not what it *really* is bring the *I* into being?

One can discern now the direction which will be taken by those who exploit the weak point of materialism. For the materialist, the conscious subject is not a reality worth mentioning; for the spiritualist, thinking about reality begins with the affirmation of the subject. As soon, however, as one really sees the importance of the subject, there is a danger that the subject's importance will be exaggerated. Without the *I*, the world of things is not what it *really* is, viz., non-*I*. Without the *I*, it is simply impossible to speak about the world of things, and the term "to be" loses all meaning. Only a slight exaggeration is needed now to reduce the being of material things to that of the subject. This is the direction taken by spiritualistic monism. While materialism simply omits the meaning of

[17] J.-P. Sartre, *L'existentialisme est un humanisme*, Paris, 1954, p. 65.
[18] M. Merleau-Ponty, *Phénoménologie de la perception*, Paris, 1945[14], Avant-propos, p. II.
[19] J.-P. Sartre, *L'imagination*, Paris, 1948, p. 1.

the subject, or at most views the subject as not worth mentioning, spiritualistic monism lets the density of material things evaporate into thin air; they become mere contents of consciousness.[20]

Thus spiritualism takes seriously the "originality" of the subject. As a subject, man cannot be the result of material processes and forces; he is "himself". If this point is exaggerated, one does not merely eliminate the subject's receptivity with respect to the dense world of material things, but also the possibility of recognizing that other subjects are subjects. How could a self-absolutizing subject recognize and accept that another subject is an *other* subject, has an identity *of his own*? The self-absolutizing subject is forced to reduce the other subject's distinctness and own identity to that of himself; he thus does away with the other's own identity. But as soon as the I conceives itself as, "strictly speaking", containing all other I's in itself, it can no longer conceive itself as the little finite I, distinct from other I's, which every real I *de facto* is. I, the author of this book, do not include all other I's. Spiritualistic monism, then, is obliged to sacrifice the distinct ownness of the little subject to an absolute Subject. The place of the little subject which every real subject is, is taken by the "great" impersonal Subject, of which the many, mutually distinct, subjects are viewed as particularizations, dialectic moments or functions. Fichte's absolute Ego and Hegel's absolute Spirit eloquently illustrate where this trend of thinking ultimately leads.[21]

This metaphysics also contains a theory of "God", but it is a very special theory, for the metaphysics in question is that of a self-absolutizing subject. Obviously, such a subject can never accept the divine God since that would mean the negation of the subject's self-absolutizing. A self-absolutizing subject can only recognize a "God" who is conceived as the absolutized Subject himself. Actually, the qualifications of the absolute Subject in spiritualistic monism become so fantastic that they coincide with the "names" traditionally ascribed to God. The "God" of spiritualistic monism is the deified Subject.[22]

The absolutized Subject who is called the Absolute Truth and the Absolute Good is a danger for the *real* subject, for the searching for *real*

---

[20] M. Merleau-Ponty, *o.c.*, Avant-propos, p. x.

[21] A. Dondeyne, *Beschouwingen bij het atheïstisch existentialisme*, in : Tijdschrift voor Philosophie, XII (1951), pp. 27-28.

[22] J. Ortega y Gasset, *De mens en de mensen*, Ned. van G.J. Geers, The Hague, 1958, pp. 57-58.

truth and the establishing of *real* goodness. While in spiritualistic monism the "little" I is, strictly speaking, not supposed to count, the *reality* of the I is that it is a "little" I; and the *reality* of truth and goodness is a relative, precarious and risky truth and goodness. The absolute Subjectivity of spiritualistic monism is the Subjectivity of *no one*; its absolute Truth is true for *no one*; its absolute Good is the good of *no one*. Nothing is more tempting in such a situation than that one or the other "little" subject falls for the temptation to take the "place" of the absolute Subject and to "take care" of absolute Truth and absolute Goodness.[23] First, of course, the claim is made that the "little" subject does not count and that it is exclusively the absolute Subject which thinks and acts in the "little" subject. *In reality*, however, only the "little" subject, or a group of "little" subjects, such as a nation or a state, exist. That is why the assertion that the absolute Subject thinks and acts in and thought the "little" subject, *de facto* amounts to the claim of the "little" subject to speak "divine" truth and establish "divine" goodness. The "little" subject thinks that he can speak with "divine" authority and act with a "divine" guarantee. He attaches so much weight to *his* assertions and actions that he can no longer listen to anyone else, and any resistance becomes in his eyes *lèse majesté*. He imagines that he speaks for the absolute Subject, he fancies that his truth is "God's plan" for man and world, and he claims that his actions execute this plan with a "divine" guarantee.[24]

The preceding section could also have been placed in Chapter Three, where the rejection of metaphysics was discussed. It would then have been necessary to speak also of Marx because the "God" rejected by Marx is the "God" of Hegel. The Prussian State had placed itself on the standpoint of this "God" in order to be above all criticism.[25] Marx viewed this as intolerable and therefore rejected the "God" of metaphysics *tout court*. His intention, however, was not to arrive at an authentic "affirmation" of God. The same is true for Merleau-Ponty,[26] but not for Gusdorf[27] in his discussion with Brunschvicq.[28]

[23] A. Dondeyne, *Inleiding tot het denken van E. Levinas*, in : Tijdschrift voor Philosophie, XXV (1963), p. 562.

[24] G. Gusdorf, *Traité de Métaphysique*, Paris, 1956, pp. 102-132.

[25] J.-Y. Calvez, *La pensée de Karl Marx*, Paris, 1956, pp. 55-78.

[26] M. Merleau-Ponty, *Eloge de la philosophie*, Paris, 1953[12].

[27] G. Gusdorf, *Mythe et métaphysique*, Paris, 1953.

[28] G. Gusdorf, *Traité de metaphysique*, p. 104.

3. LOGICAL EMPIRICISM

The latest developments in the domain of analytic philosophy have shown an unexpected turn in this way of thinking. The oldest representatives of analytic philosophy did not recognize the language in which metaphysics spoke "about" God as cognitively meaningful. They viewed such language as a simple misuse of speech because the truth or untruth of statements "about" God was, in their eyes, beyond verification.

All this seemed rather simple until analytic thinkers began to realize the presuppositions implied in this standpoint. It then became apparent that they had started with the conviction that language is meaningful only if it is *cognitively* meaningful. Furthermore, it also became obvious that if the verifiability of statements was insisted upon, a certain conception of "verification" *de facto* always played a role and was assumed to be *the* conception.

For this reason analytic philosophy searched for and found new ways. A different evaluation of "metaphysical" language was one result of all this. It is my intention to trace here the main stages of this development.

Empiricism and Rationalism

Anyone who is somewhat familiar with the thought of analytical philosophers must have been struck by the fact that in their philosophy nothing at all remains of the inspiration living in rationalism. One can see this readily in the ease with which the verification principle is used and which, as a matter of fact, implies an *a priori* option in favor of empiricism. The only kind of statements judged to be verifiable are such propositions as "this stain is green", "a cat sits on the mat", and "there are craters on the backside of the moon". And only these statement are called verifiable *because* the analysts have opted for the absolutism of sense experience. The rationalist, too, would demand that statements be "verified", but for him this would mean that it must be possible to *think* them in a coherent way. Things which can merely be verified by sense experience cannot be, for him, truths of any importance.

The Principle of Verification

Nevertheless, it would be wrong to present matters as if there had been no struggle at all about the principle of verification among the analysts. The fact that their struggle remained within the fundamental option for empiricism has in no way diminished its spectacular character.[29]

The issues was to formulate the verification principle in such a way that it could really function as a criterion to distinguish the cognitively meaningless use of language from its cognitively meaningful use. The question arising here was where to find the criterion by which one could establish the criterion separating meaningful and meaningless uses of language. For it turned out that in the attempts to answer this question one always made a *choice*. Let us give an example.

Ayer makes a distinction between the "strong" and the "weak" sense of verifiability. A statement is verifiable in the strong sense if—and only if—the truth of this statement can be decisively and *conclusively* established in experience.[30] The opposite of this conclusive verifiability is verifiability in the weak sense, for which it suffices that it be possible for experience to render it probable.[31] Ayer rejects the demand of conclusive verifiability because of the consequences flowing from such a demand. For it would imply that general scientific statements, such as "arsenic is poisonous" and statements about the remote past must be called meaningless. Since the series of observations by which these statements must be verified is unavoidably finite, their truth can never be decisively and conclusively established.[32]

It is rather obvious that an option is involved here. General scientific statements and statements about the remote past apparently *must* not be allowed to become meaningless. But why not? And why is a criterion for the meaningfulness of statements *not* rejected if it eliminates metaphysical statements? Metaphysical statements apparently *must* not be allowed to become meaningful.[33] In other words, the search for a criterion for the meaningfulness of propositions is already guided by a criterion which actually decides beforehand about the criterion one is supposedly still looking for. How can anyone justify such a procedure? One pretends to "conclude" that metaphysical propositions are meaningless, but there is no question here at all of really *concluding* anything. All that happens

---

[29] Carl G. Hempel, *Problems and changes in the empiricist criterion of meaning*, in : Revue internationale de Philosophie, IV (1950), pp. 41-63.

[30] "... if, and only if, its truth could be conclusively established in experience". A.J. Ayer, o.c., p. 37.

[31] "But it is verifiable, in the weak sense, if it is possible for experience to render it probable". A.J. Ayer, *o.c.*, p. 37.

[32] A.J. Ayer, *o.c.*, pp. 37-38.

[33] Of course I don't pretend without "reason" that metaphysical statements are meaningful.

is that one gives expression to one's presuppositions and *a priori* decrees. Thus it is no surprise that many analysts can so readily dispose of metaphysics : "It can be quickly shown" to be meaningless.[34] No wonder; the whole matter had already been decided beforehand.

The example of Ayer is only one among many—so many that with W. de Pater one can say that the principle of verification has died the death of its "one thousand qualifications".

The verification principle, however, has not merely died from its "one thousand qualifications". The main cause of its demise was contained in its own inner constitution : it turned out that it could not live up to the demands imposed by itself. At present, this view is accepted rather generally, but a remark made by Ludwig Wittgenstein in his TRACTATUS had laid the groundwork for it. Wittgenstein defends there the idea that language expressions are meaningful only if they are directly or indirectly a picture of the reality spoken of. But everything Wittgenstein says to make the relation of picture to reality acceptable is not itself a picture of reality. And so he does not hesitate to say that his sentences are meaningless.[35]

Wittgenstein's remark dates from the time when he himself still adhered to logical atomism, but its result was that the requirements for the meaningful use of language, as posited by the verification principle of logical positivism, also became demands which had to be satisfied by the language in which the principle itself is formulated. And then it turned out that this language itself could not be called meaningful.[36] For if the cognitively meaningful use of language is restricted to the analytical judgments of logic and mathematics and the statements of the empirical sciences, then the language in which the verification principle is formulated itself is not cognitively meaningful; it doesn't satisfy its own requirements. The statement in which this principle is formulated is a "metaphysical proposition".[37]

[34] A.J. Ayer, *Demonstration of the impossibility of metaphysics*, in : Mind, 43 (1934), p. 339.

[35] "Meine Sätze erläutern dadurch, dass sie der, welcher mich versteht, am Ende als unsinnig erkennt, wenn er durch sie —auf ihnen—über sie hinausgestiegen ist. ... Er muss die Sätze überwinden, dann sieht er die Welt richtig". L. Wittgenstein, *Tractatus Logico-Philosophicus*, 6.54.

[36] C.B. Daly, *Metaphysics and the limits of language*, in : Prospects for Metaphysics, Essays of Metaphysical Exploration, ed. by Ian Ramsey, London, 1961, p. 179.

[37] "The fact is, the verification principle is a metaphysical proposition—a 'smashing' one if I may be permitted the expression". John Wisdom, *Philosophy and Psycho-Analysis*, Oxford, 1953, pp. 245-246.

Interlude : Phenomenology and Analytic Philosophy

I would like to "define" metaphysics as the attempt to render explicit the implicit "saying"-of-*is* which human existence itself is.[38] Such a metaphysics, then, would bear a phenomenological character. It was Edmund Husserl who gave the impetus to such a metaphysics when he launched phenomenology as an attempt to find the ground for any statement whatsoever. For statements do not have a ground without any further ado; one does not know without any further ado what they are about. It is only as explicitation of the subject's immediate presence to an appearing reality that a statement can be called "grounded". Thus a statement must be "verifiable", and it is verified by bringing it back to "what presents itself ... in its bodily reality",[39] by indicating "that which shows itself, ... the manifest".[40]

One can readily see here that there is a clear resemblance between the search for a foundation of statements as made by phenomenology and, on the other hand, the search of analytical philosophy for a criterion of cognitively meaningful use of language. This similarity can be illustrated by comparing one of Husserl's most important texts with a decisive passage from Moritz Schlick. Husserl says :

No theory can mislead us in regard to the principle of all principles : that every primordial dator intuition is a source of authority for knowledge, that whatever presents itself in "intuition" in primordial form (as it were in its bodily reality), is simply to be accepted as it gives itself out to be, though only within the limits in which it then presents itself.[41]

And speaking about the "first step of all philosophizing", Schlick says :

The first step of all philosophizing and the foundation of all reflection is to realize that it is utterly impossible to indicate the meaning of any assertion whatsoever in any other way than by describing the state of affairs that must exist if the assertion should be true. If this state does not exist, then the assertion is false. For the meaning of an assertion obviously lies only in this that it expresses a certain state of affairs. One must precisely indicate this state of affairs to indicate the meaning of the assertion. True, one can say that the proposition itself already indicates this state of affairs, but this is so only for one who *understands* the proposition. When, however, do I understand a proposition? When I know the meaning of the words occurring in it? This meaning can be clarified by definitions. But in these definitions new words occur and I must

---

[38] W. Luijpen, *Existential Phenomenology*, rev. ed., Pittsburgh, 1969, pp. 178-185.
[39] E. Husserl, *Ideen* I (Husserliana III), p. 52.
[40] M. Heidegger, *Sein und Zeit*, p. 28.
[41] E. Husserl, *Ideen I*, p. 52.

again know their meaning. One cannot go on to infinity in defining; sooner
or later we arrive at words the meaning of which cannot be again described
by a proposition. This meaning has to be immediately indicated, the sense of
the word must ultimately be *shown*, it must be *given*. This is done by an act
of pointing, of showing, and what is shown must be given, for otherwise it
cannot be pointed out to me.[42]

The similarity between phenomenology and analytical philosophy with
respect to "the first step of all philosophizing" is indeed striking. But
let us add one other text of Husserl. In his LOGICAL INVESTIGATIONS he
says:

> Evidence is ... nothing but the "experience" (*Erlebnis*) of the truth .... The
> evident judgment ... is a consciousness of originary givenness .... Evidence
> is called a seeing, perceiving, grasping of the self-given ("true") state of affairs.[43]

The endeavor to find a ground for any statement whatsoever has been
developed in different directions by phenomenology and by analytical
philosophy. Husserl ultimately founds all our statements in the experience of the life-world, that is to say, in the implicit "affirmation" which
existence itself is.[44] And in my opinion, the restless search of analytical
philosophy for a criterion for the cognitive meaningfulness of language
is animated by the same intention and concern as is phenomenology
when the latter tries to make explicit the implicit "saying"-of-*is* which
human existence is. The "one thousand qualifications" which the
verification principle has received bear witness to this. True, the analysts
study only *explicit* statements, but the failure of the attempt to formulate
a simple criterion to distinguish between meaningful and meaningless
sentences shows that the implicit "saying"-of-*is* is too rich and too powerful in the eyes of the analysts themselves to be caught in a simple catch-all
formula.

[42] Moritz Schlick, *Gesammelte Aufsätze*, pp. 89-90.

[43] E. Husserl, *Logische Untersuchungen*, Halle, 1928[4], I, p. 190.

[44] "... Allen Zwecken, auch den theoretischen der 'objektiven' Wissenschaften,
denn darin liegen ja die 'Selbstverständlichkeiten', die der Wissenschaftler beständig
gebraucht—universal gesprochen, die Welt dieser selbstverständlich verständlich
seienden und in der Weise der als wahr und wirklich auszuweisenden Dinge ist der
Boden, auf dem alle objektive Wissenschaft erst sich entfalten kann; mit einem Worte
die Lebenswelt, diese 'bloss' subjektive und relative, in ihrem nie stillhaltenden Fluss
der Seinsgeltungen, deren Verwandlungen und Korrekturen ist—so paradox das
erscheinen mag—der Boden, auf dem die objektive Wissenschaft ihre Gebilde 'end-
gültiger', 'ewiger' Wahrheiten, der ein für allemal und für jedermann absolut gültigen
Urteile aufbaut". E. Husserl, *Die Krisis der Europäischen Wissenschaften und die
transzendentale Phänomenologie*, (Husserliana VI), p. 465.

Language Games

The preceding considerations were almost exclusively guided by the ideas of those representatives of analytical philosophy who adhere to the logical positivism of the Vienna Circle. Wittgenstein's logical atomism was touched only in passing, and Bertrand Russell was not even mentioned. In connection with the latest developments in the realm of analytical philosophy, Wittgenstein must now be explicitly considered, but as the later Wittgenstein, the author of PHILOSOPHICAL INVESTIGATIONS.[45]

Like Russell, Wittgenstein in his TRACTATUS had started from the assumption that the meaningful use of language admits only one form, viz., the cognitive-descriptive use. Moreover, he had assumed that this one meaningful form of language contained the accurate picture of reality (the so-called "picture theory"). To investigate what a word means thus meant to search for one available object coupled as meaning to one word.[46] It was the extremely abstract form of the question : what is the meaning of a word?, that gave rise to the illusion that this question could always be answered by referring to one entity—just as the question, what is the capital of France?, is answered by referring to one entity in reality. As soon, however, as such a conception about the meaning of a word is accepted, there is no reason not to extend it to include also the meaning of sentences. Wittgenstein assumed that one complex entity corresponded to one sentence.[47]

Although Wittgenstein thought that only the cognitive-descriptive form of language use could be admitted as meaningful, he was not blind to what he called "the problems of life".[48] But how could one speak about them? There simply is no language in which it can be done, and it is, as a matter of principle, impossible that a statement about them could be true.[49] Yet there are "things that cannot be put into words";

---

[45] L. Wittgenstein, *Philosophische Untersuchungen*, Frankfurt a.M., 1967.

[46] G. Nuchelmans, *Overzicht van de analytische wijsbegeerte*, p. 176.

[47] G. Nuchelmans, *o.c.*, pp. 174-176.

[48] "Wir fühlen, dass selbst, wenn alle möglichen wissenschaftlichen Fragen beantwortet sind, unsere Lebensprobleme noch gar nicht berührt sind". L. Wittgenstein, *Tractatus Logico-Philosophicus*, 6.52.

[49] "Die Gesamtheit der wahren Sätze ist die gesamte Naturwissenschaft (oder die Gesamtheit der Naturwissenschaften)". L. Wittgenstein, *o.c.*, 4.11.

they are what is "mystical".[50] But "what we cannot speak about we must pass over in silence".[51]

In his later works Wittgenstein himself rejected the presuppositions of his TRACTATUS. A closer examination of "actual language" led him to the conclusion that the "crystalline purity of logic" had not resulted from investigation but had simply been imposed on language as a demand. He had not investigated how language is actually used but prescribed how it ought to be used.[52]

Gradually Wittgenstein began to realize that the meaning of a word is only understood when its use in a specific context, in all kinds of particular circumstances, is indicated.[53] There is not just one given object coupled to one word as its meaning, but one and the same word acts differently in different contexts. This means that there exists not merely the one language game of describing the states of affairs, but many language games must be distinguished, such as giving orders, reporting, making a joke, proposing riddles, asking, thanking, cursing, greeting, praying and so on.[54] There is the language of science, the novel and poetry, of commerce, politics and love, of education, penal law and probation, of prophetism, anarchism and religion.[55] Sentences may be grammatically similar, but this does not mean *per se* that the way language is used in them is always the same. For example, the statement, "Christ rose

---

[50] "Es gibt allerdings Unaussprechliches. Dies zeigt sich, es ist das Mystische", L. Wittgenstein, *o.c.*, 6.522.

[51] "Wovon man nicht sprechen kann, darüber muss man schweigen". L. Wittgenstein, *o.c.*, 7.

[52] "Je genauer wir die tatsächliche Sprache betrachten, desto stärker wird der Widerstreit zwischen ihr und unsrer Forderung. (Die Kristallreinheit der Logik hatte sich mir ja nicht *ergeben*; sondern sie war eine Forderung)". L. Wittgenstein, *Philosophische Untersuchungen*, par. 107.

[53] "Die Bedeutung eines Wortes ist sein Gebrauch in der Sprache". L. Wittgenstein, *o.c.*, par. 43.

[54] "Wieviele Arten der Sätze gibt es? Etwa Behauptung, Frage und Befehl?—Es gibt unzählige solcher Arten : unzählige verschiedene Arten der Verwendung alles dessen, was wir 'Zeichen', 'Worte', 'Sätze' nennen. Und diese Mannigfaltigkeit ist nichts Festes, ein für allemal Gegebenes; sondern neue Typen der Sprache, neue Sprachspiele, wie wir sagen können, entstehen und andre veralten und werden vergessen". L. Wittgenstein, *o.c.*, par. 32.

[55] Cl. Schoonbrood, *Theologisch taalgebruik in het licht van de wijsgerige betekenisanalyse*, Jaarboek 1965-66, Werkgenootschap van katholieke theologen in Nederland, p. 107.

from the grave", is grammatically similar to the statement, "Chris rose from his deck-chair", and "we have laid Mother in the grave" does not grammatically differ from "we have laid the goat in the ditch"; yet the use of language is different. What is meaningless in one language game can still be meaningful in another. In arithmetic the statement, "3 is red", is meaningless, but this same statement is meaningful for one who wishes to classify paints by means of numbers.[56]

Under the influence of the later Wittgenstein analytical philosophy has greatly changed. The fundamental principles of both logical atomism and logical positivism could not be maintained.

First of all, the picture theory of logical atomism was rejected.[57] It could perhaps still be used as a model to clarify the cognitive or descriptive use of language, but as soon as one admits that other uses of language can also be meaningful, the theory turns out to be faulty. One need only to think here of a sentence like, "scram or I'll get you!"

Secondly, the monopoly of the verification principle advocated by logical positivism was broken.[58] The task of logical positivism was to indicate the experiential situation within which it is, at least in principle, possible to establish whether a statement is true or false; and only then can an assertion become meaningful. But the situation becomes entirely different when the use principle decides whether a statement is meaningful.[59] One then no longer inquires only about the conditions in which it is possible to determine whether a statement is true, but looks for the specific logic contained in the actual use of language. Every language game "has its own kind of logic",[60] and only in the cognitive or descriptive use of language one can ask whether a statement is true or false.

---

[56] H. Hubbeling, *De betekenis van de analytische filosofie voor de wijsgerige theologie*, in : Tijdschrift voor Filosofie, 29 (1967), p. 748.

[57] W. de Pater, *Analytische Wijsbegeerte*, in : Catholica, I, p. 117.

[58] W. de Pater, *a.c.*, p. 117.

[59] "So the verificational principle of meaning in the hands of empiricist philosophers in the 1930's became modified either by a glossing of the term 'verification' or by a change of the verification principle into the use principle : the meaning of any statement is given by the way in which it is used". R.B. Braithwaite, *An empiricist's view of the nature of religious belief*, in : The Existence of God, ed. by John Hick, New York-London, 1964, p. 235.

[60] "The 'Wittgenstein I' slogan, 'The meaning of a proposition is the method of its verification' has been replaced by the 'Wittgenstein II' slogans, 'Don't ask for the meaning, ask for the use', and 'Every kind of statement has its own kind of logic' ". C.B. Daly, *Metaphysics and the limits of language*, in : Prospects for Metaphysics, Essays of Metaphysical Exploration, ed. by Ian Ramsey, London, 1961, pp. 179-180.

Thirdly, as soon as the verification principle is replaced by the use principle, it becomes evident that, in principle, one cannot object to the ethical and religious use of language. The language of ethics and of religion also has a specific kind of logic, and this logic can be disclosed by analysis. It is enough that a language game is actually played to make it the possible object of investigation. No actually used language may be rejected as an object of inquiry.

The Religious Use of Language

The introduction of the use principle in the analysis of the logic of a language did not merely allow analytical philosophy to investigate also the religious use of language; it also led to results which drew the attention of those philosophers who at first had rejected all analytical philosophy on the ground that it did not appear to be authentic philosophy. Perhaps Wittgenstein himself had been responsible for that rejection because in his TRACTATUS he had explicitly stated that philosophy is nothing but "logical clarification", and that it doesn't result in "philosophical propositions" but in "clear propositions".[61]

It is undeniable, however, that the requirements imposed to guarantee the intended clarity presuppose a philosophy. One who on the basis of clarity defends the demand that only statements of the physical sciences are clear and therefore meaningful, makes use of a philosophical theory of knowledge which is in principle "complete", even if he himself doesn't realize this. Thus it could happen that the opponents of analytical philosophy often refused to view it as an *authentic* philosophy and at most recognized it as that "philosophy" which one needs to reject philosophy.

The application of the use principle in the analysis of the religious use of language has made a profound impression on those philosophers whom, for brevity's sake, we may call "metaphysicians", that is to say, thinkers outside analytical philosophy who considered it possible to speak "about" God. The analysts' investigations made these metaphysicians realize that in their speaking "about" God they used exclusively a cognitive-descriptive language, and now the question arose whether such an exclusivism was tenable. Doubts in this matter were raised mainly through the works of Austin[62] and Evans.[63]

---

[61] "Ein philosophisches Werk besteht wesentlich aus Erläuterungen. Das Resultat der Philosophie sind nicht 'philosophische Sätze', sondern das Klarwerden von Sätzen". L. Wittgenstein, *Tractatus Logico-Philosophicus*, 4.112.

[62] J.L. Austin, *How to do things with words*, The William James Lectures delivered at Harvard University in 1955, Cambridge, Mass., 1962.

[63] Donald D. Evans, *The Logic of Self-Involvement*, A philosophical study of

Austin and Evans

John L. Austin began by asking himself whether it is really true that philosophers simply assume that a statement is always intended to describe a particular state of affairs or establish a fact in such a way that the statement is either true or false.[64] Grammarians, Austin adds, knew, of course, that there are also questions and exclamations, as well as statements which express an order, a wish or a concession. In recent times, however, both grammarians and philosophers have devoted more careful attention to the investigation of what used to be called rather thoughtlessly "statements". The first result of this attention was the conviction that a statement must be verifiable; and many statements then turned out to have been merely pseudo-statements. The philosophers were willing to admit that they had produced quite a bit of nonsense. Yet this willingness had its limits; one could also go too far in reducing statements to pseudo-statements.[65] Thus they began to ask themselves whether those statements so lightheartedly reduced to pseudo-statements were really intended to be statements in the sense of "straightforward information about facts".[66] Is this really the case, for instance, in ethical propositions?

These reflections led Austin to make a distinction between "constative" and "performative" sentences.[67] Performative sentences look like constative sentences or descriptions of states of affairs, but this is not at all what they are. Austin gives several examples of performative utterances : "I do take this woman to be my lawful wedded wife", "I name this ship the *Queen Elisabeth*", "I give and bequeath my watch to my brother", "I bet you sixpence it will rain tomorrow".[68] In such sentences I do not *describe* what I am doing, but I *do* what I am saying in them.[69] If I say, "I promise it to you", I do not give an external descrip-

---

everyday language with special reference to the christian use of language about God as Creator, London, 1963.

[64] J.L. Austin, *o.c.*, p. 1.

[65] "Yet we, that is, even philosophers, set some limits to the amount of nonsense that we are prepared to admit we talk". J.L. Austin, *o.c.*, p. 2.

[66] J.L. Austin, *o.c.*, p. 2.

[67] J.L. Austin, *o.c.*, pp. 2-7.

[68] J.L. Austin, *o.c.*, p. 5.

[69] "In these examples it seems clear that to utter the sentence (in, of course, the appropriate circumstances) is not to *describe* my doing of what I should be said in so uttering to be doing or to state that I am doing it : it is to do it". L.L. Austin, *o.c.*, p. 6.

tion of an internal act, but my act of speaking itself *is* the promise.[70]

A certain manner of speaking, then, *is* itself *doing* something, and the term "performative language" aptly expresses this. That is why performative language is not, like constative language, either true or false. This cannot be proved—just as it cannot be proved that the expression "damn"! is true or false.[71]

Nevertheless, all kinds of things can be wrong with performative language.[72] A performative utterance, such as "I appoint you Secretary of Defense", is *invalid* if *I* make it. It is an *abuse* to say. "I promise you that I will do it", if I have no intention of doing it. It is "inconsistent" to tell someone, "I transfer my power to you", if next I treat him as a usurper of my power. Such language utterances are not untrue but "unfortunate", they suffer from "infelicities".[73]

At first, it may seem as if the distinction between constative and performative acts of speech is watertight and convincing. But Austin himself later criticized it. Initially he had thought it possible to call certain acts of speech exclusively constative and others exclusively performative. This would have meant that the former would then have been exclusively either true or false and the latter exclusively either fortunate and felicitous or unfortunate and infelicitous. Austin, however, discovered that the infelicities which at first he had regarded as characteristic of performative speech, can also be found in the constative use of language.[74] Constative utterance also can be infected with invalidity,[75] abuse[76] and inconsistency.[77] To limit ourselves to an example of invalidity in both the performative and the constative uses of language, one who says, "I donate my books to you", while he has just sold the

---

[70] J.L. Austin, *o.c.*, pp. 9-11, 13.

[71] J.L. Austin, *o.c.*, p. 6.

[72] Cf. G. Nuchelmans, *Overzicht van de analytische wijsbegeerte*, pp. 218-226.

[73] "... the utterance is then, we may say, not indeed false but in general *unhappy*. And for this reason we call the doctrine of the *things that can be and go wrong* on the occasion of such utterances, the doctrine of the Infelicities". J.L. Austin, *o.c.*, p. 14.

[74] "... we find that statements *are* liable to every kind of infelicity to which performatives are liable". J.L. Austin, *o.c.*, p. 135.

[75] J.L. Austin, *o.c.*, pp. 136-137.

[76] J.L. Austin, *o.c.*, pp. 135-136.

[77] "If I have stated something, then that commits me to other statements : other statements made by me will be in order or out of order. Also some statements or remarks made by you will be henceforward contradicting me or not contradicting me, rebutting me or not rebutting me, and so forth". J.L. Austin, *o.c.*, p. 138.

same books to someone else, makes an utterance that is not valid. But this is also the case when someone says, "the present king of France is bald". His utterance is not merely false but nul and void.[78]

At the same time, the idea that only constative utterances are either true or false also turned out to be untenable. The language of advice or a verdict obviously has a specific logic; nevertheless, advice or a verdict calls for a kind of checking which resembles the checking of facts and the speaking of truth or untruth in constative utterances.[79]

These remarks briefly indicate why Austin dropped his original distinction between constative and performative acts of speaking. He replaced it by distinguishing in "every genuine speech act" the "locutionary act" and the "illocutionary act".[80] The locutionary act is the aspect of referring to facts or states of affairs that can be called true or false; the illocutionary act is the aspect of *doing* by *speaking*. Considered in themselves, both aspects of the speech act are abstractions.[81]

Donald Evan's work lies in line with that of Austin and continues it by the analysis of self-involving speech, applied to biblical language and, in particular, biblical speaking about creation. Evans begins with a classification of performative utterances, but he does not conceive the term "performative" in Austin's original sense as opposed to constative utterances. He calls any "speech-act-with-its-illocutionary-force" performative.[82] Constative utterances fall under this heading as "a class of performatives".[83] Where Austin speaks of the illocutionary force" of utterances, Evans speaks of their "performative force".[84]

The scope of Evans's investigation can be indicated in the form of a question : does the statement, "the Creator made the world", mean something like the statement, "Jones built the house"? Or, does the for-

---

[78] See : G. Nuchelmans, *o.c.*, pp. 220-226.

[79] "Can we be sure that stating truly is a different *class* of assessment from arguing soundly, advising well, judging fairly, and blaming justifiably? Do these not have something to do in complicated ways with facts? The same is true also of exercitives such as naming, appointing, bequeathing, and betting. Facts come in as well as our knowledge or opinion about facts". J.L. Austin, *o.c.*, p. 141.

[80] "... every genuine speech act is both". J.L. Austin, *o.c.*, p. 146.

[81] J.L. Austin, *o.c.*, p. 146.

[82] Donald D. Evans, *The Logic of Self-Involvement*, p. 39, footnote.

[83] "Thus when I say that constatives form a class of performatives, there might seem to be no genuine difference from Austin". Donald D. Evans, *o.c.*, p. 39, footnote.

[84] "Austin pointed out that this illocutionary force (which I call 'performative force') ...". Donald D. Evans, *o.c.*, p. 81, footnote 1.

mer statement, in opposition to the latter, imply a kind of commitment and is it the expression of a personal feeling and a personal attitude? According to Bultmann, an assertion about God as creator can never be a neutral statement but always is an act of thanksgiving and a surrender; one who fails to realize this misunderstands the biblical and existential character of the affirmation of creation. Such a way of speaking is then no longer the "language of faith".[85] While agreeing with this, Evans adds that there exists no adequate study of how a language can "involve" the speaking subject if more is understood by this expression than the subjective assent to a fact expressed in that language.

The topic of Evans's study is precisely the self-involving character which occurs in certain forms of language use. In a performative speech act such as, "I submit to your authority", I commit myself to certain actions in the future; and in a performative speech act such as, "thank you for your kindness", I imply a subjective act of gratitude. Viewed from the side of the speaking subject, this is more than mere assent to a fact. Such statements imply a "commissive" and "behabitative" on the part of the subject.[86]

Alongside self-involving utterances which are performative uses of language, Evans places self-involving expressions of feelings.[87] An utterance like "terrific!" contains the expression of the subject's feelings; and "I look on life as a play" implies the expression of a subject's attitude.[88] Evans calls utterances "self-involving" if they imply a "behabitative" or "commissive".

In his opinion, biblical theology badly needs a logic of self-involving language. For this biblical theology itself emphasizes the importance of non-propositional speech with respect to both God's revelation—God's word to man—and man's religious language—man's word to God. In both cases language or the "word" is not, or not purely, propositional but primarily a "self-involving activity".[90] God does not merely supply supernatural information about himself, expressed in flat affirmations

---

[85] Donald D. Evans, *o.c.*, p. 11.

"Thus no flat Constative entails a Behabitive or Commissive; that is, no flat Constative entails a self-involving utterance". Donald D. Evans, *o.c.*, p. 57.

[87] "We shall see that verbal expressions of feeling, like Behabitive and Commissive utterances, are self-involving, and that they involve a distinct use of language, alongside the performative and causal uses". Donald D. Evans, *o.c.*, p. 79.

[88] Donald D. Evans, *o.c.*, pp. 115-141.

[89] Donald D. Evans, *o.c.*, p. 14.

[90] Donald D. Evans, *o.c.*, pp. 14-15.

of facts, but he "addresses" man in an "event" or "deed" by which he commits himself to man and in which he expresses his inner "self". Similarly, man does not merely assert facts "about" God, but he addresses God in worship, committing himself to God and expressing his attitude to God. Because and to the extent that God's self-revelation and man's religious speaking are a "self-involving verbal activity", biblical theology cannot do without an understanding of the various ways in which language is self-involving and an activity.[90]

Evans views his endeavor as perfectly justified, both from the standpoint of theology and from that of analytical philosophy. Theologians intend to give verbal expression to Christian faith, and analytical philosophers devote themselves to ordinary language. Now, the "ordinary language" to be investigated by those who wish to discuss Christian faith is the language of the Bible itself.[91] For the "ordinary language" which is the object of analytical investigation, is the language that is actually used in its natural environment;[92] and this "natural habitat" of the actually used Christian language is the Bible.[93] Biblical language, then, is what analytical philosophers call "ordinary language".[94]

---

[91] "Analytic philosophers insist on an appeal to *ordinary* language; and if a philosopher who studies christian beliefs wants to use the same method that he employs elsewhere ... the ordinary language to which he *should* appeal is biblical language". Donald D. Evans, *o.c.*, p. 15.

[92] Donald D. Evans, *o.c.*, p. 16.

[93] Donald D. Evans, *o.c.*, pp. 16-18.

[94] "My main point, in any case, is that 'ordinary' language to which an analytic philosopher should appeal when he considers *christian* conceptions is biblical language". Donald D. Evans, *o.c.*, p. 17.

CHAPTER FIVE

HERMENEUTICS OF RELIGIOUS EXISTENCE

From the preceding chapters it should be evident that one cannot glibly dispose of the whole matter by saying : "We, modern men, 'obviously' are no longer able to do anything with a mythical or metaphysical conception of God". At least, I hope to have succeeded in showing that such a statement does not mean anything at all unless the meaning of the terms "mythical" and "metaphysical" is very precisely indicated.

A second reason to distrust such a statement is this : who and what are "we, modern men", and what is so "obvious" about us? Harvey Cox defines "us" as secularized city-dwellers, characterized by pragmatism and profaneness.[1] Herbert Marcuse may be said to agree with this "definition" but thinks that it is rendered more profound if we add that modern man is a consumer lulled to sleep and too degenerate to retain the ability to realize what could make his existence authentic.[2] Such a type of man may no longer be able to "do anything" with a certain conception or a certain way of life. But why on earth should anyone wish to measure the meaningfulness or meaninglessness of that conception or way of life by such a type of man?

This difficulty is largely or even totally disregarded by some thinkers who try to interpret religious existence. In Paul Van Buren's eyes, all speaking "about" God is meaningless.[3] He is greatly irritated by the fact that theologians of existence refuse to admit this and counters whatever they say by asking whether they really think that this still means anything to modern man.[4] He wonders where they have found

---

[1] Harvey Cox, *The Secular City*, London, 1967, p. 62.

[2] Herbert Marcuse, *One-Dimensional Man*, London, 1968, pp. 9-31.

[3] "The empiricist in us finds the heart of the difficulty not in what is said about God, but in the very talking about God at all". Paul van Buren, *The Secular Meaning of the Gospel*, London, 1966³, p. 84.

[4] Paul van Buren, *o.c.*, pp. 68, 71, 74, 83.

their "modern man" because, for Van Buren, modern man is the man who has given in to the absolutism of the "empirical spirit of our age",[5] while for the theologians of existence modern man appears to be something else.

That is why I should like to express myself with greater reserve than Ogden, who says that the demand to demythologize, arising from man's modern situation, must be *unconditionally* accepted.[6] It is this qualification "unconditionally" that gives rise to reservations. For if the situation of modern man includes the absolutism of the scientific-technological attitude, then one who is conscious of the narrow-mindedness of this absolutism cannot accept the situation of modern man "without qualification"[7] as the norm for what is relevant or irrelevant to man.[8] I consider it relevant that a young man calls his girl a "rose". If modern man no longer understands this and demands that the young man use exclusively the models created by psycho-diagnosis when he and his girl become "ingredients" of a psychological test, then "modern man" is lost, and the young man can no longer say what he intends to say.

In a similar way, when religious existence is rejected by postulatory atheism, a role is played in this rejection by both an interpretation of religious existence and an over-all view of man. It is on the basis of this over-all view of man that religious existence, *tout court*, is rejected by postulatory atheism.

It also happens, however, that the same over-all view of man does not lead to a rejection of religious existence, *tout court*, but only to that of its proposed or presupposed interpretation. In that case it is granted that the truth of a certain view of man forces us to reject religious existence in the proposed or assumed interpretation. What is not granted, however, is that therefore religious existence, *tout court*, must be rejected because the proposed interpretation is judged to contain only an inauthentic form of religious existence. A few examples may serve to clarify the point. It has been said that the term "religious" must be applied to the following :

[5] Paul van Buren, *o.c.*, p. 83.

[6] "The first principle ... is that the demand for demythologisation that arises with necessity from the situation of modern man must be accepted without condition". Schubert M. Ogden, *Christ without Myth*, A study based on the theology of Rudolf Bultmann, London, 1962, p. 148.

[7] Paul van Buren, *o.c.*, p. 102.

[8] Gabriel Vahanian, *No Other God*, New York, 1966.

1. One who separates the best and most precious of his own being in order to project it as an alien being and then kneels down before this alien being, without realizing that he is, strictly speaking, adoring himself (Feuerbach).[9]
2. One who lives in the illusion that his desire to be a child again and enjoy the protection of a father is fulfilled (Freud).[10]
3. One who thinks that he will realize himself and receive justice in a kingdom that is not of this world because society leaves him no room for his *real* self-realization (Marx).[11]
4. One who tries to make "in itself" and "for itself" coincide in and through his self-transcendence (Sartre).[12]
5. One who views all searching for truth and value as superfluous because he thinks that he possesses God as Truth itself and Goodness itself (Merleau-Ponty).[13]

Postulatory atheism claims that there should not be any religious people and that the God spoken of by the religious man does not exist. Others, however, give a different interpretation to religious existence. They agree in whole or in part with the reasons adduced by postulatory atheism to reject what it does reject, but defend the position that all this does not oblige us to demand the rejection of religious existence, *tout court.*

---

[9] "Die Religion, wenigstens die Christliche, ist das Verhalten des Menschen zu sich selbst, oder richtiger : zu seinem Wesen, aber das Verhalten zu seinem Wesen als zu einem anderen Wesen. Das göttliche Wesen ist nichts anderes als das menschliche Wesen, oder besser : das Wesen des Menschen, abgesondert von den Schranken des individuellen, d.h. wirklichen, leiblichen Menschen, vergegenständlicht, d.h. angeschaut und verehrt als ein anderes, von ihm unterschiedenes, eigenes Wesen—alle Bestimmungen des göttlichen Wesens sind darum Bestimmungen des menschlichen Wesens". L. Feuerbach, *Das Wesen des Christentums*, Sämtliche Werke, newly edited by Wilhelm Bolin und Friedrich Jodl. Stuttgart, 1903, p. 17.

[10] S. Freud, *Die Zukunft einer Illusion*, Gesammelte Werke chronologisch geordnet, London, Band XIV, pp. 325-380.

[11] "Die Religion ist die allgemeine Theorie dieser Welt, ihr enzyklopädisches Kompendium, ihre Logik in populärer Form, ihr spiritualistischer Point d'honneur, ihr Enthusiasmus, ihre moralische Sanktion, ihre feierliche Ergänzung, ihr allgemeiner Trost- und Rechtfertigungsgrund. Sie ist die *phantastiche Verwirklichung* des menschlichen Wesens, weil das *menschliche Wesen* keine wahre Wirklichkeit besitzt". K. Marx, *Zur Kritik der Hegelschen Rechtsphilosophie*, in : Die heilige Familie, Berlin, 1953, p. 11.

[12] J.-P. Sartre, *L'Etre et le Néant*, Paris, 1950²⁹, p. 653.

[13] M. Merleau-Ponty, *Sens et non-sens*, Paris, 1948, pp. 165-196, 351-370; *L'homme et l'adversité*, and *Deuxième entretien privé*, in : La connaissance de l'homme au xxe siècle, Rencontres internationales de Genève, Neuchâtel, 1952, pp. 51-75, 215-252.

This "defense", as we will see later in greater detail, cannot *exclusively* consist in the analysis of the specific logic proper to religious language. Since Wittgenstein launched his theory of "language games", the logic of any *de facto* used language has qualified for analysis. Such an analysis can also be made by an adherent of postulatory atheism. He then analyzes a certain way of speaking simply because this way *de facto* exists; at the same time, he is of the opinion that this speaking is not worth while because it is "about nothing".

This leads us to the conclusion that the religious man must indeed show that his speaking is "about something". He must not merely analyze the specific *logic* of his language game but also justify the specific *truth* of his language. In other words, he must "point out" a specific "reality".

1. THE CALLING OF THE NAME "GOD"

What is it that the religious man means when he calls the name "God"? There are people who sincerely think that there should not be any believers in God. Similarly, there are people who are convinced that there should not be any artists. But, there is no escape from the fact that there are artists. That is why I may and even must ask what an artist intends when he creates a work of art. For there cannot be any doubt that the artist does intend something, even if some people are convinced that he should not intend anything. The same holds for the man of faith. He intends something when he calls the name "God", even though others are convinced that the religious man has no right to exist. So, what does he mean when he calls "God"?

Let me note at once that the believer does indeed intend to *call* the name "God". He does not intend to "establish" that God exists, to "describe" what God is or to "explain" anything by accepting God's existence. The religious man *calls* the name "God", and this "calling" can be a shouting, a whispering of his name. It can be a prayer, a song, an alleluia, a complaining, a sorrowing, a cursing : God! Thank God! God be praised! God Almighty! Goddamn!

When things are expressed in this way, it should be evident that any interpretation of what it means to *call* the name of "God" should steer clear of the idea that there is question here of "establishing" or "describing" "something" or "somebody", or that an attempt is being made to "explain" "something" by means of "something" or "somebody" by means of "somebody".

When the religious man calls, shouts, whispers the name "God", he expresses the mystery of his existence. Under certain conditions he discovers in his existence a "depth"[14] the reality of which cannot be indicated in "flat descriptive" terms[15] functioning as particularizations of what in ordinary speech we call "something" or "somebody". In calling the name "God", the religious man does not intend to describe "something" or "somebody" just as he can describe a geological layer or John. Let us give a few examples :

A child is born, and the religious man exclaims "God"!

In health or illness, the religious man shouts "God"!

He sexually unites with another human being, and in his ecstasy the religious man calls "God"!

He is dying and his lips whisper "God"!

At the rising and the setting of the sun, in the pale shine of the moon and the stars, before the roar of the sea, at the gentle waving of the wheat stalks, the threat of a storm and the menace of a flood, at the welling up of a spring and the germinating of the seed, the religious man exclaims "God"!

When he conquers in battle or suffers defeat, when he lives in poverty or in prosperity, when he suffers injustice or is vindicated, the religious man calls "God"!

When he is reduced to slavery in Egypt, rises against his oppressors, overcomes the terrible risk of his revolt against his masters, the religious man exclaims "God"!

When, wandering through the desert with his people, he meets ethical demands imposing themselves on him as inescapable conditions of humanity, the religious man calls "God"!

When he must go into exile, he complains "God"!

And when he can return again from his exile, he joyfully shouts "God"!

The religious man calls, shouts, whispers the name "God"! He prays, he sings, he shouts for joy and laments, he sorrows and curses.

---

[14] "The name of this infinite and inexhaustible depth and ground of all being is *God*. That depth is what the word *God* means. ... He who knows about depth knows about God". Paul Tillich, *The Shaking of the Foundations*, London, 1949, p. 57.

[15] "Let us first recall that in my view, belief in God arises from what I have called cosmic disclosures, situations where the Universe 'comes alive', where a 'dead', 'dull', 'flat' existence takes on 'depth' or another 'dimension' ". Ian T. Ramsey, *Talking about God : Models, ancient and modern*, in : Myth and Symbol, ed. by F.W. Dillistone, London, 1970[2], p. 87.

Situations of Existence

To understand what the religious man means when he calls the name "God", the above-mentioned situations must be conceived as situations of existence, i.e., as situations of *man* viewed as an existent subject. This point must be stressed, for it is possible to speak about man without conceiving "man" as existent subject and, consequently, without conceiving him really as *man*. Let us illustrate what this means.

When a young man calls his girl "sweet", he calls her so as an existent subject. But he could also make her an "ingredient" of mechanics. He would do this by putting her on a scale. The scale says : "One hundred pounds", just as it would have done if he had put a bag of cement on it. The scale cannot say : "sweet". As "ingredients" of mechanics, girls are never sweet. In a similar way people are never religious as "ingredients" of the sciences.

The religious man, we said, sexually unites with another person and in his ecstasy he calls "God"! This is nonsense, of course, for anyone who reduces sexuality to a mere object of science. It is possible to describe sexual intercourse in terms of the working of certain glands, increase of blood pressure, depth and volume of breathing—panting in ordinary language—etc. But one who thinks of sexual intercourse *only* in such terms had better not get married in church or even before a justice of peace, for the only place where he belongs is in the laboratory.

"A child is born", we said, "and the believer exclaims 'God' "! That is why, soon after birth, the child is carried to the temple or church. This is done even if the child is stillborn. But when in an abortion clinic the physician kills the unborn child, it is simply dropped into the waste disposal unit. Things like this can happen only if the unborn child is reduced to a mere object of the sciences. In such a case nothing reveals itself of that mysterious "depth" which the religious man tries to express when he calls "God"!

For an understanding of existence as religious it is necessary that philosophy reject the services offered by the sciences, no matter how well-intentioned they may be. The religious man cannot occur in the sciences, just as "lovely girls" cannot occur in mechanics or physiology.

The preceding ideas have often been interpreted as an attempt to devaluate or even reject the positive sciences. But this is not at all my intention here. I merely point out that the undivided and unreduced wealth of existence, conceived as "subjectivity immersed in the body and involved in the world",[16] cannot be discussed by the sciences because they have *chosen*—and for their purpose, rightly so—a standpoint of questioning and answering by which existence undergoes a "reduction". *Only* philosophy speaks about the essence of man as existence; the sciences do *not*,[17] and this includes psychology, sociology and linguistics.

This statement does *not* mean that philosophy devalues the positive sciences when it says that they are unable to speak of man as existence. But it *does* mean that when the pursuers of the positive sciences have made man an "ingredient" of their discipline in and through their empirically verifiable laws, the question about man's *essence* has not yet been raised. Calling man's essence "existence" is possible only on the basis of a philosophical reflection.

In the same line of thought, one can see that reflection on scientific knowledge is not *itself* scientific knowledge.[18] To reflect on physics, biology, chemistry, sociology, psychology and linguistics is *not the same* as to pursue these sciences. Such a reflection is philosophical, and philosophy conceives the sciences as modes of being-man, as modes of existence.[19] Not, however, the ingredients of these sciences, but the *pursuers* of them should be called modes of existence. The linguistic structures spoken of by linguists are not existences, but the linguists themselves are.

If the sciences do not speak of man as existence, neither do they speak of the essence of religiousness, for this essence is a specific mode of existing. The specific character of religiousness consists in experiencing "depth" in existence, and this experience makes man call "God".[20]

---

[16] W. Luijpen, *Existential Phenomenology*, rev. ed., Pittsburgh, 1974⁴, pp. 54-68.

[17] "Les vues scientifiques selon lesquelles je suis un moment du monde sont toujours naïves et hypocrites, parce qu'elles sous-entendent, sans la mentionner, cette autre vue, celle de la conscience, par laquelle d'abord un monde se dispose autour de moi et commence à exister pour moi". M. Merleau-Ponty, *Phénoménologie de la perception*, Paris, 1945¹⁴, Avant-Propos, p. III.

[18] "Die Physik kann als Physik über die Physik keine Aussagen machen. Alle Aussagen der Physik sprechen physikalisch. Die Physik selbst ist kein möglicher Gegenstand eines physikalischen Experimentes. Dasselbe gilt von der Philologie. Als Theorie der Sprache und Literatur ist sie niemals ein möglicher Gegenstand philologischer Betrachtung. Das Gesagte gilt für jede Wissenschaft". M. Heidegger, *Vorträge und Aufsätze*, Pfullingen, 1954, p. 65.

[19] "Wissenschaften sind Seinsweisen des Daseins". M. Heidegger, *Sein und Zeit*, p. 13.

[20] "The necessity for the name 'God' lies in the fact that our being has depths which naturalism, whether evolutionary, mechanistic, dialectical or humanistic, cannot or will not recognize. And the nemesis which has overtaken naturalism in

If this idea is accepted, then we must inevitably look critically at the eagerness with which some theological schools call upon the behavioral sciences as auxiliary disciplines of theology. For it is beyond dispute that the specific standpoint from which, e.g., sociology asks questions does not allow anything to appear of what philosophy tries to express when it speaks about the esence of religious existence. Let us give an example.

A religious-sociological investigation recently asked the question, "Is the Bible for you God's word"? About sixty percent of the people questioned answered in the affirmative.[21] *But no one knows what this statistic means.* The religious sociologist can communicate the result of his inquiry to the theologian. The latter, however, is not entitled to conclude from this that for sixty percent of the repliers the Bible is God's word. All he knows is that a certain percentage of people answered a certain kind of question in a certain way. That is all! He does not know *what they mean* with their affirmation. He should even add that the sociologist as sociologist does not know what he himself means when he asks people to answer this question. And if he thinks that he does know what he means with his question, then, as a sociologist, he still does not know whether he *rightly* means this. One who asks, "Is the Bible for you God's word"? only knows what he is asking if he has at his disposal the necessary means to interpret the statement : "This is God's word". But most certainly sociology is not in the possession of such means.

Calling the Name "God" and "Describing"

As soon as man began to reflect explicitly on himself, he also tried to speak about the mystery, the "depth" in his existence to which he gave expression by the name "God". Sometimes he managed to do so in a truly ingenious way; there are geniuses not only in physical science and ethics but also in religion. The religious genius makes it possible for other people to "see" the mystery in their own existence, and it is this "seeing" of the mystery that makes man call out "God"! This "seeing" is known as "believing", and the disclosure of this ' depth" is known as 'revelation."

---

our day has revealed the peril of trying to suppress them". John A.T. Robinson, *Honest to God*, London, 1963[9], p. 54.

[21] *God in Nederland*, Introduction by G.H.L. Zeegers, commentary by G. Dekker and J.W.M. Peters, Amsterdam, 1967, p. 128.

Once again, full emphasis is to be placed on the term "calling", for the mystery in human existence is not recognized when this "calling" is *replaced* by a "constative describing" in which the name "God" becomes the subject of a judgment in which a predicate is added to the subject. The calling of the name "God" may not be replaced by such statements as :

God gives us a child.

God restores my health.

God sends me an illness.

God has attached intense pleasure to sexual intercourse.

God makes the sun rise and set and he has put the stars in the firmament.

God makes the sea roar, the wheat undulate, the storm burst, the spring well up and the seed germinate.

God gives us victory in battle.

God inflicts a defeat on us.

God sends me poverty and want.

God gives me prosperity.

God permits that I suffer injustice.

God vindicates my rights.

God intervenes in history.

God rewards the good.

God punishes evil.

God sends us into exile.

God brings us back from exile.

The calling of the name "God", I said, cannot be *replaced* by a constative description in which the name "God" becomes the subject of a judgment.[22] The preceding series of sentences all are judgments. Everyone, however, knows that the religious man, in whatever phase of history he lived or still lives, does use such sentences. The religious man expresses himself in the way I have said that it *cannot* be done. What, then, is the meaning of this?

Anthony Flew's Parable

What it means that the religious man *does* make the name "God" the subject of a judgment can only be understood if one realizes that the

---

[22] "Theological assertions are not flat or uniform as we might say 'The cat is on the mat' is flat and uniform". Ian T. Ramsey, *Talking about God* : *Models, ancient and modern*, in : Myth and Symbol, ed. By F.W. Dillistone, p. 97.

religious man is also wholly insensitive to anything that can be brought
to bear against his statements. He is like one of the two explorers spoken
of in Flew's parable. To avoid repetition, the parable essentially amounts
to this that the religious explorer's statement, "A gardener must have
been at work here", appears to be beyond falsification. When no gardener
is to be seen, the believer says that he is invisible; when no one gets hurt
by the barbed wire and no one touches the electric fence, the religious
man is not surprised because the gardener has no body. No matter what
his unbelieving companion says to falsify the claim that "a gardener must
have been at work here", the believing explorer always finds an answer
and disregards all objections.[23] His statement simply cannot be falsified
and appears capable of being harmonized with whatever happens or
does not happen.

The religious man is indeed like that explorer. "God stands on our
side", he says. If it is pointed out to him that, nevertheless, he will be
humiliated and made to suffer, he says, "God chastizes him whom he
loves".

"God stands on our side", he says. But the "other side" lives in
prosperity and enjoys good fortune. The religious man replies : "Do not
fear. God sends his blessings to both the just and the unjust".

"God stands on our side", the religious man sings. But he still needs
to prepare himself for all possibilities, he may not put any conditions,
issue any ultimatum and, above all, set no time limit within which his
statement must be verified. For, "we must not put God to the test".[24]

The religious man simply does not allow his statements to be falsified.
"God, give us a child", he prays or "God, restore my health". What
the modern man of science tells him about the reproduction of man,
health, disease and death, fertility and lust, does not seem to touch him.
"God makes the sun rise and set", he says, even though he knows what
the astronomer can tell him about the sun and is familiar with the fact
that the meteorologist can predict when the sea will be roaring, a thunderstorm break loose or the sun shine bright. "God inflicted a defeat on
us" or "God blesses us with wealth", he says, even though he is not
ignorant of the fact that strategists can explain victories and defeats
and that economists predict when periods of poverty or prosperity will
occur. The religious man does not deny what the modern men of science
tell him, but it does not seem to touch his faith. What does this mean?

---

[23] A. Flew, *Theology and falsification*, in : New Essays in Philosophical Theology,
ed. by A. Flew and A. MacIntyre, London, 1969[7], pp. 96-99.

[24] Fr. Ferré, *Basic Modern Philosophy of Religion*, London, 1967, p. 340.

No "Flat Descriptions"

It means that the religious man does *not* conceive his statements "about" God, despite their external appearance and grammatical form, as "flat descriptions" of God's essence and deeds.[25] Despite the external appearance, he intends to convey in those statements the "depth" of his existent subjectivity. The very standpoint from which the sciences raise their questions makes it *impossible* to let the "depth" of existence appear to the pursuers of the sciences as such. That is why the religious man can disregard the statements of science as long as he himself in his seemingly "flat descriptions" really does intend to give expression to the "depth" of his existent subjectivity.

This idea is utterly beyond Flew's understanding. While he is willing to grant that language does not exclusively consist of assertions and explanations, he cannot accept that religious language does not really intend to give "flat descriptions" of God's essence and deeds. Flew himself views all religious language as meaningless, but he demands that those who use this language conceive their statements as "flat descriptions". And if they do not, then they are, in his eyes, no longer orthodox. Thus, according to Flew, one becomes a heretic if one does not put the statements, "God loves his children" and "God causes a fountain to spring up" on a par with "Joe loves his children" and "geological conditions cause a fountain to spring up".[26]

2. THE PROPER CHARACTER OF RELIGIOUS LANGUAGE

The Symbolic Use of Language

If religious language is not a "flat description", what, then is its character? Religious language is symbolic language.[27] This assertion would be misun-

---

[25] "We seem, then, to be driven to the conclusion that theistic expressions like 'God is on our side' or 'God made the World' do not typically function among modern theists as empirical hypotheses, despite their superficial resemblances to "The sheriff is on our side' or 'The universe began with a big bang' ". Fr. Ferré, *o.c.*, p. 341.

[26] "... I nevertheless want to insist that any attempt to analyse Christian religious utterances as expressions of affirmations of a *blik* rather than as (at least would-be) assertions about the cosmos is fundamentally misguided. First, because thus interpreted they would be entirely unorthodox". A. Flew, in : *o.c.*, pp. 107-108.

[27] "Aus dem Gesagten folgt, dass alles, was die Religion über Gott, über seine Eigenschaften, sein Handeln und seine Manifestationen aussagt, symbolischen Charakter hat und dass man den Sinn des Begriffs Gott völlig verfehlt, wenn man die symbolische Ausdrucksweise wörtlich versteht". P. Tillich, *Systematische Theologie*, II, Stuttgart, 1958[3], p. 15; *Dynamics of Faith*, London, 1957, pp. 41-54.

derstood if it is taken to mean that religious language is *only* symbolic,[28] in the sense of saying "less" than the language of "flat description". On the contrary, symbolic language says "more", precisely because it makes use of the *special* way in which symbols point beyond themselves.[29] Mere signs also point beyond themselves to a signified reality,[30] but symbols are used to show meanings which cannot be disclosed by any other means.[31] Not only religious symbols do this. When artistic experience expresses itself symbolically, this expression can never be replaced by the signs which the sciences use to express their experiences.[32] The same is true for religious language. Precisely because of the *special* way in which the symbols used refer beyond themselves, religious language cannot be replaced by the language of philosophers and theologians.[33]

The way symbols point beyond themselves is *special* because in the use of symbolic language the words, without denying the referential intentionality which they directly and immediately possess, nonetheless transcend this intentionality. "From afar" they make present meanings whose "presence" cannot be put on a par with the presence of that which is intended and called forth in their direct and immediate referential intentionality.[34] This, however, does *not* mean that the symbolized is *not* present. Let us use the term "absent presence" for this *special* kind of presence. Religious symbols make the holy present, but not in the same way as they make present that which is intended and called forth in the direct and immediate intentionality of the symbols used. Thus the symbols have a "double intentionality".[35] The "first intentionality" refers to what is literally signified, something that could be called "clear" if this term is not misunderstood. The "second intentionality" points to an "absent presence" by way of the symbol's lack of transparency.[36]

---

[28] P. Tillich, *Systematische Theologie*, II, p. 15; *Dynamics of Faith*, p. 45.

[29] P. Tillich, *Symbol und Wirklichkeit*, Göttingen, 1962, p. 4.

[30] P. Tillich, *Dynamics of Faith*, pp. 41-42.

[31] P. Tillich, *Symbol und Wirklichkeit*, p. 5.

[32] P. Tillich, *Dynamics of Faith*, pp. 42-43, 45.

[33] "In der Begegnung mit heiligen Orten, heiligen Zeiten, heiligen Personen und heiligen Bildern erfährt der Mensch etwas vom Heiligen selbst—eine Erfahrung, die durch keine Erkenntnis vermittels philosophischer oder theologischer Begriffe ersetzt werden kann". P. Tillich, *Symbol und Wirklichkeit*, p. 5.

[34] J. Macquarrie, *Principles of Christian Theology*, New York, 1966, pp. 122-123.

[35] "Nous dirons que le symbole recèle dans sa visée une intentionalité double". P. Ricoeur, *Finitude et Culpabilité*, II, La symbolique du mal, Paris, 1960, p. 22.

[36] "Ainsi, à l'opposé des signes techniques parfaitement transparents qui ne disent que ce qu'ils veulent dire en posant le signifié, les signes symboliques sont opaques,

It would be misleading to say that symbols point beyond themselves in a special way if this assertion is taken to refer to symbols detached from the speaking subject. For the "coming to pass" of the "absent presence" of the holy in and through the symbol's "second intentionality" is equiprimordially the "coming to pass" of the existent subject in a "second dimension", the dimension of "depth" within existence.[37] Once this is understood, one also understands why so many symbols say nothing at all or very little to Western man. For to the extent that Western man has become the victim of the absolutism of the sciences, his existence "comes to pass" only in the "first dimension". He merely understands the language of signs, not that of symbols. Signs "tell" him something and "do" something for him : they make him realize himself, but only in the "first dimension" of his existence. Thus he dwells exclusively in a profane world and understands only the language of "flat descriptions".

This implies that, strictly speaking, modern man leads a truncated existence.[38] He relegates symbolic language to the domain of children, poets and the psychically disturbed, and then thinks that he is justified in dismissing symbols.[39] Thus it escapes him that the symbolizing "moment" of his existence is an essential "moment" thereof.[40] He is cut off from the "depth" of his existence and from the holy in the world.[41]

A consequence of this is that he no longer understands myths. For the victims of scientism myths are nothing but pseudo-scientific chatter, they are not "true" in any sense. As we saw, however, myths do not belong to the "first dimension" of existence, their language is not the

---

parce que le sens premier littéral, patent vise lui-même analogiquement un sens second qui n'est pas donné autrement qu'en lui.... Cette opacité fait la profondeur même du symbole, inépuisable comme on dira". P. Ricoeur, o.c., p. 22.

[37] "Aber der menschliche Geist könnte diese neuen Dimensionen nicht ergreifen, wenn das Symbol nicht gleichzeitig auch in ihm eine neue Dimension öffnete". P. Tillich, Symbol und Wirklichkeit, p. 5.

[38] Mircea Eliade, Das Heilige und das Profane, Vom Wesen des Religiösen, Hamburg, 1957, pp. 119-126.

[39] Mircea Eliade, Images et Symboles, Essais sur le symbolisme magico-religieux. Paris, 1952, p. 13.

[40] "On est en train de comprendre aujourd'hui une chose que le XIXe siècle ne pouvait même pas pressentir : que le symbole, le mythe, l'image appartiennent à la substance de la vie spirituelle, qu'on peut les camoufler, les mutiler, les dégrader, mais qu'on ne les extirpera jamais". Mircea Eliade, o.c., p. 12.

[41] "... il est coupé de la réalité profonde de la vie et de sa propre âme". Mircea Eliade, o.c., p. 24.

language of *signs* but that of *symbols*.[42] Myths belong to the "second dimension" of existence, for in them the symbol receives the form of the story.[43] These stories are "stories of the gods";[44] they tell sacred stories, primordial events which happened "once upon a time". They talk about what the gods and heroes have done and have revealed. The deeds of gods and heroes reveal the holiness of human actions and behavior, of objects, places and times. That is why human deeds are never purely profane, for they repeat divine examples. That is why the history of the mythical man is always sacred history. In the telling of myths the sacred primordial events are recalled and made present again. Mythical history is true history; the mythical story discloses a "second dimension" in actions, behavior, history, cosmos, objects, time and space,[45] by this that man lets the holy speak to him.

How can modern man still put himself in the myths and let them speak to him? For modern man myth and history have gone their separate ways. The time of the myth and the time of events in the sense of the science of history cannot be coordinated, and the space of myth does not occur in geography. For modern man the world is not sacred, but the domain of his ever-increasing power. For modern man actions and behavior have no divine exemplars, and objects are for him objects of

---

[42] The careful reader will not fail to notice that I do not "use" Vergote's conception of the myth, explained in Chapter One, but make use of the ideas of Ricoeur, which Vergote doesn't share, and those of Tillich, whom Vergote doesn't name. According to these two authors, the symbol assumes the form of a story in the myth. Thus they interpret the myth symbolically, which, in Vergote's view, is hermeneutically wrong (cf. his article, *De mythe als manifestatie*, in : Tijdschrift voor Filosofie, 34 (1972), p. 210). Yet, I wonder whether the two views are really opposed to each other. Vergote's position is so unique that many stories which others call "mythical" do not qualify for this label in his view. I've heard him say that the Bible contains no myths. When Bultmann, on the other hand, began to speak of myths, he was not particularly interested in determining the exact boundaries of genres of stories on the basis of their literary character, but was simply concerned with certain *biblical* stories. These he called "myths". Vergote, however, investigates the literary character of certain stories which *he* calls "myths", and, on the basis of his investigation, arrives at the conclusion that there are no myths in the Bible. In other words, Vergote and Bultmann are talking about different stories. Vergote may now be right when he refuses to give a symbolic interpretation to the stories which *he* is concerned with and which *he* calls "mythical". But this doesn't tell us anything yet about other stories, such as those which Bultmann calls "mythical".

[43] "Il faut en effet rendre compte de deux caractères du mythe : qu'il est une parole et qu'en lui le symbole prend la forme du récit". P. Ricoeur, *o.c.*, p. 158.

[44] P. Tillich, *Dynamics of Faith*, pp. 48-54.

[45] Mircea Eliade, *Das Heilige und das Profane*, pp. 56-62.

scientific language and technological know-how. That is why we must ask, how can modern man still put himself in the myths and let them speak to him?

To the extent that modern man has become the victim of the absolutism of his "modernity", there is no such possibility. And to the extent that this is the case, modern man's existence is truncated. Man is estranged from his own essence when he thinks that mythical consciousness suffices to establish him in an environment that has been so enormously enlarged by science and technology. But he is similarly self-estranged when the absolutism of his scientific and technological attitude makes him insensitive to what happened to man in myths, viz., that the holy speaks to him.[46]

The mythical moment of human existence is not easily suppressed or eliminated.[47] If the "really" holy is not holy for man, then something else will be.[48] If man does not adore a divine God, he will bend his knee for a non-divine god. The degeneration of anything which violates man's mythical consciousness is, itself, pseudo-mythical;[49] it uses a pseudo-mythical and pseudo-symbolic language to suggest a pseudo-depth in human existence.[50] The "myth" of the twentieth century and the "myth" of National Socialism are pseudo-myths which exploit and falsify the authentic mythical moment in human existence.[51] Insofar, however, as modern man has not yet become a victim of the absolutism of his "modernity", he retains the ability to understand myths as "true".[52] Not, of course, as true in the etiological, i.e., scientifically explanatory, sense, for the sciences makes this sense impossible, and rightly so. But the truth about man is not exhausted by speaking scientifically about him.[53] On the contrary, scientific language is "superficial". It

[46] G. Gusdorf, *Mythe et métaphysique*, Paris, 1953, p. 189.

[47] "So ist die Mehrzahl der Religionslosen immer noch an Pseudoreligionen und abgesunkenen Mythologien beteiligt. Das wundert uns nicht, denn wir haben bereits gesehen, dass der profane Mensch der Abkömmling des *homo religiosus* und ausserstande ist, seine eigene Geschichte zu annulieren". Mircea Eliade, *Das Heilige und das Profane*, p. 124.

[48] p. Tillich, *Dynamics of Faith*, pp. 1-4.

[49] G. Gusdorf, *o.c.*, p. 190.

[50] Mircea Eliade, *Images et Symboles*, pp. 18-24.

[51] "... symbol and myth are forms of the human consciousness which are always present. One can replace one myth by another, but one cannot remove the myth from man's spiritual life. For the myth is the combination of symbols of our ultimate concern". P. Tillich, *Dynamics of Faith*, p. 50.

[52] Mircea Eliade, *Images et Symboles*, p. 76.

[53] R. Bultmann, in : Kerygma und Mythos, I, pp. 22-23; II, p. 183; VI-i, p. 24.

does not let the holy appear because it cannot speak about human existence and its "depth". This "depth" is voiced only in symbolic and mythical speech.

Because religious language is essentially symbolic and mythical, the
program of demythologization should never be conceived as an attempt
to eliminate mythical speech altogether.[54] There should never be any
"demythification" because the time of myths is not past.[55] What *is*
past is the time in which it was possible to conceive myths as a kind of
pseudo-scientific knowledge. But precisely because this time is past,
modern man is offered the possibility of recognizing the *truth* of mythical
speech,[56] and realizing its irreplaceable character.[57]

According to Paul Ricoeur, we are the *first* people in the history of
civilization who are able to realize the truth of the mythical dimension.[58]
He seems to suggest with this that, before our modern time, the myth
was always misunderstood because an etiological function was assigned
to it. While there is no need to deny that such a function was ascribed
to it, it does not follow that for the non-modern man the myth had *exclusively* an etiological role. *One* inauthentic moment in the understanding
of the myth does not eliminate *all* authenticity. If the religious man uses
"flat descriptive" language and is insensitive to the objections raised
against his "flat descriptions", this insensitivity *can* hide a moment of
authentic understanding.

Obviously, this does not imply that authentic understanding is *per se*
present. It can also happen that resistance to the task of demythologization is a form of fanaticism and arises from the refusal to give up a
kind of truth and certainty to which no man is entitled. The religious man
calls the name "God" and thereby gives voice to the "depth" of this
existence. But he may not *replace* this calling by "flat descriptions",
in which God is made the subject of a judgment and a predicate is added
to this subject. Not every *seemingly* "flat description", however, is

---

[54] "What does this negative and artificial term mean? It must be accepted and
supported if it points to the necessity of recognizing a symbol as a symbol and a myth
as a myth. It must be attacked and rejected if it means the removal of symbols and
myths altogether". P. Tillich, *Dynamics of Faith*, p. 50.

[55] P. Ricoeur, *Finitude et Culpabilité*, II, La symbolique du mal, p. 154.

[56] "Ce qui est perdu c'est le pseudo-savoir, le faux logos du mythe, tel qu'il s'ex-
prime par exemple dans la fonction étiologique du mythe. Mais perdre le mythe comme
logos immédiat, c'est le retrouver comme mythos". P. Ricoeur, *o.c.*, p. 154.

[57] "There is no substitute for the use of symbols and myths : they are the language
of faith". P. Tillich, *Dynamics of Faith*, p. 51.

[58] P. Ricoeur, *o.c.*, p. 154.

really a "flat description". Mythical language *seemingly* has the form of the "flat description". But this semblance deceives only one who fails to recognize the meaning of symbolic language. Usually such a person will reject religious language, but if he does not do this and conceives religious language as "flatly descriptive", then this language loses its religious dimension. The holy is then lowered to the domain of the profane, the "second dimension" of existence is reduced to the first, religiousness degenerates into an absolutistic ideology, and an idol is adored instead of God.

This kind of fanaticism can only be prevented by letting the myth function as a "broken myth", i.e., a myth which is understood as a myth.[59] This expression has been introduced by Paul Tillich, but I do not consider it very felicitous because it insinuates that the "unbroken myth" cannot function properly, except for those who have entered the historical phase of demythologization. This idea is objectionable to me for the same reason for which above I objected to the the view that we are the first people in the history of civilization who can recognize the truth of the mythical dimension.

"Object Language and More" : *Ian T. Ramsey*

The preceding hermeneutical study of symbols and myths is an attempt to satisfy, at least partly, the demand made at the beginning of this chapter. The religious man, I said there, must show that his speaking "is about something"; he must justify the specific "truth of the religious language game" and thus "point to" a specific "reality". Such an attempt is made in the contemporary hermeneutics of symbols and myths, but not only there. In the philosophy of linguistic analysis also there exists now a reflection which leads to results that are very similar to those of existential thinking. To show this, I shall begin with the ideas of Evans.

The presuppositions of logical atomism and the ways in which logical positivism handled the principle of verification made all religious propositions pseudo-statements. But this situation changed when Wittgenstein launched his theory of the "language games". The *fact* that a language game is played, is enough to make it the object of an investigation, for the meaning of words and sentences is determined by their *use* in a specific context and in all kinds of special circumstances. From the

---

[59] "A myth which is understood as a myth, but not removed or replaced, can be called a 'broken myth'." P. Tillich, *Dynamics of Faith*, p. 50.

standpoint of this use principle, it is not possible to reject the religious use of language.

A question, however, arises here which could shake the importance of the entire analytical philosophy *as philosophy* down to its very foundation. It is obvious that, on the basis of the use principle of analytical philosophy, religious language can no longer be rejected. But the question is whether such a rejection is now *altogether impossible* by the simple fact that it cannot be based on the use principle. If a certain language game is *de facto* played, the logic of such a language can be analyzed. But if I play the religious language game, does this *de facto* use *per se* imply that it is *impossible* for anyone to tell me : "Do not indulge in such nonsense"! to indicate that my speaking "is about nothing"? The objector knows that I have read Austin and Evans, that I do not intend to give "flat descriptions" of God; he knows that I interpret my speaking as performative, self-involving and expressive, that I conceive it as adoration, blessing and thanking, and that I wish to give expression to an attitude and a way of acting by which I intend to commit myself to God. He knows all this. Nevertheless, does this make it logically impossible to say : "Do not indulge in this nonsense, for your language speaks about nothing"?

There are analysts who say that this is indeed impossible. No one, they hold, can meaningfully say that there is no God because "God", in the Judeo-Christian language use, means "necessarily existing being".[60] Evans relates that he has "occasionally encountered" this view and explicitly ascribes it to Norman Malcolm.[61] Any attempt to justify or reject a language game in its totality from a standpoint outside that game would thus be a logical error.[62] For if people *de facto* speak in a particular way, their words have a "use and hence a meaning"; thus there is no further

---

[60] "I have occasionally encountered it in philosophical discussion with followers of Wittgenstein, and Malcolm's article does exemplify it to some extent". Donald D. Evans, *The Logic of Self-Involvement,* A philosophical study of everyday language with special reference to the Christian use of language about God as Creator, London, 1963, p. 23, footnote 4.

[61] "The only effect (Anselm's ontological argument) could have on the fool of the Psalm would be that he stopped saying in his heart 'There is no God', because he would now realize that this is something he cannot meaningfully say or think". Norman Malcolm, *Anselm's ontological arguments*, in : The Philosophical Review 69 (1960), p. 61.

[62] "A language-game is neither open to any attack from outside itself, nor dependent on any justification from outside itself". Donald D. Evans, *o.c.*, p. 22.

question as to whether anything real or existing is referred to in the language game as a whole.[63]

Evans rejects this view, which he puts on a par with Karl Barth's conception of God's word. According to Barth, God's word is decisive for man's knowledge of God because this knowledge is based on God's word. That is why this knowledge of God cannot possibly put itself into question or allow that it be put into question from any standpoint outside God's word.[64] There simply is no standpoint from which someone or something can compete with God's word as the foundation of man's knowledge of God.[65] There exists, indeed, a striking similarity between Malcolm and Barth in this matter.[66]

In my opinion analytical philosophy has reached a point in its development where its limitations as a *philosophy* can no longer remain hidden. Logical atomism and logical positivism still were metaphysical ways of thinking because, at least implicitly, they contained a certain conception about "reality" and "truth" *as such*. But through the works of the later Wittgenstein the analysis of "ordinary language" became the focus of attention, every *de facto* used language game was accepted as an object of logical analysis, but the question whether a particular language game was worth playing fell into the background. The crucial issue, however, is whether this question can really stay in the background. Is it really impossible to say to someone who plays the religious language game : "Stop that nonsense!"? Certainly not. But in defense against such an order one cannot be satisfied with saying that one's speaking is performative, self-involving and expressive and therefore has a logic of its own. He will have to *justify* the *use* of his language by showing that it is "about something", and this brings back the question about "reality" and "truth".[67] Now, the attempt to answer this question is entirely different

---

[63] "... There is accordingly no further question as to whether anything real or existing is referred to in the language-game as a whole". Donald D. Evans, *o.c.*, p. 22.

[64] "Aber eben darum kann Erkenntnis Gottes sich selbst nicht in Frage stellen, kann sie, will sie sich selbst verstehen, nicht von einem Ort ausserhalb ihrer selbst her fragen : ob sie wirklich sei?" Karl Barth, *Die Kirchliche Dogmatik*, Zürich, 1948, II-1, p. 2.

"Es gibt keinen solchen andern Ort, von dem aus jemand oder etwas mit dem die Erkenntnis Gottes begründenden Worte Gottes konkurrieren könnte". Karl Barth, *o.c.*, p. 2.

[66] Donald D. Evans, *o.c.*, pp. 22-23.

[67] "But the fact that a word has a meaning does not guarantee that it refers to anything; and the fact that a word has a use does not justify the use". Donald D. Evans, *o.c.*, p. 24.

from analyzing the logic of the religious language game; it is metaphysics.

The question of "reality" and "truth", I may add, does not arise only in connection with the justification of the religious language game. If in a particular situation or in encountering someone, I get angry and shout, "damn!" no one can say that my utterance is untrue. But it is possible for someone to show that my choice of language is not justified—for example, by indicating that I was wholly mistaken in my appreciation of the situation, that the meaning of certain words in the encounter escaped me or was entirely misunderstood by me. Showing me the "reality" and "truth" of the situation or the encounter in the form of a cognitive-descriptive language game, then makes me realize that my language game was unjustified in the actual situation. My cursing was "about nothing", for on closer inspection, it turned out that I stood in the un-reality and the untruth of the situation or the encounter which gave rise to my curses. I then apologize for my language game on the basis of the investigation of the "reality" and the "truth". Such an investigation is entirely different from an analysis of the logic of cursing.

Evans is very much aware of the above-mentioned distinction with respect to the use of religious language.[68] Questions about the "reality" and the "truth" of religious language cannot be replaced by questions concerning its brand of logic.[69] Evans makes the logical questions the topic of his book because their study appears most necessary to him and he carefully avoids apologetic issues.[70] But he realizes that these isues still remain to be considered.

Ian T. Ramsey, on the other hand, so it appears to me, makes an attempt to raise both types of issues. He is not satisfied with the observation that religious language has a logic of its own and with an analysis of this logic, but tries to find the "empirical anchorage" of that language and asks himself "to what kind of situation" religious language appeals.[71] In

---

[68] "I reject the theological view that the existence of God and the possibility of knowing God are questions which need not and must not be raised once we have noted that the biblical 'language-game' is in fact played". Donald D. Evans, *o.c.*, pp. 23-24.

[69] "Questions of theological truth are not replaceable by questions concerning the internal logical 'grammar' of biblical language". Donald D. Evans, *o.c.*, p. 24.

[70] "I have avoided Christian apologetics". Donald D. Evans, *o.c.*, p. 24.

[71] "To what kind of situation does religion appeal? What kind of empirical anchorage have theological words?" Ian T. Ramsey, *Religious Language*, An Empirical Placing of Theological Phrases, London, 1957, p. 14.

other words, he wishes to show that the specific religious use of language, with its own peculiar logic, "is about something".

Ramsey calls these specific situations "disclosure situations". Disclosure situations are not *per se* religious. Generally speaking, they are situations whose observable reality can, in the first instance, be seized in "flat" descriptions accessible to anyone; for example, the situation of a court in session or of a first-aid station. They have no "depth". But it can happen that the judge suddenly realizes that the delinquent he is judging is a former school friend, or the surgeon who performs an emergency operation on a traffic victim can suddenly recognize his own wife in the victim.[72] In such a case the situation "discloses" a "depth" whose reality can no longer be grasped in "flat" descriptions accessible to all. The situation now comprises "observables and more than observables".[73] A disclosure situation can only be "described" with the aid of a language which is "object language and more" and which exhibits a logic of its own, different from that of "flat" descriptions.[74] "Flat" descriptions cannot evoke the specific "discernment" contained in a disclosure situation.

According to Ramsey, religious language also is such a more-than-descriptive language. It is rooted in that "odd kind of a situation" in which the religious man discerns an "odd depth". Thus this language can only be understood when this depth is evoked.[75] If this does not happen or does not succeed, then the religious language is misunderstood.

A disclosure can be evoked only through the use of appropriate models. A model is a "situation with which we are familiar and which can be used for reaching another situation with which we are not familiar".[76] For example, if the religious man wishes to indicate what he means by

[72] See : W. de Pater, *Taalanalytische perspectieven op godsdienst en kunst*, Antwerpen, 1970, pp. 15-55; R. Veldhuis, *Ian T. Ramsey's analyse van de religieuze taal*, in : Kerk en Theologie, 18 (1967), pp. 135-151.

[73] Ian T. Ramsey, *Freedom and Immortality*, London, 1960, p. 152.

[74] "... its language will be object language and more, i.e. object language which has been given very special qualifications, object language, which exhibits logical peculiarities, logical impropriety". Ian T. Ramsey, *Religious Language*, p. 38.

[75] "We can note that to understand religious language or theology we must first evoke the odd kind of situation to which I have given various parallels above. This is plainly a *conditio sine qua non* for any religious apologetic". Ian T. Ramsey, *o.c.*, p. 47.

[76] "Now, what is a 'model' in this context? It is a situation with which we are all familiar, and which can be used for reaching another situation with which we are not familiar". Ian T. Ramsey, *o.c.*, p. 61.

the statement, "God is all-powerful", he uses "powerful" as a model because it places him in a familiar situation, even in many familiar situations. The model "powerful" makes us think of the "power" of an army. But an able pen is mightier, more "powerful" than the army. And the able pen of one who lives by his conviction is "more powerful" again than that of one whose deeds undermine his words. Doing one's duty is "powerful" because of the good example it gives; yet love is more "powerful" again than merely doing one's duty. Which love? The story should continue, go on and on until it "begins to dawn" and a disclosure situation is reached in which the statement, "God is all-powerful", becomes meaningful.[77]

While "powerful" functions as a model, "all" acts as a qualifier. It is a directive which prescribes a special way of developing the model.[78] The development must continue until the situation comes alive and assumes depth, until "it rings a bell", "the ice breaks", "the penny drops".[79] The qualifier also warns us not to forget the odd logic of religious language once the disclosure situation has been reached.[80] It reminds us that the language is no longer a "flat" description. The religious use of language is *never* "flat"-descriptive. The statement, "God is up there", does not mean something like "Peter is up there" (on the 88th floor). And the statement, "God is infinite", should not be understood in the same way as the statement, "The leaf is green".[81] "God is my rock and my refuge" has an entirely different meaning than "Gibraltar is my rock and my refuge". Religious statements imply a minimum of "descriptive" meaning; thus they "say" little. A statement such as "the cat sits on the mat" says a lot.[82] That is why, as a "flat" description, it has no religious meaning.

The "odd" logic of religious language also prohibits us from asking questions based on the assumption that religious language is "flat" descriptive language. One cannot ask, "How does God influence history"?

[77] W. de Pater, *o.c.*, p. 27.

[78] "It is a directive which prescribes a special way of developing those 'model' situations". Ian T. Ramsey, *o.c.*, p. 62.

[79] Ian T. Ramsey, *o.c.*, pp. 19, 49, 90.

[80] "We must expect religious language to be appropriately odd and to have a distinctive logical behaviour". Ian T. Ramsey, *o.c.*, p. 49.

[81] Ian T. Ramsey, *Christian Discourse*, Some logical explorations, London, 1965, pp. 79-80.

[82] "Qualifier-sentences being, as I have suggested, slogans or mnemonics 'say' virtually nothing in the sense in which 'The cat is on the mat' 'says' a very great deal". Ian T. Ramsey, *o.c.*, p. 80.

if this question is understood on a par with the question, "How does the sea act on the dike"? Speaking "about" God is possible only when one uses a descriptive form of speech—no matter what kind it is—in such a way that it evokes a disclosure and thus tells more than the descriptive story.[83] Similarly, the conclusions from the "proofs" for God's existence must not be conceived as "flat" descriptions of God's essence;[84] they are merely "techniques to evoke disclosures".[85]

Ramsey, I think, has done more than what the "philosophers of ordinary language" were accustomed to do. He has gone beyond the investigation of the logic implied in the *de facto* used religious language game. He has tried to anchor this language game in empirical situations and to show that this language game is worth playing because "it is about something".

Let us dwell a little on this expression : "it is about something". Ramsey realizes, of course, that there is no guarantee for the success of the attempt to evoke disclosure situations and thereby showing that religious language "is about something". This matter is quite obvious to him. One who thinks that he can guarantee the success of such an attempt must assume that he has power over God and that the initiative of the disclosure or revelation lies with him and not with God. Such a person is guilty of "semantic magic".[86]

On the other hand, Ramsey emphasizes that the discernment arising from a disclosure situation is not something *purely* subjective. While it may be true that the coming about of disclosures and the birth of discernment rooted in them can never be guaranteed, nevertheless, Ramsey is convinced that, once discernment has arisen, it implies an "objective reference" and that disclosure situations have a subject-object structure.[87] Expressed in phenomenological terms, the birth of discern-

---

[83] Ian T. Ramsey, *On the possibility and purpose of a metaphysical theology*, in : Prospects for Metaphysics, Essays of Metaphysical Exploration, ed. by Ian Ramsey, London, 1961, p. 173.

[84] "All I need remark now is that talk about God is certainly *never* apt, if it is in terms of plain descriptions alone". Ian T. Ramsey, *o.c.*, p. 173.

[85] Ian T. Ramsey, *o.c.*, p. 172.

[86] Ian T. Ramsey, *Religious Language*, p. 79.

[87] "Let us emphasize, without any possibility of misunderstanding, that all these situations, all these characteristically different situations, when they occur, have an *objective* reference and are, as all situations, subject-object in structure". Ian T. Ramsey, *o.c.*, p. 28; Ian T. Ramsey, *Talking about God : Models, ancient and modern*, in : Myth and Symbol, pp. 86-92.

ment in religious situations means for Ramsey a certain "event", viz., the "coming about" of existence [88] in an entirely new dimension, one which can no longer be seized in terms of a "flat" descriptive language game. Ramsey comes here very close to Bultmann, for whom thinking about man is not exhausted by the "objectifying" approach of the sciences of nature and of history. There is also another kind of thinking, mythical thinking, which intends "to speak of the proper reality of man", his "understanding of existence".[89] Myths speak about man as existence,[90] and are misunderstood if they are conceived as "flat" descriptions.

Thus the evolutions within analytical philosophy turn out to be very striking. This form of philosophy has turned away from Russell, the early Wittgenstein, Moritz Schlick, Carnap and Ayer—to limit ourselves to a few representatives of logical atomism and logical positivism. Ramsey turns out to be very close to the existence theology of Bultmann. For both, "speaking 'about" God" is "speaking about man".[91] And for neither does this imply subjectivism.[92]

Nevertheless, there remains an urgent question. Let us grant that myths do not speak in an "objectifying" way but give expression to man as existence; let us grant that the religious use of language is evocative and intended to call forth the specific "depth" of a religious disclosure;[93] and let us also grant that the term "objective reference" is applicable to such an existential situation. But even then it remains true that myths can go awry and that the evocative use of language can be deceptive. There is no guarantee that the mythical and evocative use of language will not cause illusions and hallucinations.[94] The mythical and evocative use of language *can* suggest a "depth" that does not exist, it *can* recommend a path that leads nowhere, it *can* point to a future that is not really

---

[88] "When situations 'come alive', or the 'ice breaks', there is an objective 'depth' in these situations along with and alongside any subjective changes". Ian T. Ramsey, *Religious Language*, p. 28.

[89] R. Bultmann, in : Kerygma und Mythos, VI-1, pp. 24-25.

[90] "Der Mythos will nicht kosmologisch, sondern anthropologisch — besser : existential interpretiert werden". R. Bultmann, in : Kerygma und Mythos, I, p. 22.

[91] Ian T. Ramsey, *On the possibility and purpose of a metaphysical theology*, pp. 174-177; R. Bultmann, *Glauben und Verstehen*, II, Tübingen, 1961³, p. 86.

[92] Ian T. Ramsey, *Religious Language*, p. 27; R. Bultmann, *Glauben und Verstehen*, II, Tübingen, 1961³, pp. 233-234.

[93] "The language we use about God will always have to be so constructed that it is potentially generative of, evocative of, a disclosure". Ian T. Ramsey, *o.c.*, p. 174.

[94] F. Ferré, *Language, Logic and God*, pp. 139-143.

accessible. This means that the question about the "reality" and "truth" of the religious use of language returns here again, and this brings back the issue of a "critical resort".

In the past, metaphysics with its much-disputed "proofs" of God's existence used to function as the "critical resort" with respect to religious speech. In my opinion, metaphysics still has to fill this function. I will explain this later after first discussing a difficulty that can be made in connection with what we have seen thus far.

3. SPEAKING "ABOUT" GOD IS SPEAKING ABOUT MAN

Barth Versus Bultmann

Saying that the religious man gives voice to the "depth" of his existence when he calls the name "God", and saying that this is also the case when he makes the name "God" the subject of a judgment makes it possible to understand the statement that speaking "about" God is speaking about man.[95] Frequently, however, this induces people to draw the conclusion that God, therefore, is "really nothing", i.e., "nothing objective" but, at most, "something subjective". This is approximately the terminology in which Karl Barth formulated his main objection to Bultmann's view. Barth says :

The entire body of the statements of the Christian creed ... refers to human existence. They make possible, and give a foundation to a Christian understanding of this existence, and thus they become—indirectly—also determinations of human existence. But this is not what they are fundamentally. Fundamentally they determine the being and acting of a God who is *different* from man and who *comes to the encounter* of man : The Father, the Son and the Holy Spirit. This alone is enough to make it impossible to reduce those statements to sentences about man's inner life.[96]

Bultmann himself quotes this passage to show that he cannot really have a dialogue with Barth as long as the latter holds that existential thinkers speak about "man's inner life" when they talk about man as existence. Barth's last sentence, he says :

[95] "Das Wissen um Gott ist zunächst ein Wissen des Menschen um sich selbst". R. Bultmann, *Glauben und Verstehen*, II, Tübingen, 1968[5], p. 86; *Jesus Christ and Mythology*, London, 1966[4], p. 53; Schubert M. Ogden, *Christ without Myth*, A study based on the theology of Rudolf Bultmann, London, 1962, p. 137.

[96] K. Barth, *Die Kirchliche Dogmatik*. Zürich, 1948, II-2, p. 534.

... betrays a complete misunderstanding of what existential interpretation is and what the meaning of existence is which this interpretation has in mind. It does not at all refer to the "inner life of man" which, divorced from what differs from it and is encountered by it (whether the world, fellowman or God) can be seized, let us say, by a religious-psychological consideration, but certainly not by an existential consideration. For the latter wants to seize and understand the real (historical) existence of man, and this man exists only in the interconnection of his life with what is "different" from him; he exists only in encounters.[97]

The statement, "speaking 'about' God is speaking about man" was also used by Feuerbach and Carl Jung, but they attached a different meaning to it than the one given to it by thinkers who conceive man as "existence". For those who call man "existence", "something" is not "something" because it is *either* "something objective" *or* "something subjective", in the tacit supposition that the "subjective" is divorced from the "objective". One who calls man "existence" affirms the subject who man is, but as permeated with that which is not the subject himself. Calling man "existence" affirms the reciprocal implication of the "subjective" and the "objective".[98] This is not what Feuerbach and Jung had in mind. I should like to discuss this here briefly, one of the reasons being that it shows how the denial of objectivism leads to the danger of falling into subjectivism, and vise versa.

Feuerbach

For Ludwig Feuerbach, speaking about God is speaking about man. The essence of man consists in knowing, willing and loving. Man knows in order to know, wills in order to will, and loves in order to love. Now, that which is for its own sake is essentially divine.[99] The unity of reason, will and love is the divine Trinity in man,[100] and man cannot be con-

---

[97] R. Bultmann, *Glauben und Verstehen*, II, Tübingen, 1968[5], pp. 233-234.

[98] This model is totally unknown to Paul van Buren. That's why he cannot understand Bultmann and Ogden. "If in the language of faith a statement about God is really a statement about man, if what faith speaks of is, 'exhaustively and without remainder', man and his selfunderstanding, then to say that this is equally language about 'God and his activities' is to assert that the same words refer to man, where they are verifiable, and to God, where they are not". Paul van Buren, *The Secular Meaning of the Gospel*, p. 67.

[99] L. Feuerbach, *Das Wesen des Christentums*, Sämtliche Werke, neu herausgegeben von Wilhelm Bolin und Friedrich Jodl, Stuttgart, 1903, pp. 3-4.

[100] "Die göttliche Dreieinigkeit im Menschen ... ist die Einheit von Vernunft, Liebe, Wille". L. Feuerbach, *o.c.*, p. 3.

scious of the Trinity without experiencing infinite joy over it.[101]

According to Feuerbach, man does not realize at once that his consciousness of God is his own self-consciousness. That's why it is better to say that religious consciousness is the *first* consciousness of man. For man projects his own essence outside himself before he finds it in himself. He begins by making his own essence an object which he views as a different being.[102] Thus religious consciousness is man's childish consciousness, for, in the eyes of a child, the man who the child itself is, is like another man.[103] That is why the history of religions consists in this that things which in an earlier religion were held to be objective are viewed as something subjective in a later religion. What was first adored as God is later recognized as something human. In this way every forward step of religion is a forward step in man's self-knowledge. But every religion which views its elder sisters as idolatrous makes an exception for itself with respect to the common essence of religion. Having a different object, a different content, one loftier than that of earlier religions, it lives in the illusion that its content is something superhuman. The philosopher, however, studies the essence of religion which is hidden from religion itself; for him, religion itself is the object, which it never is for religion itself.[104]

There is no sense whatsoever, says Feuerbach, in distinguishing between God-in-himself and God-for-me. Man cannot determine whether God-in-himself is different from what he is-for-me.[105] The distinction between an object-in-itself and an object-for-me can only be made if the object *can* really appear to me different from the way it does appear, but not if an object appears to me as it *has to* appear to me. Now, God has to appear to me as a human being or as a being resembling man. Every religion views the gods of other religions as mere representations of God but values its own conception as representing God as he is in himself. It is evident, however, says Feuerbach, that what is for man

---

[101] L. Feuerbach, *o.c.*, p. 7.

[102] "Der Mensch verlegt sein Wesen zuerst ausser sich, ehe er es in sich findet. Das eigene Wesen ist ihm zuerst als ein anderes Wesen Gegenstand." L. Feuerbach, *o.c.*, p. 16.

[103] L. Feuerbach, *o.c.*, pp. 16-17.

[104] L. Feuerbach, *o.c.*, p. 17.

[105] "Ich kann gar nicht wissen, ob Gott etwas anderes an sich oder für sich ist, als er für mich ist; wie er für mich ist, so ist er alles für mich. Für mich liegt eben in diesen Bestimmungen, unter welchen er für mich ist, sein Ansichselbstsein, sein Wesen selbst; er ist für mich so, wie er für mich nur immer sein kann". L. Feuerbach, *o.c.*, pp. 19-20.

the highest being is also for him the divine being. With respect to such a being, how could he then still ask what this is "in itself"? If God were the object of a bird, he would be for the bird a winged being, for a bird knows nothing loftier and more blessed than being-winged. It would be ridiculous for the bird to say : "God appears to me as a bird, but I do not know what he is in himself".[106] It is ridiculous because God cannot possibly appear otherwise to a bird than as a bird. Man believes in love as a divine quality because he himself has love; he calls God wise and good because he knows nothing better than wisdom and goodness— just as the bird knows nothing better than being-winged. Accordingly, religious consciousness is nothing but man's consciousness of the best of himself.[107]

Feuerbach's critics have answered him by pointing out that according to his view God is "really nothing", i.e., nothing "objective", but at most something "subjective". This was indeed what Feuerbach had wanted to say and this is why his opponents called him an atheist.

Carl Jung

With respect to Jung, matters are fundamentally the same although the accent is somewhat different. Jung also holds that speaking "about" God is speaking about man.[108] It is a speaking about the human psyche, the collective unconscious, archetypes, that which is psychically most powerful.[109] Jung emphasizes the "relativity of God", by which he means that God never exists "absolutely" and "divorced" from human subjectivity and human conditions. In a certain sense God is dependent on the human subject. There exists a mutual relationship between man and God, so that, on the one hand, man can be conceived as a function of God and, on the other, God as a psychical function of man.[110] The

---

[106] L. Feuerbach, o.c., p. 21.

[107] "Im Wesen und Bewusstsein der Religion ist nichts anderes, als was überhaupt im Wesen und im Bewusstsein des Menschen von sich und von der Welt liegt". L. Feuerbach, o.c., p. 27.

[108] "Die Entdeckung und ausführliche Formulierung der Relativität Gottes zum Menschen und seiner Seele scheint mir einer der wichtigsten Schritte auf dem Wege zu einer psychologischen Erfassung des religiösen Phänomens zu sein". C.G. Jung, Psychologische Typen, Zürich, 1921, p. 340.

[109] C.G. Jung, o.c., pp. 337-362; Psychologie und Religion, in : Zur Psychologie westlicher und östlicher Religion, Gesammelte Werke, Band 11, Zürich-Stuttgart, 1963, p. 64; Psychologie und Alchemie, Zürich, 1952², pp. 13-62; Symbolik des Geistes, Zürich, 1953, p. 394; Das Geheimnis der goldenen Blüte, Zürich, 1948, p. 58.

[110] "Unter Relativität Gottes verstehe ich eine Ansicht, nach der Gott nicht 'abso-

idea of God is the symbolic expression of a psychical condition or function which is characterized by the fact that in this condition conscious willing is totally overpowered, and this leads to deeds and accomplishments beyond the power of conscious efforts.[111] This overpowering impulse or inspiration originates in an accumulation of energy in the unconscious. It gives rise to symbols, which the collective unconscious contains as hidden possibilities.

In the orthodox view God is "absolute", i.e., "existing for himself.[112] This view expresses a total separation between God and the unconscious. Psychologically speaking, this means that one is unconscious of the fact that the divine power originates in one's own self.[113] Those who lack this consciousness project God outside themselves.

According to Jung, primitive religions[114] and Catholic Christianity as a matter of fact do make such a projection.[115] They externalize that which is really an internal process. Such an externalization, however, must not be rejected without any further ado. The experience of the numinous, which overpoweringly arises from the unconscious, is the experience of the "awe-inspiring" (*tremendum*) and "fascinating" (*fascinosum*), and this can be too much for the individual psyche.[116] The individual psyche will then endeavor to defend and shield itself against individual religious experience. It can effectively do so by adhering to a religion in general and Catholic Christianity in particular. Religious

---

lut', d.h. losgelöst vom menschlichen Subject und jenseits aller menschlichen Bedingungen existiert, sondern nach der er vom menschlichen Subjekt in gewissem Sinne abhängig, und eine wechselseitige und unerlässliche Beziehung zwischen Mensch und Gott vorhanden ist, so dass man einerseits den Menschen als eine Funktion Gottes und andererseits Gott als eine psychologische Funktion des Menschen verstehen kann". C.G. Jung, *Psychologische Typen*, p. 340.

[111] C.G. Jung, *Psychologie und Religion*, Gesammelte Werke, Band 11, p. 88.

[112] C.G. Jung, *Psychologische Typen*, p. 341.

[113] C.G. Jung, *o.c.*, pp. 340-341.

[114] "Geister und Zauberei sind die Ursachen der Krankheiten beim Primitiven. Die autonomen Inhalte haben sich bei ihm in diese übernatürlichen Figuren projeziert". C.G. Jung, *Seelenprobleme der Gegenwart*, Zürich, 1946, p. 316.

[115] "Diese gewaltige Projektion erlaubt dem Katholiken, ein beträchtliches Stück seines kollektiven Unbewussten in tastbarer Wirklichkeit zu erleben". C.G. Jung, *o.c.*, p. 172.

[116] "Der Ersatz hat den offensichtlichen Zweck, *unmittelbare Erfahrung* zu ersetzen durch eine Auswahl passender Symbole, die in ein fest organisiertes Dogma und Ritual eingekleidet sind". C.G. Jung, *Psychologie und Religion*, Gesammelte Werke, Band 11, p. 46.

experience is dogmatically and ritually channeled there, and this gives a feeling of certainty, security and tranquillity. The dogma is like a dream which mirrors the spontaneous and autonomous activities of the objective psyche, the unconscious. As objectified expressions of the unconscious, dogma and ritual offer a certain protection against the "awe-inspiring" and "fascinating" of the individual religious experience. The dogmatic expression, moreover, is much more effective than a scientific theory.[117] The scientific theory neglects the affective aspect of experience, while this aspect precisely finds expression in the dogma. Thus scientific theories become much more quickly antiquated than dogmas. The idea of the suffering God-man may well be five thousand years old, and that of the Trinity is probably even older.[118]

Although Jung shows appreciation for "confessions"—primitive religions and Catholic Christianity—he thinks that religious experience occurs in them only in a very impoverished form. For the "confessions" give religious experience the form of a projection. They transfer the content of the religious experience from "within" to "without". God, the Trinity, Christ, Mary, angels, devils, sin, redemption and salvation are put down as "metaphysical entities", divorced and isolated from man. In this way the authentic religious experience is reduced to "faith", i.e., to a certain holding to be true. This faith blocks the road to self-consciousness, self-understanding and autonomy demanded by the modern mind. Modern consciousness abhors faith,[119] it wants to know, i.e., to experience.[120]

According to Jung, it is especially in Christianity—and particularly in Catholicism—that the original religious experience of the archetypes has shrivelled up through the overpowering influence of dogma and ritual. This impoverishment is a kind of stagnation and regression of the archetypical unconscious.[121] Because the Christian located his

---

[117] "Das Dogma ist wie ein Traum, der die spontane und autonome Tätigkeit der objektiven Psyche, des Unbewussten, spiegelt. Solch ein Ausdruck des Unbewussten ist ein sehr viel wirksameres Schutzmittel gegen weitere unmittelbare Erfahrungen als eine wissenschaftliche Theorie". C.G. Jung, o.c., p. 49.

[118] C.G. Jung, o.c., pp. 49-50.

[119] "Das moderne Bewusstsein perhorresziert den Glauben". C.G. Jung, Seelen-probleme der Gegenwart, p. 417.

[120] C.G. Jung, o.c., p. 417.

[121] "Eine ausschliesslich religiöse Projektion kann die Seele ihrer Werte berauben, so dass sie sich infolge der Inanition nicht mehr weiter zu entwickeln vermag und in einem unbewussten Zustand stecken bleibt". C.G. Jung, Psychologie und Alchemie, p. 22.

God wholly "outside" himself, his interiority remained untouched and undeveloped. It could even happen that he would in the unconscious revert to earlier phases of development, so that he would "officially" be a Christian but psychically a pagan.[122] Official Christianity, Jung thinks, is really a failure. It has not succeeded in Christianizing the soul in such a way that Christian ethics have exercised a real influence on "Christian" Europe. Christian missionaries preach the gospel to poor naked heathens, but the "inner" Christians populating Europe have not yet understood anything at all of Christianity. Christianity would have to start all over again. As long as religiousness is nothing but "faith" and ritual and does not become the soul's own experience, nothing has really happened as yet. One who does not understand this may be a very learned theologian, but he lacks the most elementary notions of authentic religiousness and education.[123]

Only psychology, Jung holds, can offer a way out of the impasse. Psychology can reactivate the archetypical unconscious, the original religious function of the soul. It can make modern man "see". Theologians devote all their intelligence to the endeavor of proving the existence of the "light", but they ought to realize that there are "blind" men who don't know that their eyes can "see" something.[124] To "see" means to realize that the outwardly projected images are symbols of the soul's unconscious life. Psychology can restore to dogma and ritual their original meaning. What dogmas express and what rituals celebrate is the archetypical unconscious of the human soul.[125]

Is Jung Agnostic?

From the preceding pages it should be clear that Jung conceives religious experience exclusively as the experience of the "interior God". He does not wish anyone to make the mistake of interpreting his psychological considerations as a kind of proof for God's existence. All they prove is that there exists an archetypical image of the divinity.[126] The

---

[122] C.G. Jung, o.c., p. 24.

[123] C.G. Jung, o.c., p. 25.

[124] "… dass es Blinde gibt, die nicht wissen dass ihre Augen etwas sehen könnten". C.G. Jung, o.c., p. 26.

[125] "Die Archetypen des Unbewussten sind empirisch nachweisbare Entsprechungen der religiösen Dogmen". C.G. Jung, o.c., p. 32.

[126] "Es wäre ein bedauerlicher Irrtum, wenn jemand meine Beobachtungen als eine Art Beweis für die Existenz Gottes auffassen wollte. Sie beweisen nur das Vorhandensein eines archetypischen Bildes der Gottheit". C.G. Jung, Psychologie und Religion, Gesammelte Werke, Band 11, p. 64.

experience of this image has a numinous character; that is why it is a religious experience.

Critics have argued that for Jung, too, God is "really nothing", i.e., nothing "objective", but at most something "subjective". Jung's answer was that no one should be surprised by this since he wished to speak about "God" solely as a psychologist. Such a standpoint implies methodological limitations; any pursuer of any empirical science whatsoever has to accept such limitations and he need not apologize for them.[127] The psychologist of religion speaks exclusively about psychical facts and regularities, which he describes just as the mineralogist and the botanist describe their own objects.[128] In other words, the psychologist of religion does not intend to enter the realm of the theologian. Even if the language used by the psychologist and the theologian seems the same, what they speak about is different. When the theologian speaks about God, he refers to the "metaphysical Absolute Being",[129] but when the psychologist uses the same term, he is concerned with the archetypical unconscious.

Jung bitterly complains that his critics appear unable to make the necessary methodological distinctions. When he speaks about God as archetypical image—"and this is all we can say about God from a psychological standpoint"[130]—when he calls gods personifications of unconscious psychical contents,[131] his critics imagine that he is trying to replace theology by psychology or reduce it to this.[132] Jung objects to philosophers and theologians who view his empirical-psychological concepts, hypotheses and models as attempts to make metaphysical statements. He reminds philosophers and theologians that he is not at all ignorant of the fact that, philosophically speaking, his empirical concepts

---

[127] "Ich muss mich damit begnügen, den Standpunkt, den Glauben, das Streben, die Hoffnung und die Liebe des Empirikers, die allesamt in der Auffindung und Feststellung beweisbarer Tatsachen und deren hypothetischer Erklärung gipfeln, zu schildern und verweise für den theologischen Standpunkt auf ...." C.G. Jung, Vorwort zu V. White : *Gott und das Unbewusste*, in : Gesammelte Werke, Band 11, p. 332.

[128] C.G. Jung, *o.c.*, p. 331.

[129] C.G. Jung, *o.c.*, p. 331.

[130] C.G. Jung, *Psychologie und Religion*, Gesammelte Werke, Band II, p. 64.

[131] C.G. Jung, *Symbolik des Geistes*, p. 394.

[132] "Ich begegne immer wieder dem Missverständnis, dass die psychologische Behandlung oder Erklärung Gott auf nichts als Psychologie reduziere. Es handelt sich aber gar nicht um Gott, sondern um Vorstellungen von Gott, wie ich immer betont habe". C.G. Jung, *o.c.*, p. 394, footnote 16.

are logical monstrosities. "As a philosopher, I would be a sorry figure".[133] But he does not wish to be a philosopher. Neither does he wish to be called a heretic, for heretics make theological statements. If anyone has to be called a heretic, says Jung, it will have to be my patients.

Accordingly, Jung intends to speak only about the psyche and objects if his opponents conclude from this that God is for him *"merely* something psychical". This "merely" is too much. Although the psychologist cannot make metaphysical statements without going beyond the boundaries of his competence,[134] this does not give anyone the right, he holds, to add a qualifying "merely" to what the psychologist can talk about.[135] One who does this anyhow shows that he underrates the psychical or the soul. This is a typical Western deviation.[136] The soul should be spoken about with reverence because of its intrinsic dignity. But the soul has been "emptied", which the result that "every God is outside".[137] Everything the Christian believes in stands outside him in image and word, in the Church and the Bible, "but it does not stand within him".[138] Theologians, says Jung, should really be grateful to him because he shows that the soul is naturally religious; yet this is precisely why they accuse him of psychologism.[139] Jung argues that he would not be interested in psychology at all if he were not convinced that the supreme values lie in the soul in a way that can be experienced. But when he says this, he is accused of deifying the soul. His rebuttal is : "Not I but God himself has deified the soul".[140] Jung himself merely points to the facts which prove that the soul is "naturally religious". He is convinced that he does not thereby do an injustice to dogmas or destroy anything; on

---

[133] C.G. Jung, Vorwort zu C. White : *Gott und das Unbewusste*, in : Gesammelte Werke, Band 11, p. 334.

[134] "Psychologie als Wissenschaft von der Seele hat sich auf ihren Gegenstand zu beschränken und sich davor zu hüten, ihre Grenzen etwa durch metaphysiche Behauptungen oder sonstige Glaubensbekenntnisse zu überschreiten. Sollte sie einen Gott auch nur als hypothetische Ursache setzen, so hätte sie implizite die Möglichkeit eines Gottesbeweises gefordert, womit sie ihre Kompetenz in absolut unzulässiger Weise überschreiten würde". C.G. Jung, *Psychologie und Alchemie*, p. 28.

[135] C.G. Jung, *o.c.*, p. 21.

[136] C.G. Jung, *Das Geheimnis der goldenen Blüte*, p. 58.

[137] C.G. Jung, *Psychologie und Alchemie*, p. 21.

[138] C.G. Jung, *o.c.*, p. 24.

[139] "Wenn ich aber nachweise, dass die Seele natürlicherweise eine religiöse Funktion besitzt ... da fällt mir eben gerade die Theologie in den Arm und überführt mich des 'Psychologismus' ". C.G. Jung, *o.c.*, pp. 25-26.

[140] C.G. Jung, *o.c.*, p. 26.

the contrary, he shows that the dogmas are meaningful and provides new dwellers for an empty home.[141]

Is Jung's complaint about being misunderstood exclusively to be attributed to his critics's inability to make a simple methodological distinction? This does not seem to be the case. Jung did not merely say that he wished to speak about God exclusively as a psychologist, but he also asserted that psychological speaking was the *only* way to speak about God. He claimed that, since the development of consciousness demands the withdrawal of all projections, doctrine about God which defends the non-psychical existence of God is impossible,[142] and that only psychology still allows us to approach religious matters.[143] He asserted that anyone who intends to speak about a God "outside" man is naive because he fails to recognize that his idea of God has the character of a projection. From the time of his earliest works he assumed the standpoint of Kant and held that a God-in-himself can be neither affirmed nor denied.[144] He ridiculed those "metaphysicians" who "think that they have knowledge of unknowable matters of the world to come".[145] He explicitly stated that he mercilessly intended to do away with the metaphysical claims of all "mystery doctrines".[146] He proclaimed that in metaphysics nothing can be understood, but that what metaphysics talks about can be psychologically understood.[147] He called the aspirations of meta-

---

[141] "Die Psychologie verschafft Möglichkeiten zum besseren Verständnis des Vorhandenen, sie öffnet das Auge für die Sinnerfülltheit der Dogmen; sie zerstört eben gerade nicht, sondern bietet einem leeren Haus neue Bewohner". C.G. Jung, *o.c.*, p. 29.

[142] "Da nun die Entwicklung des Bewusstseins die Zurückziehung aller erreichbaren Projektionen verlangt, so kann auch keine Götterlehre im Sinne nicht-psychologischer Existenz aufrechterhalten werden". C.G. Jung, *Psychologie und Religion*, Gesammelte Werke, Band 11, p. 93.

[143] "Zum Verständnis der religiösen Dinge gibt es heute wohl nur noch den psychologischen Zugang". C.G. Jung, *o.c.*, p. 97.

[144] "Wir bewegen uns hier, was nicht zu vergessen ist, ganz im Gebiete der Psychologie, der bekanntlich keinerlei transzendente Bedeutung weder in positiver noch in negativer Beziehung zukommt. Es handelt sich hier um ein schonungsloses Wahrmachen des durch Kant fixierten erkenntnistheoretischen Standpunktes nicht bloss für die Theorie, sondern, was wichtiger ist, auch für die Praxis". C.G. Jung, *Wandlungen und Symbole der Libido*, Leipzig-Wien, 1912, pp. 224-225, footnote 3; *Das Geheimnis der goldenen Blüte*, p. 64.

[145] C.G. Jung, *Antwort an Martin Buber*, Gesammelte Werke, Band 11, p. 658.

[146] C.G. Jung, *Das Geheimnis der goldenen Blüte*, p. 56.

[147] "Metaphysisch ist nichts zu begreifen, wohl aber psychologisch". C.G. Jung, *o.c.*, p. 57.

physics arrogant, pretentious and ridiculous[148] because metaphysics is ignorant of our not-knowing. He defended the need for a new world-view and defined its newness as the victory over the superstition that this worldview has objective validity.[149] For all these reasons Jung's critics address to him the reproach that he merely *says* that he only wishes to pursue psychology while, as a matter of fact, he goes far beyond its limits.[150] This is why he is called an agnostic.[151]

Unavoidable Misunderstandings About Jung's Position[152]

According to R. Hostie, Jung abandoned his agnosticism after 1940.[153] As a psychologist, Jung continued to hold fast to his empirical-scientific attitude and to accept its methodological limitations, says Hostie, but he no longer defended the idea that this attitude was the only one in which one could speak "about" God. He had come to realize and accept the specific meaning and truth of metaphysical and theological speech and of the convictions of religion and faith.

It must be admitted that there are texts in Jung which seem to support Hostie's interpretation. When Jung speaks about the work of art, he emphasizes that psychology is unable to answer the question about the essence of the work of art. Psychology can speak about the inner and external causes accounting for the form of a certain work of art, but this does not say anything about its essence. Similarly, psychology can speak about the phenomenon of religion, but it does not even touch the question concerning the essence of religion.[154] A psychologist who thinks that he can speak about its essence digs his own grave as a psychol-

---

[148] C.G. Jung, *o.c.*, pp. 58, 64.

[149] "Wenn wir uns aber nicht rückwärts entwickeln wollen, so muss eine neue Weltanschauung jeden Aberglauben an ihrer objektiven Gültigkeit von sich abtun". C.G. Jung, *Seelenprobleme der Gegenwart*, pp. 331-332.

[150] "Was Jung zum Vorwurf zu machen ist, ist vielmehr, dass er in seiner Behandlung des Religiösen die Grenzen der Psychologie in den wesentlichsten Punkten mit souveräner Freiheit, aber zumeist ohne anzumerken oder gar zu begründen, dass er es tut, überschreitet". M. Buber, *Religion und modernes Denken*, in : Merkur VI (1952), pp. 110-111.

[151] J. Goldbrunner, *Individuation*, Krailling vor München, 1949, pp. 167-168.

[152] In finding my way through Jung's enormous writings for this question I owe much to Han M.M. Fortmann, *Als ziende de onzienlijke*, Hilversum-Antwerpen, 1964, I, pp. 240-266; IIIa, pp. 51-64; J. Goldbrunner, *o.c.*, R. Hostie, *Analytische psychologie en godsdienst*, Utrecht, 1954.

[153] R. Hostie, *o.c.*, pp. 148-169.

[154] C.G. Jung, *Seelenprobleme der Gegenwart*, pp. 40-41.

ogist. For, one who makes the philosophy of religion a part of psychology becomes defenseless when others make psychology a part of physiology. Such a procedure disregards the specific character of psychology.

All this indicates that, for Jung, there are, in principle, other questions than those of psychology. But if this is so, why does Jung so often abandon this principle and lay himself open to the accusation of psychologism and agnosticism?

In my opinion, Jung's critics demand too much of him. They want him to concede that, unlike psychologists, metaphysicians and theologians are able to speak about God-in-himself. Thus the misunderstanding between Jung and his critics became inevitable. No one among his critics ever made it clear to him that the dilemma, God is either "something subjective" or "something objective", was faulty because these critics themselves tacitly accepted this dilemma. Both parties assumed that something is "something" if it is either "something subjective" or "something objective"; both took for granted the divorce between the "objective" and the "subjective". Thus the "objective" meant the "in itself", that which is not experienced, not known, of which there is no consciousness, that which is what it is, divorced and isolated from the subject. What Jung so passionately rejects is the objective understood in the objectivistic sense : "the image which we have of God is never 'divorced' from man", he says.[155] Jung asks Martin Buber "where God has made his own image, divorced from man", and how he, Buber, would be able to say anything about such an image?[156] Jung wonders how he would manage to establish that "our conception is identical with the nature of things in themselves".[157] He wonders how he would be able to distinguish between our human experience of God and God himself since, to do this, "one would have to know God in and for himself, which seems impossible to me".[158]

In the light of these remarks, what possible meaning can be attached to the overcoming of agnosticism which Hostie claims to find in Jung's later works? Jung was accused of obliterating all objectivity, of reducing to subjectivity everything which religion calls objective, and of calling it ridiculous, pretentious and arrogant that metaphysicians claimed to

[155] C.G. Jung, *Antwort an Buber*, Gesammelte Werke, Band 11, p. 661.

[156] "Kann mir Buber angeben, wo Gott sein eigenes Bild, losgelöst vom Menschen, gemacht hat? Wie kann etwas derartiges konstatiert werden und von wem"? C.G. Jung, *o.c.*, p. 661.

[157] C.G. Jung, *o.c.*, p. 658.

[158] C.G. Jung, *Bruder Klaus*, Gesammelte Werke, Band 11, p. 350.

be able to speak about the objective. Does the "overcoming of agnosticism", spoken of by Hostie, mean that Jung later conceded that there is no arrogance in wanting to speak about the "in itself" as that which is not spoken of, that it is possible for metaphysicians to have experience of the non-experienced, to know about the non-known, to be conscious of what one is not conscious of? Hardly. For if the "objective" must *per se* be interpreted in the objectivistic sense, then "agnosticism" is intellectually more respectable.

Hostie's approval of Jung's victory over agnosticism itself is suspect. It is true, indeed, that according to Jung anyone is free to "accept metaphysical explanations for the origin of" those archetypical "images".[159] In his later years he no longer objected to people who claimed that religious concepts, thanks to the inspiration of the Holy Spirit, are concrete representations of "metaphysical objects".[160] But Jung always added : "This conviction is possible only for one who possesses the charism of faith. Unfortunately, I myself cannot boast to have such a charism".[161] One who sees this as Jung's turning away from agnosticism can approve this turn only if he himself starts from the presupposition that faith must be conceived as "accepting as true", i.e., as an act by which man assumes that God-in-himself corresponds to the idea "God" and therefore really exists. He must start from the presuposition that faith is the act by which man asserts that the judgment, "God exists", is true, and this then means that this judgment is in harmony with the reality-in-itself of God. But if this is what faith is supposed to be, then the agnostic attitude is much more enlightened.

The debate between Jung and his critics was doomed to fail because both parties were victims of something that remained "unspoken", the "hidden option" which escaped discussion. This tacit option was the dichotomy between the "subjective" and the "objective". One who starts from this option faces an inevitable choice between these two. Jung

---

[159] "Es steht dem gläubigen Menschen frei, irgendwelche metaphysischen Erklärungen über den Ursprung dieser Bilder anzunehmen ... Niemand kann den Glauben daran verhindern, als erste Ursache Gott, den Purusha, den Atman oder das Tao anzunehmen". C.G. Jung, *Psychologie und Alchemie*, pp. 28-29.

[160] "Man kann glauben, dass die Begriffe des Bewusstseins vermöge der Inspiration des Heiligen Geistes unmittelbare und korrekte Darstellungen ihres metaphysischen Gegenstandes seien". C.G. Jung, *Antwort an Buber*, Gesammelte Werke, Band 11, p. 659.

[161] C.G. Jung, *o.c.*, p. 659.

opted for the "subjective"[162] because he knew no other interpretation of the "objective" than the objectivistic interpretation of this term. His opponents opted for the "objective" because they failed to see that their choice contained this objectivism. Thus the debate remained fruitless.

The "Self" of Religious Self-understanding

If the "self" of religious self-understanding is conceived as an "isolated" self, then the claim that "speaking about God is speaking about man" could justify the accusation of subjectivism. But today's proponents of this claim do not at all conceive the "self" or subjectivity as an isolated "self" or a separate subjectivity. Religious "self-understanding" is the self-understanding of an *existent* subject, i.e., a subject who is himself only in unity with that which is not the subject, viz., the body, the world, others, God.[163] It may be useful to dwell a little on this point and to give a few examples.

With respect to the things of the world, I can say that they are objectively "graspable". This means that they are graspable by *my hands*, and "my hands" should be defined as "I who grasp". One of the reasons why things are as graspable as they actually are lies in the fact that I have two hands, each with five fingers. If I had only one hand with only one finger, things would be graspable in a very different way. Our physical sciences also would be very different because, for one hand with only one finger, entirely different instruments and experimental appa-

---

[162] "Alles, was ich erfahre, ist psychisch. Selbst der physische Schmerz ist ein psychisches Abbild, das ich erfahre; alle meine Sinnesempfindungen, die mir eine Welt von raumerfüllenden, undurchdringlichen Dingen aufzwingen, sind psychische Bilder, die einzig meine unmittelbare Erfahrung darstellen, denn sie allein sind es, die mein Bewusstsein zum unmittelbaren Objekt hat. Ja, meine Psyche verändert und verfälscht die Wirklichkeit in solchem Masse, dass ich künstlicher Hilfsmittel bedarf, um feststellen zu können, was die Dinge ausser mir sind, dass z.B. ein Ton eine Luftschwingung von bestimmter Frequenz, und eine Farbe eine bestimmte Wellenlänge des Lichtes ist. Im Grunde genommen sind wir dermassen in psychische Bilder eingehüllt, dass wir zum Wesen der Dinge ausser uns überhaupt nicht vordringen können". C.G. Jung, *Wirklichkeit der Seele*, Zürich-Leipzig, 1939, p. 24.

[163] "Integral to any God-statement ... is the consciousness of being encountered, seized, held by a prevenient reality, undeniable in its objectivity .... In traditional categories, while the reality is immanent in that it speaks to him from within his own deepest being, it is also transcendent, in that it is not his to command : it comes, as it were, from beyond him with an unconditional claim upon his life". John A.T. Robinson, *Exploration into God*, London, 1967, pp. 66-67.

ratus would have been necessary. If the things in the world had handles but the human body had a spherical shape, things would *not* be graspable. And one who claims that the things, because of their handles, are graspable-in-themselves mentally attaches a couple of grasping hands to those spheres, on the basis of which he can call the things-with-handles "graspable". Accordingly, speaking about the objectively graspable world is speaking about man; there is no form of subjectivism involved in this.

When, hot and thirsty, I drink water, this liquid obviously is not H_2O for me. It becomes H_2O only when it becomes an object of chemistry. One who claims that water *was already* H_2O assumes that it was already an object of the chemist's considerations. Accordingly, speaking about the chemical world is speaking about man as a chemist.

When I go for a walk in the sunshine and smoke a cigar, I have, of course, no white blood corpuscles. I have these only when biologists make me an object of their science. One who claims that I *already had* those corpuscles assumes that the biologist had already made me an object of his science. Accordingly, speaking about the biological world is speaking about man as a biologist.

Thus the statement that speaking about the world is speaking about man should not be interpreted as if it implied that speaking about the world says "really nothing" about the world and refers only to the subjective contents of consciousness. Subject "and" world constitute a unity of reciprocal implication.[164]

Nevertheless, I do not intend to claim that the statement "speaking 'about' God is speaking about man" is now clear. All that has been shown is that the conclusion, "God, then, is 'really nothing', i.e., nothing objective but at most 'something subjective' ", does not follow. If I were simply to claim that God is "something objective", I would be giving a "flat description" of God. I shall return to this point later but would like to present here an appropriate text of Augustine :

What do I love when I love You? Not bodily beauty, nor the fair harmony of time, nor the brilliance of light which gladdens our eyes, nor the sweet melodies of varigated songs, nor the fragrant smell of flowers, ointments and spices, not manna and honey, not limbs delightful to bodily embracements. None of these I love when I love my God. And yet I love a kind of melody, of fragrance and meat, a kind of embracement when I love my God : He is light and melody and fragrance and meat and empbracement of my inner man, there where shines unto my soul that light which space does not contain,

---

[164] W. Luijpen, *Existential Phenomenology*, rev. ed., Pittsburgh, 1974[3], pp. 63-83.

where resounds that melody which time does not carry away, where lingers that fragrance which the wind does not disperse, where clings that savor which eating does not diminish, and where is given that embrace which does not slacken through satiety. This is what I love when I love my God.[165]

4. CHRISTIAN RELIGIOUSNESS

In speaking about the rejection of metaphysics, *tout court*, by those who endeavor to give authenticity to their "affirmation" of God by this rejection, Chapter Tree also mentioned the intellectualism and objectivism of scholastic metaphysics. In the present chapter I have up till now intentionally avoided to speak thematically about Christian religiousness although the topic was incidentally touched upon here and there. The reason for the delay was that I intended to use the hermeneutics of religious existence in general as a preparation for the "return to the things themselves", by which the intellectualism and objectivism of Christian religious thought are overcome. I have described religiousness or faith in general as a certain "seeing", an "experiencing" of "depth" in human existence. One should not think here of the superficial seeing or experiencing available to anyone who has eyes or scientific techniques at his disposal and thus is able to approach things and human beings in "flat descriptions". The intellectualistic and objectivistic traditions of Christian self-understanding, however, placed faith *in opposition to* all forms of "seeing" and conceived faith as "holding to be true without seeing".

The things held to be true were judgments, propositions, "articles", directly or indirectly derived from Scripture. For the Bible was viewed as containing God's revelation, *his* word about "divine reality", and God's word was held to contain "secret information" because the divine reality was called "supernatural" and as such judged to be inaccessible to man's natural "seeing". Supernatural faith, as God's gift, enabled the Christian to accept certain statements as true, i.e., in agreement with the supernatural, divine "reality"-in-itself.

Belief in Statements

It is clear, I think, that a faith reduced to a consent to "secret information" is placed wholly outside life and robbed of everything that makes it worthwhile "to have faith".[166] Once this reduction had been made,

---

[165] Augustinus, *Confessions*, X, 6.

[166] "Offensichtlich ist das Wort als Medium der Offenbarung, das 'Wort Gottes',

the question could even be asked whether it was possible to pursue theology without faith. The fact that such a question was asked eloquently illustrates how narrowly faith was conceived. If faith is nothing but a "yes" to *statements*, there is no reason why one cannot proceed as if he affirms these statements and then draw theological conclusions from them. Thus theology degenerates into a kind of logic, and faith is no longer faith in God.[167]

If faith is conceived as a "yes" to statements, I have said, it becomes wholly alienated from life. To escape this consequence, emphasis was placed on the idea that these statements contain truths guaranteed by God[168] and that, as such, they are *bound to* be meaningful for life.

It is striking that an appeal is made here to the theory that the judgment or statement is the "place" of truth. Truth was conceived as the agreement of the judgment with reality.[169] But under the influence of Greek philosophy the term "reality" was taken to refer to "reality"-divorced-from-man, "reality"-without-man, "reality"-in-itself, and of this "reality" the intellect was held to possess a faithful copy.

Abstracting here from the various theories to explain how "copies of reality" originate, I merely wish to indicate the consequences of the above-mentioned theory of truth for faith. It is simple to see them when one realizes that "reality"-in-itself means "reality" with which man has nothing to do as a matter of principle. With respect to faith this means that statements of faith also express "reality" with which man has nothing to do as a matter of principle. And even if it is granted that God's revelation guarantees the truth of such statements, this still does not

---

nicht ein Wort, das zur Information über eine Wahrheit dient, die anders verborgen bleiben würde. Wenn es so wäre, wenn Offenbarung Information wäre, so bedürfte es keiner Transparenz der Sprache. Dann könnte die alltägliche Sprache, die keinen 'Klang' des Unbedingten übermittelt, Information über 'göttliche Dinge' abgeben. Solche Information würde von erkenntnismässigem und vielleicht ethischem Interesse sein, aber alle Merkmale der Offenbarung würden ihr fehlen. Sie hätte nicht die Macht zu ergreifen, zu erschüttern und zu verwandeln, jene Macht, die wir dem 'Worte Gottes' zusprechen". P. Tillich, *Systematische Theologie*, I, pp. 149-150.

[167] S. Ogden, *De Christelijke verkondiging van God aan de mensheid van de zogenaamde "atheïstische tijd"*, in : Concilium II (1966), no. 6, p. 100.

[168] "Hanc vero fidem, quae humanae salutis initium est, Ecclesia catholica profitetur, virtutem esse supernaturalem, qua, Dei aspirante et adjuvante gratia, ab eo revelata vera esse credimus, non propter intrinsecam rerum veritatem naturali rationis lumine perspectam, sed propter auctoritatem ipsius Dei revelantis, qui nec falli nec fallere potest". Denzinger, *Enchiridion Symbolorum*, no. 1789.

[169] M. Heidegger, *Vom Wesen der Wahrheit*, Frankfurt a.M., 1954³, pp. 6-9.

imply that their truth is of importance to man as long as their truth is conceived as a mirror reflexion of "reality" with which man has nothing to do. And, how could God reveal that man has something to do with that with which he has nothing to do?

The expert reader readily recognizes in the preceding view the "hidden options" of what Husserl calls the "natural attitude". He uses this term to refer to the conviction which has become "second nature" in the West, but which cannot be justified, that knowledge consists in the mirroring-in-the subject of a reality-"divorced"-from-the-subject, a mirroring supposedly accomplished by means of a faithful "copy" of this reality. The realization that such a conviction was not tenable induced Husserl to launch phenomenology as an attempt to find a foundation on which any and all statements could be based. For it is evident that, as long as truth is located only in the judgment and as long as a statement is called "true" because the speaker is assumed to be in possession of a "faithful copy" of reality-in-itself, no real foundation for the truth of the statement can be found. The reason is that it is impossible to justify the assumption that this "copy" is truthfully a "copy" unless the knowing subject is immediately present to the reality expressed in his judgment. To justify the "copy" character of a "copy" one must be able to compare the "copy" with the original, and this presupposes that the subject is immediately present to the appearing reality. Now, the recognition of the subject's immediate presence to an appearing reality eliminates the possibility of conceiving reality as reality-in-itself.[170]

From these considerations it follows that statements of faith also do not have a foundation or ground if their truth is conceived as their agreement with God-in-himself. Not even a divine guarantee can provide such a foundation, because such a guarantee itself would also be an "object" of faith. But if faith is conceived as a "yes" to statements whose truth is taken to lie in their agreement with God-in-himself, then this same rule applies also to the belief in a divine guarantee : this belief also would be a "yes" to a statement taken to be in agreement with God-in-himself. And so on *ad infinitum*.

This infinitely re-appearing difficulty has also led to the failure of Karl Barth's thought. Barth demands that Christian thought start

---

[170] A. de Waelhens, *La philosophie et les expériences naturelles*, La Haye, 1961, pp. 48-58.

from that which God has told us about himself. Now, God's word is to be found in Scripture,[171] which contains statements about God guaranteed by God himself. Man's knowledge of God is founded on God's word. That's why this knowledge cannot possibly put itself into question or permit itself to be put into question from any standpoint outside God's word.[172]

It may seem that we have here a starting point for Christian thought which, at least for the believer, offers no problems. The statements of Scripture are guaranteed by God himself, says Barth, and therefore true. And the believer affirms these statements because they are guaranteed by God himself. But this guarantee also is an "object" of faith, and this faith also is an affirmation of a statement about God's guarantee. But why would a believer affirm such a statement? Because it is guaranteed by God—and so on *ad infinitum.*

Barth's unassailable starting point is indeed unassailable once it has been reached. But there is no justification for assuming this standpoint, and no way an approach to this standpoint can be justified.[173] Such an approach would consists of something that Barth rejects, viz., the hermeneutics of the statement, "God speaks", as a statement about the "depth" in human existence.[174] But one who takes this approach no longer arrives at the standpoint which is Barth's starting point.

Meaningless Questions and Opinion Polls

Let us dwell a little longer on one of the consequences flowing from the reduction of faith to the affirmation of a judgment or statement as "agreeing" with a divine "reality"-in-itself. That consequence is that both the affirmation and the negation of such a judgment mean exactly the same—namely, *nothing.* An example may serve to illustrate this claim.

If I take an expensive cigar in my hand, hold my hand behind my back and tell a visitor : "this cigar is expensive", he can neither affirm nor deny my statement. For him, this statement is without any *foundation,*

---

[171] "Wir sind ausgegangen von dem, was Gott selber von sich selber, von seiner Erkenntnis und seiner Wirklichkeit gesagt hat und noch sagt laut seines Selbstzeugnisses, wie es uns in der heiligen Schrift als dem Dokument des Seins und Grundes der Kirche menschlich bezeugt und insofern erreichbar und verständlich ist". K. Barth, *Die Kirchliche Dogmatik,* Zürich, 1948, II-2, p. 1.

[172] K. Barth, *o.c.,* II-1, p. 2.

[173] Fr. Ferré, *Basic Modern Philosophy of Religion,* pp. 23-26.

[174] Heinrich Ott, *Die Bedeutung von Heideggers Denken für die Theologie,* in : *Durchblicke,* Martin Heidegger zum 80. Geburtstag, Frankfurt a. M., 1970, pp. 27-38.

it does not *really tell* him anything, it does not give expression to *reality* for him. It would be foolish of him to say "yes" and equally foolish to say "no". And if he did it anyhow, his "yes" or "no" would mean the same—nothing.

Of course, I do not intend to ask anyone to affirm or deny such a statement. But, then, what are we to think of such statements as :

God exists

God has created the world

God loves man

God is almighty

God rewards the good

God punishes evil

God has become man?

It is not inconceivable that some people may want to answer these statements in the affirmative while others wish to give a negative answer. Both the "yes" and the "no", however, are meaningless here, for an isolated judgment, cut loose from the "functioning intentionality", the implicit "saying"-of-*is* which human existence is, has no foundation, it "is about nothing". A second example may clarify this point.

After a hike through the mountains, I can give an objective description of the trail's condition. Such a description contains a series of *statements* in which the passable or impassable condition of the trail is expressed by means of predicates. The judgmental statements I make are explicit modes of saying-*is*; I explicitly ascribe certain predicates to the subject of a judgment by using the verbal copula "is".[175] If, however, I present these statements to someone who has no notion whatsoever of a mountain and who is unable to arrive at any such notion, then my statements about the passable or impassable caracter of the mountain trail are, for him, "about nothing". Such statements mean something for me because my feet, my hands, my eyes, even my whole body, have already "affirmed" the passable or impassable character of the trail. My walking, crawling and climbing, my tiredness, my exhaustion, my scratches and my grim determination to go on—all these, themselves, *are* the "affirmation" of the trail. Such an "affirmation" presupposes an original "event", the "event" of breaking-through and transcending the "thing"-in-my-being, the "emergence" of the "saying"-of-*is* which being-a-subject itself is. No subjectivity "comes to pass" in a stone rolling down the mountain trail; that is why its rolling down the trail is entirely different

---

[175] Max Müller, *Sein und Geist*, Tübingen, 1940, p. 40.

from my rolling down the trail. I am the "affirmation" of the trail. My subjectivity, immersed in my body, itself is the "saying"-of-*is* which I make explicit by expressing it in judgments. What precedes such judgments is the "event" of the coming about of meaning for the subject. Attached to my hiking over the trail is the "coming to pass"[176] of the trail's truth-as-unconcealedness.[177] I can express this truth in judgments, but none of them has any meaning whatsoever if it is divorced from the "affirmation" which my existence is.[178] Cut loose from existence, a judgment is neither true nor false; it simply says nothing.

Applying this idea to the realm of religious statements, one can see that it is utterly meaningless to ask questions such as :

Does God exist or not?

Does God love us or not?

Is God almighty or not?

Does God reward the good or not?

Does God punish evil or not?

Did God become man or not?

These questions, raised in this way, are meaningless because they start from presuppositions which are simply not tenable.[179]

If this idea meets approval, a critical attitude may become necessary with respect to the eagerness with which some pastoral theologians look at the results of certain sociological investigations in order to find there a starting point for their pastoral-theological considerations. Does it make sense to compare the doctrine of the Church with the belief of its members by means of a scientific opinion poll? Such a poll selects certain questions to be submitted to the respondents in order to "gage the content of their belief".[180] The risk involved in such a procedure has been pointed out by Professor F. Haarsma. If, for example, the questions are taken from an old-fashioned handbook of theology, the very questions themselves at once frustrate the entire poll.

Let us assume, however, that the "right" questions are asked, whatever this may mean. Even then, "judgments in the form of questions" are submitted to the respondents, and the answer will have to be a positive or negative judgment. The crucial point, of course, is whether such an

---

[176] M. Heidegger, *Identität und Differenz*, Pfüllingen, 1957, pp. 24-25.

[177] M. Heidegger, *Sein und Zeit*, p. 219.

[178] M. Heidegger, *o.c.*, p. 220.

[179] John A.T. Robinson, *Exploration into God*, p. 32.

[180] Fr. Haarsma, *De leer van de kerk en het geloof van haar leden*, Rede, Utrecht: 1968, p. 7.

inquiry gives the religious sociologist really any information about the *belief* of the respondents. He can answer in the affirmative only if he, too, assumes that belief is saying "yes" to judgments or propositions. But in that case "belief" and "unbelief" mean exactly the same—nothing at all.

Christian Faith as a Way of Existence

In the beginning of this chapter I said that the religious man names, calls, whispers the name "God" and thereby expresses the "depth" of his existence; that the name "God" may not be made the subject of a judgment in which a predicate is added to this subject by means of the verbal copula "is"; that the religious man does this anyhow and, by his insensitivity to the objections that can be made to his statements shows that he does not conceive these statements, despite their constative, descriptive and explanatory form, as "flat descriptions" of God's essence and deeds. I interpreted general religiousness as a special mode of "seeing", a "seeing" which is existence itself, and I called this "seeing" "faith". Full emphasis was placed there on man as *existence*, and any idea of making man an "ingredient" of "flat descriptive" sciences was vigorously rejected. In the endeavor to interpret Christian faith nothing of all this, I think, has to be rejected, but there is something that must be added.

"Christian faith presupposes revelation", we say. What does this mean? The revelation which makes this faith possible is the disclosure, the "revelation" of a very special *way of life*. This way of life became a reality in Jesus of Nazareth. He lived man's life in a very special way before the eyes of the other. The others, at least some of them, saw his life and this was "simply a revelation" to them. They had not thought it possible for man to live in such a way, but now they saw it before their very eyes. That is why they "believed", i.e., they, too, began to *live* this way. Their faith was made possible by a revelation, for if Jesus had not shown them this life as a possibility and a reality, they would not have been able to live it.[181]

---

[181] "Es gibt keine geoffenbarten Lehren, aber es gibt Offenbarungsereignisse und Situationen, die mit lehrhaften Begriffen beschrieben werden können. Die kirchlichen Lehren sind sinnlos, wenn sie von der Offenbarungssituation, aus der heraus sie entstanden sind, losgelöst werden. Das 'Wort Gottes' enthält weder geoffenbarte Gebote noch geoffenbarte Lehren, es begleitet und deutet Offenbarungssituationen". P. Tillich, *Systematische Theologie*, I, p. 150.

Because the first Christians began to live as Jesus had done, a "depth", a mystery revealed itself in their existence; like Jesus, they gave expression to this "depth" by naming, calling and whispering the name "God". A way of existing made it possible for them to exclaim "Father"! and in this they expressed the "depth", the mystery of their *new* existence. They realized that something special had happened to them, that this new way of life had, as it were, "come over them", that they had "received" it "from on high", and they exclaimed : "God"! "Father"!

Later some people replaced this calling of "God" by the judgment : "God has revealed himself in Christ", but this statement, of course, did not have a "flat descriptive" meaning similar to the statement : "The President showed his hand through his Secretary of State".

The new existence is distinguished from the old one as freedom from unfreedom, authenticity from inauthenticity, salvation from disaster, holiness from sin, life from death. A life in which man is a captive of pride, greed, lust, arbitrariness and unavailability is not-free, inauthentic, broken, filled with evil, sin and death. But when he accepts the new life, man "sees" that he is not the arbitrary lord and master of his new life, and in gratitude he calls "God"!

Later some people replaced this grateful *calling* of the name "God" by such judgment as :

God has freed us

God has given us salvation

God has renewed us.

But these judgments did not have the "flat descriptive" meaning that is suggested by their external form. They are not on a par with other judgments which externally resemble them, such as :

Lincoln has freed us

Peter has given us an apple

The doctor has fixed me up.

In the light of their new life the first believers saw that their old life really meant nothing but death and sin. The realization that their new life had come to them "from above" disclosed a "depth" to them; and they expressed this "depth" by calling the name "God". Later this calling was replaced by statements containing a judgment. The first Christians said :

God has made us pass from death to life

God has forgiven our sins.

But, again, these judgments did not have a "flat descriptive" meaning similar to the statements :

The teacher has made us pass from the fifth to the sixth grade

The principal has remitted our punishment.

Jesus of Nazareth revealed to man the possibility and reality of an authentic human life, but in doing this he himself became the victim of those who rejected this new way of life. The first Christians realized that they themselves could have crucified Jesus if the new life had not been given to them. Jesus had become the victim of a way of living *which at one time had been also theirs*. And on the cross they heard him exclaim the name "God" : "My God, my God, why hast thou forsaken me?" Yet they knew that a new, authentically human history had begun and in gratitude they called the name "God".

Later, again, people used judgments about all this, making God the subject of certain statements, They began to say :

God has put our guilt on Christ in order that he, who himself was without guilt, might expiate our guilt for us

God has intervened for us in history.

But these statements did not have the "flat descriptive" meaning that is suggested by their external form and which makes them resemble such statements as :

The judge has condemned John, himself without guilt, to pay the debts of his neighbor

The police have intervened in the rioting.

The people who wish to lead the life made possible by Jesus belong together and they come together. This is what I should like to call the "Church". They belong together because they share the same way of life; and they come together to call the name "God" in prayer, song, rejoicing, lament and sorrow. For they realize that they can never become lord and master of their own new life, that "what has come over them" must always again be given to them "from on high", that what once has been accomplished in them must over and over again be accomplished in them.[182]

---

[182] "To say of this or that situation, as the Biblical writers did, that 'God' is in it is not to start making statements about some supposed metaphysical entity outside it or beyond it; nor is it to say simply 'This piece of history is of fundamental importance for my life'. It is to say that in and through this event or person there meets me a claim, a mystery, a grace, whose overriding, transcendent, unconditional character can only be expressed by responding, with the prophet, 'Thus saith the Lord' ".

Meanwhile they live in the conviction that their new life is "infallibly" good : "the Church is infallible". Is this what the Fathers of Vatican Council I had in mind? I do not think so, but this is what they should have meant.

"I Believe in the Cross and the Resurrection of Jesus Christ"

What is the meaning of the statement : "I believe in the cross and the resurrection of Jesus Christ"? From the preceding considerations it should be clear that this means : I am willing to live, or at least I will try to live, as Jesus Christ has lived. It has no other meaning. If, then, I do *not* really wish to live so, I do *not* believe in anything.

People who pursue various positive sciences could object and say : "As historians, we can prove, through the most reliable methods of the science of history, that Jesus died on the cross; through the medical sciences we can prove that Jesus was dead when he was taken down from the cross; moreover, we can prove that, medically speaking, he would have been asphyxiated, if he had still been alive, when he was buried wrapped up in one hundred pounds of myrrh and aloe-leaves; through the sciences of history we can also prove that three days later his grave was empty and that Jesus again discoursed with the living. All this has been absolutely established for us; therefore, we *believe.*

Those objectors would be right if faith should be reduced to a yes to statements made by the sciences of nature, of psychology and of history. But this is not what faith is. Christian statements of faith express the "depth" which is experienced in human existence on the basis of a certain way of living; the sciences speak *neither* of this existence *nor* of the depth experienced in it. Yet, in the past Christians have gone to incredible troubles to *demonstrate* their "faith" scientifically. Consider, for example, the following statements :

Christ was virginally conceived

Christ died

Christ descended into hell

Christ ascended into heaven

Christ will return on the clouds.

Efforts were made to approach such statements with the aid of all kinds of scientific and historical considerations in the assumption that these statements were "flat descriptions" just like those of the physical and

---

John A.T. Robinson, *Exploration into God*, pp. 68-69.

historical sciences. But, we must ask, is such an assumption tenable? Mythical speech is *true* speech if it is understood according to its own intention. But mythical speech was understood as if it were scientific speech; and it became obvious that, understood in this way, mythical speech had to be called pseudo-scientific.

"*My Father Is Stronger Than the Mayor*"

Many people feel ill at ease when they encounter an attempt to disengage the language of faith from the "flat descriptions" of the sciences. This is understandable because we "modern men" have simply become fascinated with the absolutism of the sciences. We are blinded by the "light" of scientific verification. How unreasonable this is may be illustrated by an example.

A twelve-year-old boy adores his father. He does not hide his admiration and is always boasting about his father to other boys. "My dad", he says, "is very strong. Why, he is stronger even than the mayor"! What that boy says is *true*.

If we were to listen to what certain authors writing about Jesus Christ say, we would be told : "That statement cannot simply be accepted. It must first be verified. So, we will have to put the boy's father in the ring together with the mayor; then we can verify whether what the boy says is true". To my mind, such an attitude is nonsense.

Sixty years later, the twelve-year-old boy has become an old man. Sitting on a bench in the park, he says to his brother who is two years younger than he : "You remember the fair in our village sixty years ago"? "Yes", replies the other. "And do you remember how the mayor then stepped into the ring and challenged all passers-by to a wrestling match and how our dad took up the challenge and in no time had the mayor flat on the floor"? "Yes, I recall that, too". This story also is *true*.

But the above-mentioned authors, I fancy, will raise objections. They would say : "Let us, with the aid of the historical sciences, try to determine whether sixty years ago there was indeed a fair in that village. Next, let us try to establish whether there were reasons, whether economic or psychological, why the mayor could have been induced to strange ways of behaving. Finally, let us try to find witnesses and possible written documentation about the results of the mayor's wrestling. For only in this way can we verify the reliability and truth of what those two old men are saying."

This, too, is sheer nonsense. There is only one way thoroughly to falsify the truth of what that boy and those two old men said, and that is to accede to the demands of those authors.

Decades after the death of Jesus Christ, the first Christians said to one another : "Do you still remember when ...". They wanted to speak about the Jesus who had taught them a new way of life, one which had made it possible for them to give up their pride, their greed, their lust, arbitrariness and unavailability. They wished to speak of the "depth" which this way of life had given to their existence, so that they were able to name, call, whisper the name "God". It is *this* that they wished to put down in writing, and not the things that could interest the pursuers of the physical and historical sciences. That is why they said :

Christ is the Word made flesh

Christ is God.

And what they said was and is *true*. But their statements did not have a "flat descriptive" meaning as is the case with the statements :

Meat loaf is bread made flesh

Nixon is President.

"Old" and "New" Ways of Speaking "About" God

The believer's statements "about" God, which according to their external form establish, describe and explain, do not have a "flat descriptive" meaning. This idea is important for our endeavor to speak better today "about" God than people used to do in former times. Such an endeavor is essentially doomed to failure if one does not realize that any "new" way of speaking about God cannot have a "flat descriptive" meaning either. Let us list here a few statements which, according to certain authors, we may no longer use today :

God fills the gaps in my power over the world [183]

God is my Shepherd and Father [184]

God is the one who does something for me [185]

God is a person [186]

---

[183] E. Schillebeeckx, *Het nieuwe Godsbeeld, secularisatie en politiek*, in : Tijdschrift voor Theologie, 8 (1968), p. 51.

[184] Harvey Cox, *The Secular City*, London, 1967, p. 262.

[185] Dorothee Sölle, *Stellvertretung*, Ein Kapittel Theologie nach dem "Tode Gottes", Stuttgart-Berlin, 1965, p. 205.

[186] John A.T. Robinson, *Honest to God*, pp. 39-44.

God is "above us"[187]

God is a powerful cause who must, on occasion, intervene [188]

God is a center drawing all of us toward him.[189]

According to the above-quoted authors, we may no longer use these statements because we "modern men" have changed so much that statements "about" God coming from different times, different sociological conditions or different human situations can no longer tell us anything. Yet they wish to speak "about" God and therefore offer us other statements. Let us put their proposals down here in the same sequence as above :

God is the future of man [190]

God is man's partner [191]

God is the one for whom I must do something [192]

God is, by definition, the ultimate reality [193]

God is "before us"[194]

God is the source from which we have the power to take our destiny into our own hands [195]

God is an expansive power inciting people to go out of themselves and transcend themselves.[196]

Again, however, such statements must not be conceived as "flat descriptions". If one does this anyhow, they are no better than the old sequence. If, on the other hand, one does *not* conceive the old sequence of statements as "flat descriptions" of God's essence or actions, then one may legitimately ask whether they are really as bad as the above-mentioned authors seem to imply.

Prospective

I have now arrived at a point where I must let others continue. I have to

---

[187] J.B. Metz, *De kerk en de wereld*, in : Het woord in de geschiedenis, ed. by T. Patrick Burke, Bilthoven, 1969, p. 83.

[188] J.H. Walgrave, *Bidden in onze tijd*, in : De Kloosterling, 36 (1968), pp. 70-71.

[189] Leslie Dewart, *The Future of Belief*, Theism in a World Come of Age, London, 1966, p. 189.

[190] E. Schillebeeckx, *o.c.*, p. 60.

[191] Harvey Cox, *o.c.*, pp. 264-265.

[192] Dorothee Sölle, *o.c.*, p. 205.

[193] John A.T. Robinson, *o.c.*, p. 29.

[194] J.B. Metz, in : *o.c.*, p. 83.

[195] J.H. Walgrave, *o.c.*, pp. 70-71.

[196] Leslie Dewart, *o.c.*, p. 189.

limit myself to the explicitation of very general but fundamental ideas about the essence of religious existence and religious language. These general and fundamental ideas are capable of considerable development, but this would require expertise in a specific field which I do not possess.

As a philosopher, however, I must still answer one important question which lies within the realm of this work. It is the question whether it is possible to exercise a *radical* critique on religious language; that is to say, whether the symbolic and mythical language of the religious man can be called before the tribunal of *critical* rationality. Obviously, I do not wish to imply that hitherto I have proceeded uncritically, but only that the possibility of being critical has not yet been *radically* exploited. At the beginning of this chapter I asked what the religious man means when he calls the name "God", and I said that this question *may*—in a sense, even *must*—be asked. For, as a matter of fact, there are religious people who mean something when they call "God", even as artists mean something when they create a work of art. Even if others think that there *should not* be any artist and any religious people, the question still needs to be asked as to what they mean for the simple reason that these people do exist. In this chapter I have tried critically to answer this question with respect to the religious man.

The critique, however, becomes *radical* only at the moment when one delves into the objection that there *should not* be any religious people. that they *should not* mean anything and *should not* say anything because all this is "much ado about nothing". The critique only becomes radical when one explicitly refuses to be sensitive to the specific expressive power of symbolic and mythical language because one deliberately wishes to leave open the possibility that precisely this specific expressive power could establish a specific illusion—the illusion that existence has "depth". The question, then, is whether it is possible, without using the specific expressive power of symbolic and mythical language, to "indicate" that which the religious man expresses by the calling of the name "God", viz., the "depth" of his existence.

Luther and Barth absolutely reject such a radical critique and appeal to what they call "faith".[197] For Barth, to think "faithfully" is to start with what God himself has said about himself, to listen to God's word. Now, human rationality demands that one ask critically what it means

---

[197] "Die natürliche Theologie ... kann nur der Theologie und Kirche des Antichrist bekömmlich sein. Die evangelische Kirche und Theologie würde an ihr nur kranken und sterben können?" K. Barth, *Nein!* Antwort an Emil Brunner, Theologische Existenz heute, Heft 14, 1934, p. 63.

to say that "God speaks". For the calling of God's name may not be replaced by "flat descriptive" statements in which God becomes the subject of the judgment : "God speaks". If statements are used anyhow, there is no objection to this provided they are not conceived as "flat descriptions" but as expressing the "depth" in the existence of the religious man who tries to speak "about" God. It is, therefore, always man who speaks,[198] even if he listens to or expresses what "has come over him" or what he has received "from on high" and what makes him call "God". But nothing is guaranteed to him in his speaking. He is not immune to any mistake, foolishness or illusion; that is why a radical critique is demanded by human rationality. One who does not assume the radical, critical attitude runs the risk of conceiving the statement "God speaks" as a "flat description", similar to "Joe speaks". One who says "God speaks" wants to warn man against self-pride in his speaking, but he runs the risk of letting his own words be taken for God's word.[199]

As a matter of fact, man has made "God" say the most foolish things. In God's name he has committed the most barbarous deeds. There have been and there are destructive forms of "religiousness", which have caused and still cause obscurantism, ignorance, poverty, disease, dereliction of duty, intolerance, cruelty and psychical disturbances. "Faith" cannot interpret all disasters as blessings; there have been and there still are also pseudo-forms of religiousness.

That is why it is not a sign of irreligiousness but a demand of human rationality that religious speech be called before the tribunal of radical critique. Man's rationality demands that the religious man impose silence on symbolic and mythical speech with its specific expressive power and that he rationally "prove" the "existence of God".

---

[198] "Dagegen vermittelt die Sprache als Medium der Offenbarung den 'Klang' und die 'Stimme' des göttlichen Mysteriums durch den Klang und die Stimme der menschlichen Sprache. Dank dieser Fähigkeit wird die Sprache zum 'Wort Gottes'. Wenn man eine optische Metapher zur Charakterisierung der Sprache heranziehen darf, so könnte man sagen, dass das 'Wort Gottes' als das Wort der Offenbarung transparante Sprache ist. Etwas scheint (genauer : tönt) durch die alltägliche Sprache hindurch, nämlich die Selbstmanifestation der Tiefe des Seins und Sinns". P. Tillich, *Systematische Theologie*, I, p. 149.

[199] "The veto rests on morally questionable assumptions. Its high intent is no doubt sincerely to warn against human pride; but, in the end, advocates of the veto must consider the possibility that they themselves are guilty of the highest form of pride : of confusing their thoughts with God's thoughts and of assuming their own relative and human prohibitions to be absolute and divine". Fr. Ferré, *Basic Modern Philosophy of Religion*, p. 25.

The terms "prove" and "existence of God" are placed between quotation marks here because so many associations are evoked by them that it is almost meaningless to use them either positively or negatively. But that which really was at stake for twenty-five centuries when "proofs" for "God's existence" were formulated must not be lost. In the following chapter I shall endeavor to show this.

CHAPTER SIX

RELIGIOUS EXISTENCE AND METAPHYSICAL SPEECH

Philosophy is "reserve personified". For the philosopher *as* philosopher it is impossible to take part in the prayerful, singing, lamenting, sorrowing and cursing calling of the name "God". A philosophical text is never a religious text because the philosopher's "attitude" implies reserve, distance and critique. A religious text uses *all available means* to overcome "recalcitrance" to the religious message and evoke the "consciousness of depth". But the philosopher as philosopher is "recalcitrance personified". *As* philosopher, he refuses to be concerned with anything but rationality; he uses only his power to let objective meaning appear; he lets himself be convinced only by what he "sees"; he is always ready to let his "seeing" be unmasked as "putative seeing".

The philosopher, however, must keep in mind that his "attitude", no matter how legitimate, is only one among many possible attitudes. *As* a philosopher, he cannot take part in the prayerful, singing, lamenting, rejoycing, sorrowing and cursing calling of the name "God". But the fact that he cannot do this *as* philosopher does not mean that he cannot do it at all. The same situation exists also elsewhere. The physicist *as* physicist never finds anything awe-inspiring, beautiful, kind or created. But this does not mean that nothing is awe-inspiring, beautiful, kind or created.

The God of Philosophers

Tradition speaks about the "God of philosophers". In what way this expression makes sense we shall see later, but we may say at once that the religious man is right when he claims that the "God of philosophers" is never the "God of the religious man". For, by virtue of his critical attitude, the philosopher is "reserve" and "recalcitrance" personified.

Let us dwell a moment on this way of speaking. I have repeatedly stressed that God may not be made the subject of a judgment if such a judgment is conceived as a "flat descriptive" statement. This rule applies also when it is said that "the God of philosophers" is not "the God of the religious man". If the religious man conceives this sentence as a "flat description", it would be better for him to remain silent. For his assertion would then be similar to the statement : "The Johnson examined by the internist is not the Johnson of the Rotary Club". But the religious man is right if he wishes to say that the experience of "depth" in human existence is different for the philosopher as philosopher than for the religious man.

Pascal has expressed this very clearly. It was obviously Christian religiousness that he had in mind when he raised religiousness high above the philosopher's metaphysical speech. The experience of "depth" in Christian religiousness implies humanity, joy, confidence and love. The experience of "depth" is consciousness of sin, grace, redemption, consolation, authentic life, salvation and hope.[1]

Other philosophers who, unlike Pascal, do not have Christian religiousness in mind when they speak of religiousness, nevertheless do not put "the God of philosophers" on a par with "the God of the religious man". Heidegger calls the "God of philosophy" a God to whom man cannot pray, for whom he cannot dance, play music or kneel down.[2]

Today it is rather generally accepted that the experience of "depth" in existence is different for the philosopher *as* philosopher than for the religious man.[3] A consequence of this is that those who take the standpoint of the religious man generally attach but little importance to what tradition calls the "proofs" for God's existence. Provisionally leaving aside the meaning which the term "proofs" used to have in the past or the present and also the correct meaning of this term, I may say at least

---

[1] "Le Dieu d'Abraham, le Dieu d'Isaac, le Dieu de Jacob, le Dieu des chrétiens, est un Dieu d'amour et de consolation; c'est un Dieu qui remplit l'âme et le coeur de ceux qu'il possède; c'est un Dieu qui leur fait sentir intérieurement leur misère, et sa miséricorde infinie; qui s'unit au fond de leur âme; qui la remplit d'humilité, de joie, de confiance, d'amour". Pascal, *Pensées*, 556.

[2] M. Heidegger, *Identität und Differenz*, p. 70.

[3] "Il s'agit si peu du Dieu auquel pensent la plupart des hommes que si, par miracle, et contre l'avis des philosophes, Dieu ainsi défini descendait dans le champ de l'expérience, personne ne le reconnaîtrait. Statique ou dynamique, en effet, la religion le tient avant tout pour un Être qui peut entrer en rapport avec nous : or c'est précisément de quoi est incapable le Dieu d'Aristote, adopté avec quelques modifications par la plupart de ses successeurs". H. Bergson, *Les deux Sources de la Morale et de la Réligion*, Editions Albert Skira, Genève, p. 231.

that these "proofs" were the work of the philosopher *as* philosopher. The religious man, then, is right when he claims that that "work" does not go beyond the "affirmation" of "the God of philosophers", who is not "the God of the religious man".[4]

Rejection of the "Proofs" for God's Existence by the Religious Man

Some believers in God do not merely minimize the importance of the "proofs" for God's existence, but absolutely reject such proofs. They are not atheists but view this "proof" as a hidden form of atheism.[5] According to them, man's very religiousness *demands* this rejection. Generally speaking, these people are the same cited in Chapter Three, where I spoke about the rejection of metaphysics, *tout court*, by thinkers who wish to let the "affirmation" of God attain an authentic level. With respect to their rejection of "proofs" for God's existence, I would like to present here a brief list of their reasons for doing this and add a short commentary to them.

Kant, again, figures first on this list. The elaboration of his theory of transcendental method had led him to the realization that the ideas of reason—including the idea "God"—must be thought *of necessity*. Man cannot escape *conceiving* absolutely everything as the result of an absolute Cause or God. Metaphysics, however, inevitably falls into a trap of "transcendental semblance" if it conceives the "I" or soul, the universe and God, not as ideas to be *thought* but as given realities or objects of knowledge. The rejection of the ontological, cosmological and physico-theological proofs of God's existence thus is a very simple matter for Kant[6]; it follows from his theory of transcendental method. Next, in a concluding and summarizing section, he proposes his critique of *all* theology,[7] taking as the starting point his distinction between theoretical and practical knowledge.

---

[4] "Der 'Gott' der Gottesbeweise ist nicht der lebendige Gott des Glaubens, sondern ein intellektuelles, ideenhaftes Ersatzgebilde, ein 'Absolutes', ein 'höchstes' oder 'notwendiges Sein', der 'unbedingte Wert' usw., eine Grösse, deren Begriff vielleicht mit dem Gott des Glaubens in Einklang gebracht werden kann, aber niemals diesen fordert". Emil Brunner, *Offenbarung und Vernunft*, Die Lehre von der christlichen Glaubenserkenntnis, Zürich, 1941, p. 336.

[5] "La théodicée, c'est l'athéisme". G. Marcel, *Journal Métaphysique*, Paris, 1935[11], p. 65.

[6] W. Luijpen, *Phenomenology and Atheism*, Pittsburgh, 1964, pp. 30-39.

[7] I. Kant, *Kritik der reinen Vernunft*, ed. Cassirer, III, pp. 433-440.

For Kant, knowledge is "theoretical" when it expresses that which *is*. Practical knowledge, on the contrary, expresses that which *ought to be*.[8] Theoretical knowledge can be either natural or speculative. It is natural when it speaks of objects given in sense experience, and speculative when its affirmations go beyond that which is given in sense experience.[9] In his terminology, then, the traditional theoretical knowledge of God is purely speculative. The speculative use of reason, however, is wholly fruitless in natural theology and its concern is entirely void.[10] This should be rather obvious now. For if the law of causality led to a Primordial Being, then this Being would have a place in the series of objects of sense experience and, consequently, would no more than any other of these objects be the Primordial Being. If, on the other hand, it is placed above the series of objects of sense experience, then the law of causality is used in a realm where it is not objectively valid.[11] Thus there is no escape : our knowledge of God is purely speculative; it has no objective validity.

Kant challenges anyone who has more confidence in the traditional proofs than in his critique to show him on what grounds it can be considered justified to transcend sense experience by way of pure ideas. He wishes to be spared new and improved proofs of God's existence because such proofs will always somehow try to go beyond sense experience through the use of pure ideas—despite the fact that the one and only important question is how such a transcendence would be possible.[12]

Nevertheless, for speculative reason the Supreme Being remains an ideal which is the capstone and crown of all human knowledge, but the objective reality of this ideal cannot be proved. On the other hand, the same reason which makes it impossible to affirm this objective reality

---

[8] I. Kant, *o.c.*, p. 435.

[9] I. Kant, *o.c.*, p. 436.

[10] "Ich behaupte nun, dass alle Versuche eines bloss spekulativen Gebrauchs der Vernunft in Ansehung der Theologie gänzlich fruchtlos und ihrer inneren Beschaffenheit nach null und nichtig sind". I. Kant, *o.c.*, pp. 436-437.

[11] "Soll das empirischgültige Gesetz der Kausalität zu dem Urwesen führen, so müsste dieses in die Kette der Gegenstände der Erfahrung mitgehören; alsdenn wäre es aber, wie alle Erscheinungen, selbst wiederum bedingt. Erlaubte man aber auch den Sprung über die Grenze der Erfahrung hinaus vermittelst des dynamischen Gesetzes der Beziehung der Wirkungen auf ihre Ursachen, welchen Begriff kann uns dieses Verfahren verschaffen? Bei weitem keinen Begriff von einem höchsten Wesen, weil uns Erfahrung niemals die grösste aller möglichen Wirkungen, (als welche das Zeugnis von ihrer Ursache anlegen soll), darreicht". I. Kant, *o.c.*, p. 437.

[12] I. Kant, *o.c.*, p. 438.

also prevents its denial.[13] The negation is as much beyond the possibilities of reason as is the affirmation. Moreover, it is not precluded that the real existence of the Supreme Being must be affirmed in another way than by theoretical reason. Kant alludes here to morality, whose existence postulates the real existence of God. The traditional doctrine about God would then be of importance for determining our concept of the Supreme Being postulated by morality. Only theoretical reason can keep away the errors of atheism, deism and anthropomorphism by showing that their affirmations go beyond the possibilities of theoretical reason.[14] Only theoretical reason, by constant censorship, can prevent itself from being deceived by the tricks of the senses.[15] If practical reason really postulates the affirmation of the Supreme Being's real existence, only theoretical reason can further determine the concept of this Being as necessary, infinite, one, transcendent, eternal, omnipotent, etc.[16]

Investigating what exactly Kant rejects when he emasculates all "proofs" for God's existence, one comes to the conclusion that he opposes all "proofs" which claim to be able to affirm the existence of God conceived as an *object given in sense experience*. For Kant, "knowledge" means the affirmation of objects given by the senses and, since "proofs" for God's existence can never lead to such an affirmation, they must be rejected, he holds, whenever they claim to lead to *knowledge*. In my opinion, the religious man must agree with his rejection of *such* "proofs" for God's existence. But does the refusal to accept such "proofs" imply the necessity to reject the attempt to "prove God's existence" *in every sense*? Is a "proof for God's existence" *per se* an attempt to "affirm" God as an object given in sense experience? This does not follow and that is why even after Kant people continued to work at these "proofs" and also why Kant himself was intensely preoccupied with the same.

In the second place, many believers reject "proofs" for God's existence which claim to lead to the affirmation of a God-in-himself. Descartes' methodic doubt had not really removed anything from human know-

---

[13] I. Kant, *o.c.*, p. 440.

[14] I. Kant, *o.c.*, p. 439.

[15] "Und wenn es eine Moraltheologie geben sollte ... so beweiset alsdenn die vorher nur problematische transzendentale Theologie ihre Unentbehrlichkeit durch Bestimmung ihres Begriffs und unaufhörliche Zensur einer durch Sinnlichkeit oft genug getäuschten und mit ihren eigenen Ideen nicht immer einstimmigen Vernunft". I. Kant, *o.c.*, p. 440.

[16] I. Kant, *o.c.*, p. 440.

ledge,[17] but had merely added to anything he doubted the qualifier "thought of".[18] The *human* body, the *human* world and God-for-*man* were at first reduced by him to the body-idea, the world-idea and the God-idea. Descartes realized, of course, that he had not thereby given expression to the "whole" *reality* of the human body, the human world and God-for-man. God-for-the-subject, the world-for-the-subject and the body-for-the-subject are "more" than ideas. However, after Descartes had reduced the being-for-the-subject of everything which is not the subject himself, he could no longer conceive the ontological status of this "more" as a being-for-the-subject. Thus he was forced to conceive this being-"more" as "nonhuman"— as being body-in-itself, world-in-itself, God-in-himself.

Toward the end of his third MEDITATION Descartes explains his *a posteriori* argument for God's existence. He notes that he has an idea of God as Infinite Substance, Eternal, Immutable, Independent, Omniscient and Omnipotent. Now, argues Descartes, such an idea cannot have come from myself, for as a finite being I cannot produce the idea of the Infinite. Only an Infinite Substance can have caused this idea in me. Therefore, God exists.[19]

In the light of the preceding paragraphs this "Infinite Substance" must be conceived as a God-in-himself, an "unhuman" God, who is, as a matter of principle, "separated" from man and with whom man, as a matter of principle, has no relations, for in Cartesian philosophy God-for-man is an idea of and in the subject. Whatever God is over and above an idea-in-the-subject is God-in-himself. The "affirmation" of this God-in-himself is the "metaphysical", "supernaturalistic" or "theistic" "affirmation" of God which many believers reject in order to safeguard the authentic character of man's "affirmation" of God.

Carefully considered, the theory of the "metaphysical God" antedates Cartesianism, for it is *implied* in the "proofs" of God's existence offered by medieval Scholasticism. As has already been explained, Scholasticism's objectivistic philosophy of order assigned a place in brute reality to every essence, including that of man. "Being", the "totality of reality", was represented as a collection of essences which were in themselves

[17] W. Luijpen, *Existential Phenomenology*, rev. ed., Pittsburgh 1974³, p. 49.

[18] M. Merleau-Ponty, *Phénoménologie de la Perception*, Avant-propos, p. III.

[19] René Descartes, *Meditationes de prima philosophia*, Introduction et notes par Geneviève Lewis, Paris, 1946, pp. 45-46.

necessarily, universally, immutably and eternally "true", and this was so *outside* the "encounter" which human existence is. They were supposed to be "true" in themselves and outside this encounter because they were created by God. Scholasticism tried to prove all this. Starting from the experience of "motion", "efficient causes", "contingency", "grades of perfection" and "design" in the "totality of reality", Scholastic philosophy concluded to the existence of a "First Mover", a "First Efficient Cause", a "Necessary Being", a "Supreme Being", and an "Intelligent Designer".[20]

After what we have seen in Chapter Three about Christian metaphysics, there is no need to dwell at length on the Scholastic "proofs" for God's existence. In my opinion, the believer owes it to his religiousness to reject the objectivism presupposed by those proofs. One who "affirms" God as the creative origin of the order of being, conceived as reality-divorced-from-man, implicitly also conceives God as God-in-himself and, consequently, as a God with whom man, as a matter of principle, has no relationship whatsoever. God is then the "Transcendent-in-himself", "metaphysically out there".[21] If, "after" this, one persists in speaking of God's revelation about himself or of his action toward man, then the implication is that it refers to the revelation of action of a Being with whom man, *as a matter of principle, does not have anything to do*. One who, in spite of this, still "believes" is forced to conceive faith as accepting, on authority, the "truth" of judgments, propositions and "articles" about God, while conceiving the truth of these judgments as their agreement with God-in-himself. This is what some thinkers reject when they reject the "metaphysical",[22] "theistic"[23] and "supernaturalistic" God. They object to what we have called the objectivism of Christian metaphysics. The question, however, is whether what this

---

[20] Thomas Aquinas, *S. Th.*, I, q. 2, a. 3; G.J. Oltheten and C.G.F. Braun, *Hij die is*, Proeve van een wijsgerige Godsleer, Utrecht-Nijmegen, 1963, pp. 62-82; J. Peters, *Metaphysica*, Een systematisch overzicht, Utrecht-Antwerpen, 1957, pp. 455-461; R. Garrigou-Lagrange, *Dieu*, Son existence et sa nature, Paris, 1919, pp. 241-338; A.D. Sertillanges, *Les grandes thèses de la philosophie thomiste*, Paris, 1928, pp. 41-80; F. van Steenbergen, *Dieu caché*, Comment savons-nous que Dieu existe?, Louvain-Paris, 1961.

[21] J. Robinson, *Honest to God*, p. 13.

[22] M. Heidegger, *Holzwege*, p. 200.

[23] "For, to the ordinary way of thinking, to believe in God means to be convinced of the existence of such a supreme and separate Being. 'Theists' are those who believe that such a Being exists, 'atheists' those who deny that he does". J. Robinson, *o.c.*, p. 17.

metaphysics called the "proof" of God's existence is *necessarily* infected with objectivism.

The objections which some thinkers voice to the "proofs" for God's existence become even more vehement when they notice that the "affirmation" of God as Cause no longer differs from the affirmation of causes by the sciences.[24] As soon as metaphysics wants to be a "science" in order to maintain itself *vis-à-vis* the sciences[25] and as soon as it calls the "Supreme Being"[26] the "First Cause"[27] in the same way as the sciences use the term "cause" in reference to the things they discuss, God is presented as the first in a series of causes. But then, the objectors say, the denial of the "metaphysical God" is closer to the divine God than is the affirmation.[28]

Again, I agree with this objection to the "proofs" for God's existence. As soon as God is conceived as first in a series of causes, the religious man is right when he views this as the negation of religiousness.[29] Nevertheless, the question must be asked whether the metaphysics of the past did really intend to "affirm" God as the first in a series of causes or that one cannot avoid doing this as soon as the term "cause" is used. Marcel, it seems, is too quickly convinced that this is the case.[30]

Next, there is the objection raised by those believers who view any "proof" for God's existence as scandalous because God is for them the one who is most intimately present to them in love. Why, they say, would I ever conceive the notion of proving my "most beloved" "straight to his face" that he exists? Such an attempt destroys my love and makes a mockery of my beloved. "It is no proof of love for his wife if a man seriously tries to prove her existence. As long as God is a reality, I

---

[24] M. Heidegger, *Identität und Differenz*, p. 55.

[25] M. Heidegger, *Über den Humanismus*, p. 6.

[26] M. Heidegger, *Was ist Metaphysik?*, p. 19.

[27] M. Heidegger, *Nietzsche*, II, p. 415.

[28] M. Heidegger, *Identität und Differenz*, p. 71.

[29] "Pour aller tout de suite à ce qui me paraît être l'essentiel, il me semble qu'il faudrait en finir avec l'idée d'un Dieu Cause, d'un Dieu concentrant en soi toute causalité, ou encore, en un langage plus rigoureux, avec l'usage théologique de la notion de causalité". G. Marcel, *L'homme problématique*, Paris, 1955, pp. 62-63.

[30] "Il est à craindre en effet que l'idée de causalité, quelque effort qu'aient tenté les philosophes modernes pour la spiritualiser, pour la délier, pour la détacher de ses ancres primitives, est inséparable de l'existence d'un être pourvu de pouvoirs instrumentaux : elle est en somme bio-téléologique". G. Marcel, *o.c.*, p. 64.

do not try to prove his existence ... A faith that wishes to prove itself demonstrates that it is an unbelief", says Cornelis Verhoeven.[31]

More or less the same line is taken by those who think that the religious man does not need the "proof" for God's existence and that for the unbeliever such a proof is useless.[32] The fact that this "proof" is useless for the unbeliever shows that the "proof" is unconvincing. And the fact that the believer does not need it indicates that the "proof" does not say enough. For these reasons some thinkers argue that any attempt to "prove" the existence of God must be rejected.

I have already expressed my adherence to the view that the "proof" for God's existence does not say enough for the believer. For I agreed with the claim that "the God of philosophy" is not "the God of the religious man". The question, however, is whether this compels us to reject the *radically* critical attitude of philosophical rationality. Next, we must ask, isn't it a consequence of such a rejection that there remains no longer any criterion to distinguish authentic religiousness from its most gruesome degenerations? Can symbolic and mythical speech afford the luxury of rejecting every critical resort? The issue is what the religious man can answer when he is told : "Do not be a fool. What you are saying is much ado about *nothing*".

Verhoeven simply omits these questions. It stands to reason that no one intends to prove the existence of his "beloved wife" *straight to her face*. But the "absent presence" of God may not be put on a par with the "present presence" of a beloved wife to her husband. It is precisely this "absence" that can lead to the degeneration of the believer's symbolic and mythical speech. Verhoeven would be right if the statement, "God is the one who in his love is most intimately present to me", stood on a par with the statement, "Genny is the one who in her love is most intimately present to me".

"The Conclusion of a 'Proof' for God's Existence Can Never Be True"

Whatever way a "proof" for God's existence is conceived, those who

---

[31] C. Verhoeven, *Rondom de leegte*, Utrecht, 1969[6], pp. 168-169.

[32] "On aboutit donc à ce paradoxe que la preuve n'est efficace d'une façon générale que là où à la rigueur on pouvait se passer d'elle; et au contraire, elle apparaîtra presque certainement comme un jeu verbal ou une pétition de principe à celui auquel elle est précisément destinée et qu'il s'agit de convaincre". G. Marcel, *De refus à l'invocation*, Paris, 1940, p. 231. "De gelovige heeft geen bewijs nodig, de ongelovige wordt er nog achterdochtiger en ongeloviger door". C. Verhoeven, *o.c.*, p. 168.

hold such a "proof" possible will end it with the conclusion : therefore, God exists, or, therefore, God *is*.

As we have seen already, this conclusion is not true in one *particular* interpretation of the saying-of-*is*. For, what *exists*? of what can one say that it *is*? Kant answers : of objects that are given in sense experienc. Consequently, not of God. The fact that, for Kant, man's saying-of-*is* has objective validity only with respect to what is given in sense experience can be understood in the light of his theory of transcendental method : it is supposed to be concerned with human knowledge, *tout court*, but in actual fact he does not analyze human knowledge, *tout court*, but only that knowledge we have in physical science. A consequence of this is that Kant held it impossible not only to "affirm" God but even to "affirm" the "I". Even of the "I", he says, we may not say that it *is* or that it is *known*.[33] This stands to reason if *the* saying-of-*is* and knowledge, *tout court*, are conceived as the saying-of-*is* and as the kind of knowledge we have in physical science.

What happens, however, when knowledge, *tout court*, is not conceived as this kind of scientific knowledge, but as the immediate presence of the existent subject-as-*cogito* to a present, appearing reality? In this view, this existent subject is the most original "saying"-of-*is* which underlies every saying-of-*is* that assumes the form of a judgment. In terms of this view, one can also ask, what exists? or what *is*? And the answer then is : every *present, appearing* reality, every *present, appearing* be-ing.

Paul Tillich sees here the reason why there cannot be any *proof* for the "existence of God",[34] and I agree with him. For, if a proof really wants to be a *proof*, it must be able and willing to conclude : therefore, God exists, or, therefore, God *is*.[35] If, however, this conclusion is really drawn it would imply that God is conceived as a *present, appearing* be-ing; and then it misjudges precisely that which the believer intends to say when he calls the name "God". The believer doesn't intend to affirm the essence or deeds of God or to assert the existence of God because otherwise there would be something that he could not explain. But he calls the name "God" and thereby gives voice to the "depth" of his existence, to his "dwelling in an absent presence". This calling

---

[33] "Die obigen drei Ideen der spekulativen Vernunft sind an sich noch keine Erkenntnisse". I. Kant, *Kritik der praktischen Vernunft*, ed. Cassirer, V, p. 146.

[34] "Beweisen wollen dass Gott existiert, heisst—ihn leugnen". P. Tillich, *Systematische Theologie*, I, p. 239.

[35] "Es wäre ein grosser Sieg für die christliche Apologetik, wenn die Worte 'Gott' und ' Existenz' endgültig getrennt würden". P. Tillich, *o.c.*, p. 239.

may not be replaced by "flat descriptions" in which God is made the subject of a judgment, such as "God *is*" or "God exists". The language of the religious man is symbolic and mythical, it makes use of the "second dimension" of intentionality. In the "first dimension" of intentionality language is a sign language, it points to the immediately *present* and *appearing* be-ing. With respect to this be-ing, one can say that it *is*. In the "second dimension" of intentionality language points to an "absent presence", to "what is hidden in what appears". With respect to this, one cannot say that it *is* even as a present and appearing reality *is*.

Because a "proof" can only intend to make use of the "first dimension" of the intentionality of language, and because a "proof" of God's existence can never result in the "flat descriptive" conclusion that "God exists" or "God *is*", such a "proof" can never be a *proof*. But does this mean that it is *nothing*? According to Tillich, a "proof" of God's existence is not a *proof* but the expression of "concern" about God.[36] Tillich, I think, just does not say enough here; a real concern can present itself as a concern only on the basis of a hidden "affirmation". I shall try to justify this assertion by explicitating the possibility of metaphysical speech.

The Metaphysical "Proof" for the Existence of "God"

There should be little danger of misunderstanding now if the centuries-old tradition of using the term "proof" for "God's" existence is followed here in the attempt to explore what can be accomplished by metaphysical rationality in the matter of "affirming the existence of God". And, because the "God of metaphysics" may not be put on a par with the "God for the religious man", I shall use quotation marks when the word "God" is used.

Asking what possible meaning the "proof" for "God's" existence has, I metaphysically inquire into the possibility of giving a radically critical justification for what the believer intends, viz., the expression of the "depth" of his existence. For the philosophy *as* philosopher must allow the possibility that the specific expression of the believer's symbolic and mythical speech could create a specific illusion, viz., the illusion that man's existence has a "depth". This inquiry, I said, is "metaphysical", but a brief explanation of what this means may be appropriate.

---

[36] "Die Beweise für die Existenz Gottes sind weder Beweise noch führen sie zur Existenz Gottes. Sie sind Ausdruck der *Frage* nach Gott, die in der menschlichen Endlichkeit beschlossen liegt". P. Tillich, *o.c.*, p. 240.

Metaphysics in the Sciences

The term "metaphysical" is sometimes used for ideas that are implied in the positive sciences without engaging the explicit attention of the scientists and which, as scientists, they are not called upon to make explicit. Used in this way, "metaphysics" is equivalent to "philosophy".

In the pursuit of, e.g., physical science there can be no argument about the reality of not only the scientific object but also of the subject who pursues physical science. One who does not merely pay lip service to the *reality* of the subject but takes this reality seriously sees also that it makes no sense whatsoever to explain the subject, as "projector" of physical science, by means of the same categories as are used to explain the objects of physical science. For no object of physical science every "projects" a physical science.[37] The pursuit of physical science, however, starts from the implied conviction that the subject is such that he is *able* to "project" a physical science. But this is a conviction that physical science itself cannot justify. Any attempt to speak about the subject of physical science in the same way as one speaks about the objects of this science is simply hypocritical.[38] Physical science presupposes a metaphysics of the subject who "projects" this science. The sciences are modes of being-man, and about these modes of being the sciences themselves do not and cannot speak.[39]

In any mode of human thinking the thinker establishes himself in the "wonder of all wonders" : that there is something to see and something to say. The pursuer of the positive sciences also "dwells in this wonder",[40] but it is not his task to wonder about it. In a certain sense, he speaks "thoughtlessly."[41] The metaphysician wonders about the

[37] "En effet, le *Sujet* qui construit la *Science* échappe nécessairement à la Science, puisque précisément il la construit et est toujours, comme tel, au-delà, c'est-à-dire transcendant à la Science, même achevée". R. Jolivet, *L'homme métaphysique*, Paris, 1957, p. 66.

[38] M. Merleau-Ponty, *Phénoménologie de la Perception*, Avant-propos, p. III.

[39] "Wissenschaften sind Seinsweisen des Daseins". M. Heidegger, *Sein und Zeit*, p. 13.

[40] "Der Mensch—ein Seiendes unter anderem—'treibt Wissenschaft'. In diesem 'Treiben' geschieht nichts Geringeres als der Einbruch eines Seienden, genannt Mensch, in das Ganze des Seienden, so zwar, dass in und durch diesen Einbruch das Seiende in dem, was und wie es ist, aufbricht. Der aufbrechende Einbruch verhilft in seiner Weise dem Seienden allererst zu ihm selbst". M. Heidegger, *Was ist Metaphysik?*, p. 26.

[41] "Die Wissenschaft denkt nicht. Das ist ein anstössiger Satz". M. Heidegger, *Was heisst Denken?*, p. 4.

possibility of speaking,[42] he wonders about himself, for his own existent subjectivity-as-*cogito* is the wonder through which there is something to see and to say. The "metaphysical fact", in the broad sense, is the subject-as-*cogito*.[43]

If metaphysics, but not science, speaks about the subject who pursues science, then these two can never be in competition with each other.[44] Physical science cannot make any statements about physical science; that task belongs to metaphysics.[45] The same holds for all other sciences. Metaphysics can never be eliminated by the development of scientific knowledge, for metaphysics lives *within* the very pursuit of the sciences.

Regional Ontologies

There is still another reason to speak of metaphysics *within* science. When the physicist pursues his discipline, he formulates certain laws and, in doing this, he presupposes that the specific object of his science is such that it lends itself to be spoken of by these laws. A psychologist also formulates laws, but they are not the same as those of the physicist. The psychologist starts from the assumption that the specific object of his science is such that it lends itself to be spoken of according to the laws of psychology. The same principle applies to all sciences. All men of science presuppose an understanding of the *essence* of their specific object, but it is not their task to thematize and explicitate this "understanding". This "understanding" is an implicit metaphysics.

This implicit metaphysics, however, can be made explicit. There is a metaphysics of the scientific (understood as physical science) region, the historical, the psychological, the biological, the economical, the sociological regions, etc. In such a metaphysics everything that is called "scientific" is conceived as belonging to the scientific region, everything called "historical" as belonging to the historical region, everything called "biological", "economical", "psychological" and "sociological" as belonging to the biological, the economical, the psychological and the

---

[42] "Il y a métaphysique à partir du moment où, cessant de vivre dans l'évidence de l'objet—qu'il s'agisse de l'objet sensoriel ou de l'objet de la science—nous apercevons indissolublement la subjectivité radicale de toute notre expérience et sa valeur de vérité". M. Merleau-Ponty, *Sens et non-sens*, pp. 186-187.

[43] M. Merleau-Ponty, *o.c.*, p. 187.

[44] "Entre la connaissance scientifique et le savoir métaphysique, qui la remet toujours en présence de sa tâche, il ne peut y avoir de rivalité. Une science sans philosophie ne saurait pas, à la lettre, de quoi elle parle". M. Merleau-Ponty, *o.c.*, p. 195.

[45] M. Heidegger, *Vorträge und Aufsätze*, p. 65.

sociological regions. In this way of thinking metaphysically there occurs a certain "com-prehending", to which Husserl gave expression in his project of "regional ontologies". This "com-prehension" consists in the orderly arrangement of specific objects into a specific region of being, in which the objects viewed agree with one another and differ from objects which harmonize with one another in a different region of being. Existence contains many different standpoints which cannot be reduced to one another. The result is that the "world", as correlate of existence, is not monistically constructed. "The artistic" cannot be understood as an agglomerate of physico-chemical elements, and "the juridical" is not intelligible as a series of psychological impulses.[46] The "worlds" which are connected with the different standpoints contained in existence are specific "regions of being" is which the objects agree with one another by a specific way of being this or that (*Sosein*), i.e., by "regional" characteristics, and differ from objects belonging to another region.[47] Specific "regions" are accessible to the subject only from the subject's appropriate standpoint. From the standpoint of physical science I cannot see the artistic region.[48] In Husserl's language, noetic acts and noematic correlates imply one another in unity.[49]

All sciences, then, "dwell" in specific regions of being. The specific essence of these regions is not thematized and explicitated by the sciences, although the latter presuppose a certain understanding of this essence. The historian does not thematize the historical region; biologists and jurists do not thematize the biological and the juridical regions.[50] This task is performed by the metaphysician and produces "regional ontologies".

Metaphysics in the Strict Sense

The metaphysics spoken of in the preceding paragraphs is not metaphysics in the strict sense of the term, but the philosophy of the subject who pursues science and of the specific object of a specfic science. For

---

[46] Max Müller, *Sein und Geist*, Tübingen, 1940, pp. 32-33.

[47] "Alle Gegenstände kommen darin überein, zu sein. Den Gegenständen eines bestimmten, unzurückführbaren Seinsbereichs, einer Region also, ist ein bestimmtes Sosein gemeinsam". Max Müller, *o.c.*, p. 33.

[48] "Wenn ich die ihnen entsprechende Einstellung nicht habe, die bestimmte Grundart des Verhaltens nicht betätige, so kann ich bestimmten Gegenständen nicht begegnen". Max Müller, *o.c.*, p. 33.

[49] "Phänomenologie führt die erfahrene Welt ... zurück auf das Zueinander von Grundarten des Seins und Grundarten des Bewusstseins". Max Müller, *o.c.*, p. 32.

[50] Max Müller, *o.c.*, pp. 36-38.

the great metaphysicians of the past "the" metaphysical question was more profound. It was the question of what *ultimately* does it mean that everything which is, no matter how, is said *to be*. Man generally uses the little word "is" without thinking. It goes without saying for him that being *is*. This obviousness, however, is deceptive, and its acceptance is a form of thoughtlessness. But as soon as man abandons the obviousness of being, as soon as he wonders about being and reaches the stage where he asks himself what he is saying when he affirms of anything at all that it *is*, metaphysical thinking in the strict sense is born.[51]

When in a regional ontology something is said of a specific object, in other words, when a predicate is added to the subject of a general judgment, as referring to a specific region of being, the verbal copula "is" is used. The judgment expresses that a specific object "truly" and "really" *is* what it is said to be, and implicitly the judgment also "says" that it is *not* something different.[52] This situation exists in *every* judgment, and in *every* judgment the subject who says "is" intends to express that what he affirms "truly" and "really" *is* this or that, no matter on which level and from what standpoint this affirmation is made. This point is of special importance. For the saying-of-*is* occurs on many levels; thus it is evident that the question about the possiblility of saying-*is*, *tout court*, transcends all levels. The question about the possibility of saying-*is*, *tout court*, is not concerned with the possibility of a specific positive science or a regional ontology. Similarly, the question about the "true" and the "real", *tout court*, is not a question about the "truth" and "reality" of what a specific science or regional ontology confirms as "true" and "real". This means that every positive science and every regional ontology presuppose the answer to the question about the possibility and meaning of saying-*is* and to the question about the "true" and the "real", and do not thematize these questions.[53]

---

[51] "So wird die Frage nach dem 'Sinn des Seins', danach, was damit eigentlich gemeint ist, wenn wir sagen 'es ist etwas', und 'es ist soundso', zur Grundfrage der Metaphysik". L. Landgrebe, *Der Weg der Phänomenologie*, Gütersloh, 1963, p. 78.

[52] "In einem jeden Satz gebrauchen wir das Wörtchen 'ist' als Verbindung zwischen Subjekt und Prädikat, zwischen Aussagegegenstand und Ausgesagten, und wollen damit jeweils sagen : Es ist wahrhaft und in Wirklichkeit so und nicht anders". M. Müller, *o.c.*, p. 40.

[53] "Ueber allen speziellen Regionen und Bereichen, allen Einzelwissenschaften und Einzelfragen und ihren 'regionalen' Seinsvoraussetzungen gibt es eine allgemeine Vorraussetzung eines jeden Denkens und Sprechens überhaupt". Max Müller, *o.c.*, p. 40.

The thematization of these most fundamental presuppositions is the task of metaphysics in the strict sense. Transcending all specific regions of being, metaphysics asks what exactly is affirmed when man, *on any level whatsoever*, says about *anything whatsoever* that it "truly" and "really" *is* and not *not-is* .Transcending all specific standpoints of saying-*is*, metaphysics asks what exactly is the meaning of the *is*-saying contained in every specific mode of saying-*is*. The answer to these two connected questions is presupposed in the making of any judgment whatsoever. Every judgment contains a conception of man "and" one of being.[54] This is what metaphysics in the strict sense makes its topic; it is concerned with the saying-of-*is* as such "and" with being as such. This is what many thinkers mean when they say that metaphysics raises "the question of being".

Even as the positive sciences call for regional ontologies, so these regional ontologies call for a transcendental ontology or metaphysics in the strict sense. This also shows in what sense one can and must say that metaphysics in the strict sense speaks about "everything". At first, such a claim appears fantastic, but speaking about "everything" does not mean here that metaphysics lets its gaze wander over plants, animals, rocks, machines, rivers, mountains, planets and men to say something about all these.[55] Speaking about "everything" is intelligent only when the speaking subject occupies a standpoint from which a certain "com-prehension" is possible, a com-prehension within which everything thus grasped is seized as agreeing with all that *is* and excluding only nothingness.[56] Conceived in this way, metaphysics is not a "tale told by an idiot", but the exercise of human rationality in its deepest and broadest dimensions. Everything of which it is said that it *is*, is reflected upon by metaphysics as be-ing and as not-nothing.[57]

It may seem at first that metaphysics in the strict sense, as the theory of be-ing as be-ing, busies itself with an empty word devoid of meaning.

---

[54] "Aber indem das 'ist' der Copula über alles formale Verbinden hinaus eben 'ist wirklich so', 'ist wahrhaft so' sagt, enthält es die Grundauffassung des Menschen über Sein als Wirklichkeit und Wahrheit". Max Müller, *o.c.*, p. 41.

[55] "Wir befragen nicht dieses und nicht jenes, auch nicht, es der Reihe nach durchgehend, alles Seiende, sondern im vorhinein das ganze Seiende, oder wie wir aus später zu erörternden Gründen sagen : das Seiende im Ganzen als ein solches". M. Heidegger, *Einführung in die Metaphysik*, p. 2.

[56] M. Heidegger, *o.c.*, pp. 2-3.

[57] "Der Bereich dieser Frage hat seine Grenze nur am schlechthin nicht und nie Seienden, am Nichts. Alles was nicht Nichts ist, fällt in die Frage". M. Heidegger, *o.c.*, p. 2.

Let us assume for a moment that this is true and, in order to escape the "emptiness" of the word, turn to the particular domains of be-ings.[58] There we find tools and vehicles, land and sea, mountains, rivers and forests; we find trees, birds, insects, the earth, the moon and planets. "Be-ings everywhere and however we fancy".[59] But how do we know that all these things are be-ings? We simply observe it, of course. But to do this, we must already know what "is" and "be-ing" mean.[60]

Similarly, how can we establish that a putative be-ing *is* not? To do this, we must be able to distinguish between be-ing and non-be-ing; we understand what is meant by be-ing and non-be-ing. But in that case can we still claim that "be-ing" is an empty word? In concrete cases it may happen, of course, that we doubt whether something *is* or is *not*, but we cannot doubt the distinction between be-ing and non-be-ing.[61] Accordingly, the term "be-ing" is not empty and indeterminate.

To clarify all this, Heidegger, whom I have followed in the preceding considerations, offers an example that has a certain similarity to what he intends to convey in the question about be-ing. But, as we shall see, this example, precisely because it is an example, calls for certain reservations.[62]

Let us replace, he says, the term "be-ing" by "tree" and assume that "tree" is an empty word. And to escape this emptiness, let us turn to particular kinds of trees and individual samples of these kinds. A very simple procedure, it seems, but it is not simple at all. For, if the term "tree" is empty and therefore does not tell us anything, how do we know where to go when we wish to turn to particular trees? Why do we not end up with motorcars and rabbits? The reason is that the term "tree" is not really empty but tells us something about the essence "tree", and by virtue of this essence we can identify the particular trees as trees. One who fails to appreciate this does not see the tree for the trees.[63] In an analogous way it is true that we can turn to particular be-ings

---

[58] "Also weg von dem leeren Schema dieses Wortes 'sein' ... Weg vom leeren, allgemeinen Wort 'sein' und hin zu den Besonderungen der einzelnen Bereiche des Seienden selbst!" M. Heidegger, *Einführung in die Metaphysik*, p. 58.

[59] M. Heidegger, *o.c.*, p. 58.

[60] "... dann müssen wir doch bei all dem schon wissen, was das heisst : 'ist' und 'sein'. M. Heidegger, *o.c.*, p. 59.

[61] M. Heidegger, *o.c.*, p. 59.

[62] M. Heidegger, *o.c.*, p. 60.

[63] M. Heidegger, *o.c.*, p. 61.

because we understand be-ing as be-ing and, on the basis of this understanding, distinguish it from nothing.[64]

He who claims that "be-ing" is an empty word and therefore removes it from his language does not merely diminish the number of verbs by one, but he abolishes the entire language. Man would no longer be what he is—man. For being-man means "being a speaker".[65] That man names be-ing in his speaking, then, is not simply a fact in the same sense as it is a fact that someone has this or that kind of earlobe. That man understands be-ing and gives expression to it is a necessity inasmuch as man would not exist as man if he could not do this.[66]

Parmenides

Parmenides of Elea was the first thinker in history who made the all-encompassing attitude in which the philosopher is able to speak about everything, as well as the ideas arising from this attitude, the theme of his consideration. In a didactic poem Parmenides describes how a carriage brought him to the ethereal gates where the path of the day and that of the night came together. The maidens accompanying him managed to have the gates opened for him. A goddess then appeared who revealed the truth to him. This truth contains a doctrine about be-ing and a doctrine about semblance.[67]

The doctrine about be-ing says that be-ing *is* and that outside be-ing nothing *is*. The idea that non-be-ing would be is utter nonsense. An immediate consequence of this is, says Parmenides, that be-ing is one and has not come to be. It is one because plurality implies difference, but all difference is to be excluded here. Be-ing cannot be different from be-ing by being be-ing since be-ings are precisely the same by being be-ings. And they cannot differ by non-be-ing because non-be-ing is not a source of difference. Secondly, be-ing has not come to be. For whatever comes to be comes either from be-ing or from non-be-ing. But be-ing

[64] "Wenn oben auf die Notwendigkeit aufmerksam gemacht wurde, dass wir im voraus schon wissen müssen, was 'Baum' heisst, um das Besondere der Baumarten und einzelner Bäume als solches suchen und finden zu können, dann gilt dies umso entscheidender vom Sein". M. Heidegger, *o.c.*, p. 62.

[65] M. Heidegger, *o.c.*, p. 62.

[66] "Das wir das Sein verstehen, ist nicht nur wirklich, sondern es ist notwendig. Ohne solche Eröffnung des Seins könnten wir überhaupt nicht 'die Menschen' sein". M. Heidegger, *o.c.*, p. 64.

[67] F. de Raedemaeker, *De philosophie der Voorsokratici*, Antwerpen-Amsterdam, 1953, p. 151.

cannot come to be from be-ing since it already is be-ing. And it cannot come to be from non-be-ing because non-be-ing does not contribute anything to be-ing.[68]

The idea that be-ing *is* and non-be-ing *is not* could easily be viewed as a trivial truth. In actual fact, however, the idea of Parmenides was the beginning of metaphysical thinking in the strict sense, the first exercise of man's ability to speak about "everything". This requires that be-ing be spoken of, not as tree, machine, plant, planet or animal, but as be-ing, as not-nothing. Parmenides himself represented be-ing, which is one and has not come to be, as a material substance, a perfectly round sphere.[69] Later metaphysicians did not follow him in this, but they remained faithful to the *inspiration* of his thinking. For Aristotle[70] and Aquinas[71] metaphysics was thinking about be-ing as be-ing. Those who still follow them today use exactly the same formula,[72] and Heidegger also is familiar with it.[73] One can argue, of course, about the way this formula should be interpreted and what its implications are. But it is a fact that this *inspiration* has been going strong for twenty-five centuries. This should make us pause to think. Something that *continues* to live in the history of thought can, philosophically speaking, not be nothing.

Affirmation in Negation

The Scholastic tradition of metaphysical thought in particular loves the above-mentioned way of formulating the character of metaphysics. There are, however, also metaphysicians, both inside and outside the

[68] H. Diels, *Die Fragmente der Vorsokratiker*, Berlin-Grünewald, 1951[6], I, pp. 234-239.

[69] H. Diels, *o.c.*, p. 238.

[70] *Metaph.*, III, c. I.

[71] "Dicit autem ('Philosophus') 'secundum quod est ens', quia scientiae aliae, quae sunt de entibus particularibus, considerant quidem de ente, cum omnia subjecta scientiarum sint entia, non tamen considerant ens secundum quod ens, sed secundum quod est hujusmodi ens, scilicet vel numerus, vel linea, vel ignis, vel aliquid hujusmodi". S. Thomas, in *Metaph.* IV, lect. 1 (Cathala 530).

[72] "De metaphysiek is op de eerste plaats een philosophie van het zijnde als zijnde of van het zijn, d.w.z. van de intrinsieke act (of, naar een andere interpretatie, van de wezenheid) die alle 'dingen', naar alles wat ze zijn constitueert tot werkelijkheid of verwerkelijkt". D. De Petter, *Metaphysiek en fenomenologie*, in : Begrip en werkelijkheid. Aan de overzijde van het conceptualisme, Hilversum-Antwerpen, 1964, p. 137.

[73] Chapter Three explains what it means that Heidegger reproaches traditional metaphysics for its "forgetfulness of Being" because it limited itself to asking questions and thinking about be-ing as be-ing.

Scholastic tradition, who reject that formulation. Yet, precisely in their rejection, they start from the implicit conviction that the only possibility of thinking radically, of speaking about "everything", is that the subject places himself on the standpoint which Parmenides was first to see and occupy. Thus their thinking, too, is *de facto* an explicitation of be-ing as be-ing.

Scientism is one of the most eloquent examples of this attitude. No other philosophy is as antagonistic to metaphysical thought as is scientism. In its eyes, that which metaphysicians speak about is simply "nothing". But, what else does this attitude mean if not that one can only speak of "something" when that which is involved is a reality which can be disclosed by science? For the adherent of scientism be-ing is that which can be affirmed by the sciences, and what they cannot affirm is non-be-ing. Obviously, such a view contains a conception of be-ing as be-ing and as opposed to nothing. For scientistic materialism be-ing as be-ing is material be-ing, and whatever cannot be expressed in categories of things simply is non-be-ing. We find here a *metaphysical proposition in the strict sense of the term.*

Similarly, logical positivism can only reject metaphysics by implicitly admitting it. According to Ayer, all metaphysical propositions are "nonsensical" because metaphysics assumes the task of describing a reality beyond experience. Now, a proposition which cannot be verified by any experience is not a proposition.[74] We abstract here from what Ayer means by experience and verification and by the suprasensual reality which he refers to as the object of metaphysics. We merely note that Ayer lays down certain conditions which must be satisfied if a proposition is to be a real proposition, a proposition about *reality*. If these conditions are not fulfilled, then a sentence may still have the external form of a proposition, but it will not be concerned with *reality*. One can readily discern here the typical attitude of the metaphysician. *Reality* or *be-ing* is for Ayer that which can be verified in a particular way, and whatever

---

[74] "It is the aim of metaphysics to describe a reality lying beyond experience, and therefore any proposition which would be verified by empirical observation is ipso facto non metaphysical. But what no observation could verify is not a proposition. The fundamental postulate of metaphysics 'There is a super- (or hinter-) reality' is itself not a proposition. For there is no observation or series of observations we could conceivably make by which its truth or falsehood would be determined. It may seem to be a proposition, having the sensible form of a proposition. But nothing is asserted by it". A.J. Ayer, *Demonstration of the impossibility of metaphysics*, in : Mind, 43 (1934), p. 339.

cannot be verified in this fashion is *nothing*. Thus Ayer, too, has a certain conception of be-ing *as* be-ing and as opposed to nothing. In this sense he is a metaphysian.

Accordingly, the rejection of reflection on be-ing *as* be-ing and as opposed to non-be-ing is possible only if, in the very attempt to adduce reasons for this rejection, one revives metaphysical thinking. For the motivation of the rejection contains implicitly the conditions on which one is willing to admit something as something and as not nothing. That's why even the most fervent antimetaphysicians occupy a place among the metaphysicians and are studied in surveys of metaphysics with the same right as are the proponents of metaphysics.[75]

Any philosophy *de facto* contains a metaphysical moment in the sense intended here. For every philosopher has a "primitive fact", a "central reference point", from which he expects that it will enable him to throw light on the totality of reality, show its unity, com-prehend it.[76] For Descartes this central reference point is "clear and distinct ideas"— whatever cannot be understood in "clear and distinct ideas" is nothing for him. This option decides the matter of be-ing as be-ing for him. Aquinas, Marx and Bergson have other central reference points. This means that they try to understand the totality of reality by means of a different unifying principle. They are convinced that, by using a certain unifying principle, they do justice to the totality of reality, that they are not forced to reject as non-be-ing something which presents itself as be-ing. Accordingly, the use of a central reference point implies a view about the universality of be-ing as be-ing and as opposed to non-be-ing.[77]

"The Metaphysical in Man"

The metaphysical question in the strict sense of the term has not been invented by metaphysics as a "science".[78] Rather, it lies contained in the subject-as-*cogito*; better still, it is a moment of the existent subject-as-

---

[75] F. Sassen, *Wat betekent "Metaphysica"?*, in : Wijsgerig perspectief op maatschappij en wetenschap, III (1963), pp. 106-119.

[76] A. Dondeyne, *Inleiding tot het denken van E. Levinas*, in : Tijdschrift voor Philosophie, XXV (1963), p. 557.

[77] Max Müller, *Sein und Geist*, pp. 42-44.

[78] "Metaphysik ist nichts, was von Menschen nur 'geschaffen' wird in Systemen und Lehren, sondern das Seinsverständnis, sein Entwurf und seine Verwerfung geschieht im Dasein als solchem. Die 'Metaphysik' ist das Grundgeschehen beim Einbruch in das Seiende, der mit der faktischen Existenz von so-etwas wie Mensch überhaupt geschieht". M. Heidegger, *Kant und das Problem der Metaphysik*, p. 218.

cogito, a mode of being-man.[79] The subject-as-*cogito* himself is "meta-physical consciousness", "metaphysical rationality". Metaphysical ratio-nality is a kind of "knowing" of what it means that everything of which it has been, is being and will be said that it *is* belongs to the order of be-ing. Metaphysics critically and systematically explores, explicitates and develops this "knowing". Metaphysics, then, has its ground in metaphysical rationality, in a "com-prehending" dimension of the exist-ent subject's-as-*cogito* immediate presence to reality—namely, the dimension in which the subject dwells in the "universe", the universality of all be-ings as be-ings. Metaphysics presupposes "the metaphysical in man".[80] That is why metaphysics presupposes a philosophical anthro-pology and a criteriology.

"Why Is There Something Rather Than Nothing?

This is the central question of metaphysical thinking in the strict sense of the term. But it is not at once evident why this is so, and not even why this question has to be raised. To realize that it must be asked, one must first realize that every be-ing as be-ing is limited, a finite be-ing. There are many be-ings, and they differ. Every be-ing includes the non-being of all other be-ings. The "saying"-of-*is* which the existent subject-as-*cogito* is includes a "saying"-of-*is-not*. No one be-ing is the fullness of being. Be-ing is not "to be" but merely *has* "to be".

This is what metaphysicians have in mind when they call be-ing as be-ing "contingent. And it is the realization of this contingency that gives rise to the question, "Why is there something rather than nothing"?[81]

---

[79] "Hinsehen auf, Verstehen und Begreifen von, Zugang zu sind konstitutive Verhaltungen des Fragens und so selbst Seinsmodi eines bestimmten Seienden, des Seienden, das wir, die Fragenden, je selbst sind". M. Heidegger, *Sein und Zeit*, p. 7.

[80] "Wenn die Interpretation des Sinnes von Sein Aufgabe wird, ist das Dasein nicht nur das primär zu befragende Seiende, es ist überdies das Seiende, das sich je schon in seinem Sein zu dem verhält, wonach in dieser Frage gefragt wird. Die Seinsfrage ist dann aber nichts anderes als die Radikalisierung einer zum Dasein selbst gehörigen wesenhaften Seinstendenz, des vorontologischen Seinsverständnisses". M. Heidegger, *o.c.*, p. 15.

[81] "Ce fondement ultime unique est l'impossibilité pour les êtres du monde de notre expérience et non moins pour l'être humain lui-même de justifier en raison et de fonder leur être qui cependant les constitue en tout ce qu'ils sont. C'est la gratuïté radicale des êtres de ce monde en tant q'êtres. Et c'est l'évidence de cette gratuïté qui nous fait poser la question inéluctable : pourquoi y a-t-il quelque chose et non pas plutôt rien?" D. De Petter, *Le caractère métaphysique de la preuve de l'existence de Dieu et la pensée contemporaine*, in : L'existence de Dieu, Casterman, 1961, p. 167.

This question *must* be asked. Because be-ing is not by itself—which would make it the fullness of "to be"—the question about the *cause* of be-ing cannot be avoided.[82]

"Nothing is so much more simple" than be-ing. Indeed. If only one could say that nothing is, if only one could deny the metaphysical "saying"-of-*is*! But there is not nothing; the metaphysical "saying"-of-*is* cannot be eliminated. The metaphysician *must* ask about the cause of be-ing as be-ing, but this cause cannot be found within the universe of be-ings. For every be-ing which he would want to name as cause of be-ing itself gives rise to the question about the cause of be-ing. That's why "nothing" would be so much more simple. Therefore, the "Other-than-be-ing" "..."

We leave the dots and refuse to say :

"Other-than-be-ing" is, exists

"To be" is, exists

The "Infinite" is, exists

The "Absolute" is, exists

The "Necessary" is, exists

"God" is, exists.

We leave the dots, for what *is*? Be-ing is. If we were to say "Other-than-be-ing" *is*, we would have lowered the "Other-than-be-ing" to the level of be-ing.

At this stage it becomes apparent that the "saying"-of-*is* which existence is, is not what it is without that "depth" in existence whereby the "affirmation" of be-ing is transcended. The "saying"-of-*is* is undeniable and that is why the "Other-than-be-ing" "..." The refusal to replace the dots by "is" occurs in tradition as the recognition that the divine God "..." the transcendent God. God does *not* appear as be-ings appear because the divine God is *not* as be-ings are.

There are many non-divine gods but There "..." only one divine God—the God who is not, the God whose name cannot become the subject of a judgment in which a predicate is added to this subject. *In spite of this*, the religious man makes "God" the subject of such judgments. This means that he runs the risk of lapsing into inauthenticity. In the past, metaphysicians endeavored—at least, in principle—to

---

[82] In Chapter Three I've explained that Heidegger correctly blames traditional metaphysics for proceeding *at once* to a search for the cause of be-ing as be-ing. But this is no reason why the question of this cause should *not at all* be raised.

escape this danger by adding at once a negation to every affirmation "of" God.[83] One who formulates a judgment "about" God's essence and deeds denies God if he conceives his proposition as a "flat description". The religious man *calls* God's name, but what the metaphysician *describes* is the essence of *man* as a self-transcending "saying"-of-*is*.

Conclusion

This is what metaphysics can "prove". It can make us see that the existent subject-as-*cogito* implies a "depth", that the subject in his most primordial "saying"-of-*is* implies a "depth" which consists in the "affirmation' of "..." I've already indicated why I leave the dots. Yet, unlike Tillich, who speaks only of "concern", I speak of " 'affirmation' ", using double quotation marks. One set of quotation marks indicates that we are not dealing with an affirmation having the character of a judgment. Any judgment is based on an implicit "affirmation" or "saying"-of-*is* which the existent subject-as-*cogito* himself is. The second set indicates that in this primordial "affirmation" or "saying"-of-*is* a "mystery" is hidden—a mystery that can never be disclosed by the affirmation of be-ing as be-ing, a mystery that must always remain a "mystery" because the affirmation or saying-of-*is* by metaphysics is always the affirmation of *be-ing*. Nevertheless, we speak here of " 'affirmation' " because be-ing is and the "affirmation" of be-ing cannot be what it is without the " 'affirmation' " of "..."

As has been repeatedly pointed out, the philosopher is "reserve" personified. As a philosopher, he may not show himself sensitive to the *specific expressive power* of symbolic and mythical language, but uses *only* critical rationality. This critical rationality, however, enables him to reach an " 'affirmation' " which functions as a critical resort, even with respect to the symbolic and mythical language of the religious man. Symbols can run wild, myths go awry, and the religious man can degenerate. Any form of "religiousness" which affirms "God" as a be-ing is a kind of pseudo-religiousness. In a pseudo-religious attitude the "second dimension" of existence is reduced to the "first dimension"; religiousness becomes an absolutistic ideology and an idol is adored as the true God. The experience of "depth" in Christian religiousness includes humility, joy, confidence and love. The experience of "depth" is the consciousness of sin, grace, redemption, consolation, true life, salvation and hope.

---

[83] Thomas Aquinas, *S.Th.*, I, q. 1, a. 9, ad 3; *Summa contra Gentiles*, I, c. 14.

But all this is utterly counterfeited when a degenerated religious language calls man to adore an ungodly god, a god who *is*. This is what the rationality of metaphysics can, not "demonstrate", but "point out".